5O events

you really need to know

history of war

Robin Cross

Quercus

Contents

Introduction

Human history, from the empires of the ancient world to the superpowers of the 21st century, has been inextricably bound up with war and the weapons we have used to wage it. The technologies that have produced advanced civilizations have also been harnessed to the grim business of warfare. The trains that carried working people to their first seaside holidays in the 19th century also took millions of young men to war in 1914. Nearly a century later, the computer revolution, which by 2000 had come to dominate almost every aspect of life in advanced societies, has also introduced us to a new fifth dimension of warfare, in which governments jostle brutally in cyberspace.

This short history, stretching from the chariot to the Stuxnet virus that disabled Iran's nuclear enrichment programme in 2009, charts the impact of some of the most significant weapons that have been developed in the last 2,500 years. In one sense everything has changed, and in another, very little.

Throughout history, military establishments have traditionally been among the most conservative elements in society. 'If it works, don't fix it' is a rubric that served the deeply conservative Roman military machine for centuries. In 1914 the British Expeditionary Force went to war under a commander-in-chief, Sir John French, a cavalryman, who believed that 'bullets have no real stopping power against a horse'.

In the 19th and 20th centuries, the pace of technological and tactical change threatened to outstrip the ability of many military establishments to control it. In the space of little less than half a century, the first frail warplanes that took to the air before 1914, and went to war over the Western Front flown by pilots and observers improbably armed with pistols and darts, morphed into the technologically advanced B-29 Superfortress, capable in 1945 of delivering atomic weapons to the heart of the Japanese home islands. Nevertheless, it is as well to remember that the number of victims at Hiroshima and Nagasaki, grim though it was, was overshadowed by the toll exacted by the six months of B-29 fire raids on Japan's cities that preceded the A-bomb attacks.

Since 1945, the pace of change has been relentless. In the present day, the main battle tank is facing obsolescence as the master of the battlefield, and the introduction of the unmanned combat aerial vehicle (UCAV) threatens the livelihoods of many of the highly trained establishments of the world's leading air forces. In contrast, the asymmetric conflicts raging around the globe in countries of the Third World attest to the durability of one of the 20th century's most remarkable weapons: the Kalashnikov assault rifle, developed in the late 1940s and still in service worldwide.

01 The chariot
2600 BC–AD 83

The Sumerian city-states of southern Mesopotamia, which flourished in the third millennium BC, provide us with the earliest evidence of disciplined formations of heavy infantry, forerunners of the phalanx, conducting far-flung military campaigns in the beginnings of empire.

The armies of these city-states were also the first to use wheeled vehicles as mobile firing platforms. As depicted in a lyre found in the royal cemetery at Ur in southern Mesopotamia (in use around 2600–2000 BC), they were inelegant solid-wheeled wagons hauled by donkeys, or possibly the larger onager, an animal usually resistant to domestication. Perhaps these beasts of burden were mule-like hybrids, now extinct.

The animals are yoked to a draught pole and controlled by reins that run through a ring mounted on the pole. Two men ride in the chariot, a driver and a soldier wielding a spear or an axe. A quiver of spears projects from the front of the chariot. There is no indication of how these vehicles would have been deployed in battle. With their four heavy wheels, they would have been cumbersome, and the onagers would have presented an inviting target. It is likely that they provided a chauffeur service to the battlefield rather than manoeuvring on it.

Logistics The early centuries of the second millennium BC saw significant innovations in the art of war: bent-wood construction produced a lighter, more manoeuvrable chariot fitted with spoked wheels; and the development of the composite bow introduced a rapid-fire missile delivery system from the fast-moving chariot. Nevertheless, the construction of

c.2600–2000 BC	c.1600 BC	1485 BC	1274 BC
Sumerians use wheeled vehicles as mobile firing platforms	Egypt combines chariot, horse and composite bow in empire-building army	Battle of Megiddo	Battle of Qadesh

the chariots, the breeding and management of the horses, and the training of the chariot driver and warrior, were an expensive business requiring a major logistical underpinning.

To keep large bodies of charioteers in the field, armies needed substantial numbers of wheelwrights, chariot-builders, bow-makers, metal-smiths and armourers. On campaign, still more men were needed to manage the spare horses and repair damaged vehicles. Chariotry became a significant symbol of military might. The great powers of the day – Egypt, the Hittites in modern central Turkey, and the Assyrians in what is now Iraq, all became practised exponents of chariot warfare.

Egypt From about 1600 BC, Egypt turned the powerful new combination of horse, lightweight chariot and composite bow into a weapon of territorial expansion. Egypt's massive manpower and material resources stood behind an army numbering tens of thousands that could project Egyptian power well beyond its now stabilized borders.

Driving up the east Mediterranean littoral in about 1485 BC, Pharaoh Tuthmosis III found his path blocked by a coalition of local forces round

Straddle car

Surviving clay models provide evidence of smaller two-wheeled chariots and the so-called 'straddle car', consisting of an axle with two wheels, and a saddle set on a vertical post on the draught pole above the axle. We do not know how these lost war wagons were employed, but they provide ample evidence of man's unquenchable desire to devote considerable resources to the development of weapons systems – the origins of successive arms races from the ancient world to the present day.

c.500 BC	**55 and 54 BC**	**AD 83**
Scythed chariots appear in India and Persia	Julius Caesar invades Britain	Battle of Mons Graupius

the city of Megiddo (now in northern Israel), which commanded the route into southern Syria. Tuthmosis used speed and surprise to overcome the defenders of Megiddo and bottle them up in the city, which surrendered after a seven-month siege.

> **❛All the princes of all the northern countries are cooped up within it. The capture of Megiddo is the capture of a thousand towns.❜**
>
> **From Tuthmosis' inscriptions**

Egyptian chariots played a key role in the Battle of Megiddo, arriving at the critical point to shatter the federation of local forces opposing Tuthmosis. Chariotry was a high-value weapon that could only be launched at the crucial moment in a battle. Its task was to launch a drive that would break the enemy infantry. Once the tide of battle had been turned, the role of chariotry was to pursue the fleeing enemy – the phase in any engagement when most losses in men and equipment occur, and a reverse can be turned into a rout.

Battle of Qadesh The Hittite empire, originally based in central Turkey, provided the next barrier to Egyptian expansion. At the beginning of the 13th century BC, Pharaoh Ramses II led his army into western Syria to reduce the city of Qadesh, which blocked the path to confrontation with the Hittites. The two sides met at the Battle of Qadesh (1274 BC). The Egyptians were initially thrown into disarray by a Hittite chariot attack, and the situation was only retrieved by the arrival on the scene of a second Egyptian force. Qadesh was a battle of attrition, involving thousands of chariots, from which both armies emerged badly mauled. Hostilities between the two powers were ended by a non-aggression pact.

The Persians In the middle of the first millennium BC, the Persians refined the art of chariotry with scythed wheels. The Greek soldier-historian Xenophon (c.425–c.335 BC) wrote that scythed chariots were introduced into the Persian army by Cyrus the Great (d. 530 BC), although the fourth-century historian Ctesias of Cnidus places their origins earlier. Indian sources mention scythed chariots being used in the campaigns waged by the Mauryas against the Vriji confederacy during the reign of Ajatshatru (494–467 BC). However, we do not know whether scythed chariots were an Indian invention adopted by the Persians or a Persian invention adopted by the Indians.

❝And Solomon gathered chariots and horsemen: and he had one thousand four hundred chariots, and twelve thousand horsemen, which he placed in the chariot cities and with the king at Jerusalem.❞

Chronicles 1: 14

Cyrus the Younger (d. 401 BC) employed scythed chariots in large numbers. However, the days of the war chariot were now numbered. At the Battle of Gaugamela (331 BC) the army of Alexander the Great simply opened its lines to let the Persian chariots career through before attacking them from the rear.

The Celts In northern Europe, the Celts of the third century BC used chariots to fight against cavalry. When fighting from his two-horse chariot, the Celtic warrior threw his javelin first and then alighted, in Homeric fashion, to fight with his sword. Julius Caesar, who invaded Britain in 55 and 54 BC, left a description of British chariot warfare: 'Firstly they drive about in all directions and throw their weapons and generally break the ranks of the enemy with the very dread of their horses and the noise of their wheels; and when they have worked themselves in between the troops of horse, leap from their chariots and engage on foot.'

The Romans encountered Celtic chariots at the Battle of Mons Graupius, fought in northeast Scotland in AD 83. The Roman senator and historian Tacitus noted that the plain between the two armies 'resounded with the noise and with the rapid movement of chariots and cavalry'. The chariots had little effect: 'Meanwhile the enemy's cavalry had fled, and the charioteers had mingled in the engagement of the infantry.'

the condensed idea
The chariot was the ancient world's tank

02 The Macedonian phalanx 338–168 BC

The greatest military leader of the ancient world, Alexander the Great, was born in 356 BC. He was the son of another great commander, Philip II of Macedon (382–336 BC), who had transformed a weak feudal state into the dominant power in the Balkans.

As an 18-year-old, Alexander fought under his father's command at the Battle of Chaeronea (338 BC), leading the Macedonian left, which crushed the flower of the Theban army, the Sacred Band. Philip was assassinated in 336, when he was on the point of attacking Persia. By 334 his son was ready to invade the Persian empire at the head of a battle-tested army.

> **❝My boy, you must find a kingdom big enough for your ambitions. Macedonia is too small a place for you.❞**
>
> **Philip II's words to his young son, as reported by Plutarch (c.50–c.AD 120)**

The phalanx The iron core of the Macedonian army was the infantry phalanx, from whose steadiness and reliability Philip and Alexander derived much of their strength. It was almost certainly Philip who laid the foundations of the *pezhetairoi*, the 'Foot Companions', so called to stress their relationship to the king as a tactical and political counterweight to the aristocratic 'Companion' cavalry, which had started as a royal bodyguard.

Alexander embarked on his first campaign with 12,000 infantry and 1,500 cavalry. Some 9,000 of the infantry were organized on a territorial basis, in six 1,500-strong brigades (*taxeis*) of Foot Companions. The remaining 3,000 infantry formed an elite guard, the 'Shield Bearers' (*hypaspists*). The Shield Bearers and

timeline

356 BC	338 BC	334 BC	333 BC	332 BC	331 BC
Alexander born	Battle of Chaeronea – Macedonians under Philip II defeat an Athenian and Boeotian army	A combined Macedonian/ Greek army is ferried across the Dardanelles into Asia. At Granicus, Alexander defeats a combined force of Persian satraps	Alexander overwhelms the Persian army at the Battle of Issus	Alexander's siege of Tyre	Alexander seals the end of the Persian empire at the Battle of Gaugamela

Foot Companions were deployed in the centre of the Macedonian line of battle flanked by the cavalry, with whom they were trained to manoeuvre in echelon. The Companions were used in a shock role, to splinter the enemy line, which was then rolled up by the phalanx.

The *sarissa* The Macedonian heavy infantry's principal weapon was the *sarissa*, a long two-handed pike made of cornel wood, about 6.3 metres (21 ft) long, weighing about 8 kilograms (17 lb), and made in two parts joined by an iron sleeve, making it easier to carry on the march.

The phalangite wielded his *sarissa* with both hands, keeping it aligned with those of his comrades. The smallest tactical battle unit of the phalanx was the *speira* of 256 men drawn up in close order 16 deep. Phalanx drill required the *sarissas* of the first five ranks to project beyond the men in the front rank in the highly compact attack formation. The front rank held

Philip's military modernization

Macedonian infantry had originally lacked discipline, training and organization. Philip enforced a rigorous training regime that involved regular forced route marches with full equipment and baggage. He banned the use of wheeled transport and forced the infantry to carry 30 days' rations on their backs when they were campaigning. Camp followers were kept to a minimum for both infantry and cavalry, reducing the size of the baggage train and maximizing mobility. Philip also developed an efficient commissariat, which enabled him to campaign all year round, and his son provided all his campaigns with a sound logistical backup.

326 BC	**323 BC**	**281–275 BC**	**197 BC**	**168 BC**
Alexander's last and most costly victory at the Battle of the Hydaspes at the gates of India	Death of Alexander at Babylon	Pyrrhus of Epirus introduces more flexible tactics with his 'articulated' phalanx	Roman legions defeat the phalanx at Cynoscephalae	The legions, with the help of war elephants, defeat the phalanx at Pydna

their *sarissas* levelled at the enemy and projecting some 4 metres (13 ft) ahead of the man holding it. The men in the second rank, 1 metre (3.3 ft) behind the file leaders, raised their *sarissas*, extending their weapons 3 metres (10 ft) beyond the front rank. The third rank raised their *sarissas* higher and the fourth rank raised them still higher. Those in the fifth rank raised their *sarissas* towards the sky to break the force of incoming missiles while at the same time adding their weight to the force of the charge.

> **❝The strong handsome commander with one eye dark as the night and one blue as the sky.❞**
>
> Arrian (*c.*AD 90–*c.*165) on Alexander

The overall effect was a steepling hedge of *sarissas* that demoralized enemy infantry and, at this stage in the history of warfare, discouraged war elephants. Handling their *sarissas* obliged the phalangites to dispense with their heavy body armour in favour of leather corselets, helmets and greaves.

End of the phalanx As the men in the phalanx used both hands to wield the *sarissa*, they could carry only a small round bronze shield, suspended from the neck, which covered the left shoulder. In 327 those carried by the Shield Bearers were decorated with silver plates, and the formation acquired the name 'Silver Shields' (*agryraspides*).

Elephants on the battlefield

Alexander first encountered war elephants at the Battle of Gaugamela (331 BC). At the Battle of the Hydaspes (326 BC), in India, the Macedonians faced about 100 elephants lined up before the battle array at 15-metre (49-ft) intervals with the aim of stopping Alexander's cavalry. Horses do not like the smell of elephants. The Macedonian light infantry advanced against the elephants, attempting to kill their drivers with javelins, before Alexander ordered his phalanxes to attack in a tightly knit locked-shield formation, presenting the elephants with an intimidating mass of spears, which drove them off.

In the hands of a military genius like Alexander, who was able to integrate all types of troops into a seamless whole, the phalanx was a formidable weapon. But in lesser hands the phalanx had its weaknesses, and it survived in progressively degraded form. It could only operate efficiently over even ground on which there were no features to disrupt its cohesion. And when it came up against disciplined and well-led Roman armies in the second century BC, the cracks began to show.

> **❛[The men] long to again see their parents, their wives and children, their homeland.❜**
>
> **Coenus, a phalanx commander, on Alexander's expedition to India in 327–326 BC**

At Cynoscephalae in 197 BC the phalanx was defeated by the legion. At Pydna in 168 BC a Macedonian army of 4,000 cavalry and 40,000 infantry, including a 20,000-strong phalanx, was defeated by four legions commanded by Aemilius Paulus. The Macedonian line stretched for 2 miles (3.2 km), with the phalanx at its centre and cavalry on either wing. The Roman commander later recalled his alarm as the advance of the phalanx sliced through the front ranks of his army. But in the process it became disorganized, and gaps opened up to be exploited by the legionaries as the phalangites, encumbered by their heavy *sarissas*, were unable to cope with close combat. The Macedonian cavalry fled the field, leaving the phalanx to be cut up by the legions. Defeat reduced Macedonia to the status of a Roman province.

the condensed idea
The phalanx was Alexander's invincible infantry formation

03 Helepolis ('The City Taker')
305–304 BC

Demetrius Poliorcetes ('The Besieger', 337–283 BC), was one of the most colourful commanders who jostled for power over the empire of Alexander the Great after the latter's death in June 323 BC, an expert on massive siege engines. He was the son of Antigonus Monophthalmus ('One-eyed'), a Macedonian nobleman who had fought under Alexander and, with his son, was later an enthusiastic participant in the savage squabbling that tore the great Macedonian's empire apart.

The careers of both father and son ended in defeat, although Antigonus initially profited from his service with Alexander. In 319 BC he covered 287 miles (462 km) with an army of more than 4,000 infantry and 7,000 cavalry, plus war elephants, in a forced march of seven days and seven nights through the Taurus mountains, in modern Turkey, to destroy the army of his rival Seleucus, another of Alexander's generals.

Demetrius conquered Cyprus in 306, although his father's subsequent invasion of Egypt ended in failure. In 305–304 Demetrius laid siege to Rhodes, but the city's obstinate resistance obliged him to conclude a peace treaty in which the Rhodians pledged to build ships for him. In 301 father and son were defeated at the Battle of Ipsus, in which the 81-year-old Antigonus was killed by a javelin. His share of Alexander's disintegrating empire was divided between rivals. In 294, Demetrius seized control in

timeline

332 BC	306 BC	305–304 BC	302 BC	301 BC	294 BC
Alexander's siege of Tyre	Demetrius conquers Cyprus	Demetrius lays siege to Rhodes	Demetrius reinstates the Corinthian League	Battle of Ipsus	Demetrius installs himself on the throne of Macedon

Macedonia, and his descendants maintained a faltering hold over it until the Roman victory at the Battle of Pydna (168 BC).

Demetrius's last campaign, in Asia Minor, ended in disaster, capture and death as a prisoner of Seleucus in 283 BC. Demetrius was married five times and was notorious for his licentious behaviour, driving one young object of his homosexual passions to choose suicide over submission. However, it was as an exponent of siege warfare that Demetrius established an enduring reputation.

The Helepolis ('City Taker') The campaigns of Alexander the Great had seen a dramatic improvement in the techniques and technology of siege warfare. Torsion machines, powered by springs of twisted hair or sinew, were now used to shoot bolts or stones, and these came into play against the Persians in 332 BC at the siege of Tyre, the port city in what is now modern Lebanon.

The siege of Salamis

At the siege of Rhodes, many of the innovative techniques employed by Alexander were used by Demetrius Poliorcetes. Demetrius, however, was not a man accustomed to doing anything by halves, and the siege became one of the most remarkable set-pieces of warfare in the ancient world. Demetrius had built a massive siege tower during his siege of Salamis in Cyprus in 306. The first Helepolis was some 40 metres (130 ft) high and 20 metres (65 ft) square at its base, which moved on four huge solid wheels. The tower was crammed with catapults: on the lowest floor were heavy stone-throwers capable of hurling missiles weighing up to 80 kilograms (176 lb); the middle storeys heaved with heavy bolt-shooters; and at the top were lighter stone-throwers and arrow-shooters. Some 200 men operated the machines inside the tower.

288 BC	**286 BC**	**168 BC**
Demetrius leaves Macedon for Asia Minor	Demetrius imprisoned by Seleucus	Macedon conquered by Romans

Tyre was situated on a coastal island, and Alexander built a mole out towards its walls and brought up stone-throwers and siege towers. The Tyrians responded by placing padding on the walls and erecting multi-spoked wheels on the battlements to deflect incoming fire. They ran fireships aground on the mole, which set light to and destroyed Alexander's towers.

At this point the Phoenician component of the Persian fleet defected to Alexander, enabling him to establish control over the waters around Tyre. Work then began on a second mole. Alexander lashed some of his ships together and used them as platforms for battering rams. Tyrian divers attempted to cut the ships' cables but Alexander switched to chains. Eventually the battering rams brought down a section of wall and Alexander ordered a general assault on the breach and the two harbours on either side of the city. The storming of Tyre ended in bitter street fighting in which no quarter was given. The city was burnt and the 2,000 surviving Tyrians were crucified to satisfy Alexander's anger.

When Demetrius laid siege to Rhodes in 305–304, he deployed an impressive array of siege engines, including towers and floating batteries, in an attempt to take the city from the sea. A combination of determined resistance and bad weather thwarted him and he switched his attack to a land assault. The centrepiece of the renewed assault was a second, bigger Helepolis, designed by engineer Epimachus of Athens.

Helepolis 2   The City Taker's base platform, which was almost 22 square metres, was constructed of heavy timbers held together by iron spikes and mounted on eight enormous wheels. The Helepolis could be swung in any direction by pivots. The four inward-slanting corner beams were some 50 metres (164 ft) high. There were nine storeys, the first with a floor area of 430 square metres (4,628 sq ft) and the topmost 90 square metres (969 sq ft). The interior of the Helepolis was big enough to provide standing room for some 3,500 men who moved the machine forward while more pushed at the rear.

The three exposed sides of the tower were iron-plated, and in front of each storey were portholes through which missiles were propelled: rocks from the lower storeys, and lighter stones and javelins from the upper storeys. To protect the 200 soldiers manning the machines inside the Helepolis, the portholes were fitted with shutters that could be opened and closed by a mechanical device. The shutters were covered with hide and cushioned with wool to reduce the impact of counter-battery fire from the Rhodian catapults mounted on the city walls. Each storey was provided with a water tank to douse fires and two staircases for ferrying the ammunition up and down.

As it rumbled towards the city walls, Helepolis was flanked by two moveable sheds ('tortoises') from which protruded armoured battering rams 55 metres (180 ft) long, each of which was worked by 1,000 men. Eight more tortoises supported the engineers in the battering rams. The Helepolis and the battering rams brought down one of the towers and part of the wall, but a Rhodian night sortie damaged some of the siege tower's armour and set it on fire before it was dragged to safety. The resourceful Rhodians also managed to repair the breach in the wall before Demetrius brought it down for a second time, forcing an entry into the city. The incursion was driven out after a pitched battle. With his siege stalemated, and the re-provisioned Rhodians far from starvation, Demetrius was forced to come to terms with his foe after a siege that had lasted 15 months.

After the siege, the Helepolis was abandoned not far from Rhodes. But it enjoyed a subsequent half life. The resourceful Rhodians melted down its metal plating and used the material to build one of the seven wonders of the ancient world, the Colossus of Rhodes. This enormous statue, standing over 30 metres (107 ft) high and completed in 280 BC, stood guard at the entrance of the harbour at Rhodes. Modern archaeologists have speculated that the massive amount of scaffolding needed to erect the Colossus was salvaged from the looming hulk of Demetrius's City Taker. The statue was brought down by an earthquake in 226 in which tracts of Rhodes were also devastated. The legend goes that in AD 654 the surviving fragments of the Colossus were acquired by a Jewish merchant from Edessa and carried away on the backs of 900 camels. The Colossus, bastard child of the City Taker, lingered in medieval imagination as 'the brazen giant of Greek fame', words inscribed in 1903 in the base of the Statue of Liberty in New York.

the condensed idea
Helepolis was a spectacular failure of ancient war

04 The trireme
500–250 BC

The word trireme is derived from the Latin for 'three-oarer'. By the beginning of the fifth century BC, it was the standard warship of the Mediterranean. Its origins lay in the *pentekontor*, a warship with a single row of 25 oars on each side, and the bireme, which had two banks of oars. The bireme was almost certainly developed by the Phoenicians and then adopted by the Greeks.

At some point in the sixth century BC a third bank of rowers had been added to the bireme to produce the trireme, which was rowed at three levels with one man handling each oar. The Athenian naval records indicate that the oars were 4–4.5 metres (13–15 ft) long. Archaeologists excavating ship sheds at the Athenian harbour at Piraeus have established the dimensions of the trireme as 37 metres (121 ft) long and 3 metres (10 ft) wide at bottom, increasing to a width of about 6 metres (20 ft) at outrigger level.

> **❛It was decided that each sailor taking his oar, cushion and oar-strap . . .❜**
>
> **Thucydides (c.471–c.399 BC)**

Athenian records state that on the lowest level of the trireme there were 27 oarsmen (*thalamites*) on each side, working their oars through ports. Evidence that they were at some height above the waterline is provided by the tactic used by the defenders of Syracuse during its siege in 414–413 BC. The trireme's rowers were attacked as they sat on their benches by men in rowing boats who came alongside, slipping under their oars.

timeline

5th century BC	480 BC	479 BC	414–413 BC
Trireme becomes standard warship in the Mediterranean	Battle of Salamis	Battle of Mycale	Siege of Syracuse in the Peloponnesian War

There were 27 oarsmen (*zygites*) on each side in the second bank, and the third bank comprised 31 rowers (*thranites*) on each side, rowing through an outrigger, extending beyond the side of the ship, which imparted greater leverage to the oars. Triremes were steered by broad bars at the stern. They had two anchors and two landing ladders, also stored in the stern. Triremes were virtually unprotected, and there was no railing on the sides of the deck, possibly to facilitate boarding.

Sails were carried for cruising, and triremes could probably move faster under sail with a favourable wind than when powered by oars. However, a sail rig made tacking virtually impossible in a battle, as it presented the vulnerable side or stern to the enemy. Sails were lowered before battle, or even left ashore. Over long distances and under good conditions, a trireme might achieve a speed of 4 or 5 knots; over shorter distances a top speed of some 12 knots could have been sustained.

> **❝On you sons of Greece! Free your native land, free your children, your wives, the fanes of your fathers' gods and the tombs of your ancestors. Now you battle for your all.❞**
>
> **Greek battle cry at Salamis**

Artemisia I

Artemisia, queen of Halicarnassus, fought at Salamis (see overleaf) as the world's first commander of a naval fleet. Her small command sailed with the Persian fleet commanded by Xerxes. At the height of the battle, Artemisia retrieved the body of Xerxes' brother, an admiral of the fleet, from the Greeks. Her own ship was then attacked by a Greek trireme. Taking evasive action, she found herself blocked by one of her allies. She rammed and sank the Persian ship before making good her escape. Watching this bold manoeuvre, Xerxes observed, 'Truly my men are becoming women and my women, men!'

256 BC
Battle of Ecnomus

264–241 BC
The First Punic War

> **❝A king sate on the rocky brow
> Which looks o'er sea-born Salamis
> And ships, by the thousands, lay below,
> And men in nations; – all were his!
> He counted them at break of day –
> And when the sun set where were they?❞**
>
> Lord Byron, *Don Juan* (1819–24)

Salamis A trireme crew numbered 200, of whom 170 were rowers. The rowers were drawn from the lower classes but were not slaves. At the Battle of Salamis in 480 BC each trireme had a complement of heavily armed marines and some archers. Also on board was a flautist who piped time for the rowers. Salamis saw the defeat of a Persian invasion fleet of some 600 vessels by approximately 320 Greek triremes. The Greeks feigned a withdrawal and then turned on the Persians in the confined waters of the Straits of Salamis, where the latter had no room to manoeuvre and were rammed at will by the Greeks. As they struggled to extricate themselves from the narrows, the Persians were taken in the flank by triremes from Aegina. No mercy was shown to Persian sailors struggling in the water.

Salamis was a decisive defeat, which convinced the Persian king Xerxes that there was no hope of a quick victory over the Greeks. He handed over the command of his army and returned to Persia.

The trireme's tactics

Ramming was the principal tactic used by the trireme. The ram was a metal-plated 'beak' that jutted from the trireme's reinforced bows. A manoeuvre that required particular skill from the *trierarch*, the trireme's commander, was to head straight for the enemy as if intending to inflict a head-on ramming and, just before impact, veer to left or right, shipping the oars on the side closest to the enemy and smashing his oars as the two ships grazed each other. Having disabled the enemy galley, which could now row only in circles, the victorious galley would come around and ram the crippled galley in the stern. The only way to escape this fate was for the crew of the damaged trireme to board the enemy vessel before it had withdrawn its ram.

The Athenian fleet After victory over the Persians at Salamis and at Mycale (479 BC), Athens became the dominating influence in the Delian League of Ionian states, which effectively became an Athenian empire. The foundation of its power was its navy, which controlled the Aegean Sea and secured the loyalty of Athens's allies while safeguarding trade routes and the grain shipments from the Black Sea that fed the growing population of Athens.

The navy provided employment for Athens's lower classes and in turn maintained and promoted Athenian democracy. In the subsequent Peloponnesian War (431–404 BC), naval battles, fought by triremes, remained a crucial factor in the balance of power between the rival states of Athens and Sparta. During the war, the Athenians had to build some 20 triremes each year to maintain a fleet of 300.

Later warships carried more crew. At the Battle of Ecnomus, fought off Sicily in 256 BC in the First Punic War between Carthage and the Republic of Rome, the Roman quinqueremes had crews of 300, and each carried 120 marines. How they were rowed remains uncertain. It is likely that no warships had ever had more than three banks of oars, and the large numbers were accommodated by doubling up on some of the oars.

The standard warship of the Roman republic was the quinquereme. The imperial fleet, however, reverted to the trireme. The Romans were never great sailors, and tried to turn sea battles into massive boarding operations with help of a huge boarding plank (*corvus*) with a large spike on the end of it which they employed to lock their ships on to enemy vessels. The use of the *corvus* could backfire, causing the ships employing it to turn turtle.

the condensed idea
For over 200 years, the trireme was the main warship in the Mediterranean

05 The Roman legion 500 BC–AD 162

The seeds of the Roman empire were sown in the Second Punic War (218–201 BC). Prior to this, Rome's influence extended no further than the Alps. But within a hundred years Rome's influence reached into Spain, Africa and the Hellenic east.

From 500 BC, the Romans adopted the phalanx formations favoured by their Etruscan neighbours. The phalanx, however, was not well suited to the hilly topography of central Italy, and in the fourth century BC the Romans turned to the more flexible manipular formation. An army of the Roman Middle Republic (second century BC), a legion, was some 5,000 men strong supplemented with 300 cavalry. Each year the two consuls of Rome (the highest magistrates of the republic) would raise two such legions.

The legion was divided into 30 maniples, ten each of heavily armed infantry, the *hastati*, *principes* and *triarii*. Each of the maniples was accompanied by 40 lightly armed skirmishers (*velites*). The maniples of *hastati* and *principes* comprised 120 men armed with a short, thrusting sword (*gladius*), a long oval shield (*scutum*) and two heavy javelins (*pila*). The *triarii* were similarly armed but carried a thrusting spear (*hasta*). The cavalry were organized into ten *turmae* and armed with spears and circular shield. At this point, the soldiers of the legion were required to be Roman citizens and property owners.

The maniples were the basic building blocks of the Roman legion, and it was the legion that was to dominate the known world for the next 700 years. It was the most significant development in military practice

timeline

218–201 BC	**107 BC**	**31 BC–AD 14**
Second Punic War	Gaius Marius elected consul for the first of seven times	Reign of Augustus

since the time of Alexander the Great. It became the instrument of
Rome's imperial expansion and survived, in radically changed form,
until the end of the empire in the fifth century AD, and continued to
exercise an influence over military organization well into the Middle
Ages and beyond.

Marius's reforms The manipular legion was tested almost to
destruction in the two wars Rome fought against the rival Mediterranean
power of Carthage (264–241 and 218–201 BC). A rising tide of pressure,
including a declining population, later transformed the legion from an
amateur militia of conscripted men serving for six years into a professional
long-service army of volunteers. This process, long in gestation, is attributed
to the reforms introduced by Gaius Marius (157–86 BC) who was
elected consul in 107 BC. It is possible, however, that Marius may
have simply rubber-stamped developments already in place.

Significantly, the prescribed property qualifications for service in
the legion were lowered in order to draw on the reservoir of *capite
censi*, citizens who owned no property and had previously been
excused military service. In turn this involved the Roman state in
equipping the new intake. Marius's second major reform replaced
the maniple sub-unit with the cohort. A legion now consisted
of 10 cohorts rather than 30 maniples. A new cohort consisted of one
maniple each of *hastati*, *principes* and *triarii*, together with *velites*, a total of
some 400 men. The result was a unit capable of independent action. The
six centurions (NCOs) of each cohort, commanding 60–70 men, retained
the old manipular terminology, as in *hastatus* and *princeps*. The most senior
centurion was the *primus pilus*, commanding the first century of the first
cohort, the most experienced soldier when the legion was in the field.

> **⁶His temper
> was fierce
> when he came
> to exercise
> authority.⁹**
>
> **Plutarch,** *Life of Marius*,
> AD *c.*125

The training programmes ascribed to Marius, which included running
with full kit, route marching and the carrying of one's own baggage, and
the Roman army's harsh discipline, were, in all probability, a return to
the standards of an earlier generation rather than a new departure.

AD 9	43	48	117–38	122	139–42
Three legions lost in Teutoburg Forest	Invasion of Britain	Revolt of the Iceni in Britain	Reign of Hadrian	Construction of Hadrian's Wall begins	Campaign in Britain leading to the construction of Antonine Wall

> **❝Setting out on the expedition, he [Marius] laboured to perfect his army as it went along, practising the men in all kinds of running and in long marches, and in compelling them to carry their own baggage and to prepare their own food.❞**
>
> Plutarch, *Life of Marius*, AD c.125

According to Pliny the Elder (writing in the later first century AD), Marius made the eagle (*aquila*) the principal standard of each legion, replacing other symbols such as wolves, bears, minotaurs and horses. The man who carried the eagle, the *aquilifer*, ranked almost as high as a centurion. The *aquilifer* was also in charge of the pay chest.

The emperor Augustus (r. 31 BC–AD 14) inherited from Julius Caesar a superbly disciplined, staffed and led army. The immediate task facing him was to retain Caesar's creation but on a peacetime footing. He created a standing army of 28 legions, each one consisting of approximately 6,000 men plus auxiliary troops. The auxiliaries might have been troops forcibly provided by defeated or overawed enemies, volunteered by friendly rulers or hired as mercenaries. They frequently supplied cavalry support for the legionary heavy infantry, or were light infantry, archers or slingers. The extra manpower was useful, but the Romans were careful to avoid an overly large auxiliary addition to their military establishment.

Marius's Mule

The shambling gait of the heavily burdened legionary in the years after Marius's reforms earned him the nickname 'Marius's Mule'. Legionaries were now supplied with standard equipment: *gladius, scutum, pila* (one heavy, one light) and a mail shirt. Full armour, including helmet, would have weighed about 30 kilograms (66 lb), the upper limit for modern servicemen. In addition, legionaries had to carry extra baggage in the form of entrenching equipment, cooking utensils, emergency rations and personal items, all of which were strapped to a forked pole.

Rome's frontiers The frontiers of the Roman empire became permanent as conquest ceased. In about AD 100 six legions were based on the eastern frontier and two were based in the Nile delta. A single legion controlled the rest of North Africa and another was based in Spain. The bulk of the legions were stationed in garrisons along the Rhine and Danube. There were four legions in Britain, the northernmost part of the empire.

In Britain the frontier was initially marked by a barrier stretching 75 miles (120 km): Hadrian's Wall. The wall was some 5 metres (16 ft) high fronted with a broad berm and a ditch 8 metres (26 ft) wide and 3 metres (10 ft) deep. It was defended by 80 small mile castles 1,640 yards (1,500 m) apart and about 150 turrets, two of which were placed between each mile castle. Larger forts were built astride the wall about 7 miles (11 km) apart.

In AD 142, on the orders of the emperor Antoninus Pius (r. AD 138–61), construction began on the so-called Antonine Wall between the Firths of Forth and Clyde. The Antonine Wall, which took 12 years to build, was some 40 miles (64 km) long and fronted by a deep ditch (*vallum*). It was abandoned in 162 when the legions withdrew to Hadrian's Wall, although it was partially restored by the emperor Septimius Severus (r. 193–211).

> **❛Quinctilius Varus, give me back my legions!❜**
>
> **Augustus on hearing of the loss of three legions in the Teutoburg Forest, Germany (AD 9), from Suetonius, *The Lives of the Twelve Caesars***

In 1973 a fascinating insight into the lives of the legionaries policing the outer limits of the Roman empire was provided by the discovery of a cache of inscribed wooden tablets in a Roman fort at Vindolanda, a fort erected in northern England before the construction of Hadrian's Wall. The tablets record routine items of military discipline and supply, and personal messages exchanged between members of the Vindolanda garrison and their families. Poignantly, one includes an invitation to a birthday party in about AD 100. The scant references to the native Britons refer to them slightingly as Brittunculi. One of the tablets confirms that legionaries wore underpants (*subligaria*).

the condensed idea
For 700 years the legion *was* the Roman army

06 The legions in the field

*c.*203 BC–AD 113

The Jewish historian Josephus, who sided with the Romans during the Jewish revolt of AD 66–70, left a detailed description of the Roman army on the march. As a foreigner, he noted many military details familiar to Romans and thus not considered worthy of explanation. Josephus's account, *The Jewish Wars, c.*AD 75, gives us an insight into the extreme conservatism of the Roman military method.

Spread out at the head of the army were units of light-armed infantry and cavalry acting as scouts and on the alert for any sign of ambush. The vanguard of the main column consisted of a legion and a cavalry force. Every day the legions would draw lots as to which one would form the vanguard. Next came the camp surveyors, composed of ten men from each century (i.e. one man from each of the century's ten tents). In addition to their kit, they carried the tools for marking out the camp.

Behind the surveyors were the pioneer corps, tasked with clearing or bridging any obstacle in the legion's path. They were followed by the baggage of the legion's commander and that of his staff with a strong mounted escort. Then came the commander accompanied by his bodyguard, which was drawn from the ranks of the auxiliary cavalry and infantry. Next in the line of march were 120 legionary cavalry, followed by the mules carrying dismantled siege engines, towers, rams and catapults.

timeline

*c.*203–*c.*120 BC	59 BC	58–49 BC	55 BC
Polybius writes detailed history of Roman army	Julius Caesar elected consul	Caesar in Gaul	Caesar builds bridge over Rhine near Coblenz

The legion's senior officers came next: legates, tribunes and auxiliary prefects escorted by crack troops. Then came the legions, each marching behind the *aquilifer* and other standard bearers. On Trajan's Column, completed in AD 113 and commemorating Rome's wars against the Dacians, the standard bearers are preceded by trumpeters and horn blowers. Behind the standard bearers and trumpeters, came the men of the legions, marching six abreast on Roman roads and four in enemy territory, and kept in formation by their centurions. Each legion was followed by its own baggage train, as many as 2,000 mules per legion. Behind the legions were the auxiliary troops led by their own standard bearers.

The last element on the march was the rearguard – light and heavy infantry and auxiliary cavalry. Trailing close behind were the camp followers including common-law wives, prostitutes, slave dealers hoping to buy prisoners of war and a motley collection of merchants. A consular army of two legions, plus its allied contingents and cavalry, would have stretched back for 12 miles (20 km). However, if the column was marching through enemy territory or through open country, the army marched in battle order of three parallel columns that occupied some 4.5 miles (7 km). The army could cover 19 miles (30 km) a day and forced marches of 31 miles (50 km) were routinely achieved.

The marching camp Towards the end of the march a tribune and the surveying units were despatched ahead to select a site for the camp. If contact had already been made with the enemy it was important to choose

Crossing rivers

The standard Roman river crossing was achieved by ramming wooden piles into the river bed in pairs about 12 metres (40 ft) apart. They were then joined by crossbeams to form a series of trestles supporting a roadway. In 55 BC Julius Caesar built a bridge like this over the Rhine at Coblenz where the river is about 500 metres (1,640 ft) wide and 8 metres (26 ft) deep. The emperor Trajan built a more ambitious bridge over the Danube in AD 105. It was 1,135 metres (3,724 ft) long and consisted of 20 stone piers 50 metres (164 ft) high and 20 metres (66 ft) wide supporting a wooden superstructure. For a thousand years, it was the longest bridge in the world.

49 BC	44 BC	AD 74	c.75	105	113
Caesar crosses Rubicon	Caesar assassinated on the Ides of March	Fall of Masada ends Jewish revolt	Josephus's account of the Roman army underlines its conservatism	Trajan builds longest bridge in the world	Trajan's Column dedicated

Life as a legionary

Trajan's Column shows legionaries marching bareheaded with their helmets strapped to their right shoulders and their shields (which in real life would have been hide-covered) on their left. Over the left shoulder each legionary carries a pole with a crossbar at the top, to which he has tied his kit and personal items – saws, baskets, pickaxes, chains, mess tins, cooking pots, buckets, leather bags for carrying clothes and a sack for his rations. Rations might have to last anything from 3 to 15 days, and when on campaign a soldier's basic diet was wheat biscuits, supplemented by bacon, cheese and sour wine – all preserved foods. In camp his diet would improve. Archaeologists have uncovered camp rubbish dumps containing the remains of beef, mutton, pork and other meats as well as shellfish, fruit and vegetables, and quantities of salt, the sine qua non of a legionary's diet.

a site some 2.5 miles (4 km) from hostile forces that was close to a secure water supply. Ideally, the site selected would be on rising, open ground, free of cover that might be exploited by the enemy. A two-legion camp occupied an area some 700 square metres (7,535 sq ft) and would be carefully marked out by the surveying units, so that when the army arrived each unit would know where to leave its baggage while work proceeded on the defences.

A marching camp was usually surrounded by a deep ditch, the earth from which was used to build a rampart. If the camp was established close to the enemy, the cavalry, light-armed troops and half the heavy infantry were deployed in front of the ditch facing the enemy. With the baggage train secured behind the rampart, the rest of the army began to excavate the ditch and strengthen the rampart with sharpened stakes carried by the legionaries on the march.

When a marching camp was finished, it was cut down the middle by a thoroughfare, the *via principalis*, which ran in front of the consul's tent. In the camp, as in permanent legionary fortresses, the constituent units of the legion occupied the same allotted places in the camp's grid-like structure. The legionaries were housed in leather tents, eight to a tent.

Guards were mounted on the ramparts, at the stores depot and the staff officers' tents. At sunset, selected men from the infantry and cavalry were issued with the night's password inscribed on a wooden tablet (*tessera*). The password was passed on from unit to unit and the successive watches summoned by horn. The guard posts were checked throughout the night in a random fashion so that the sentries did not know when they would be paid a visit. Each man conducting the inspection would be accompanied by two or three colleagues who acted as witnesses. On being checked, the guard would present his *tessera*. If he was found asleep, he would not be disturbed and the *tessera* would be left with him to await his terrified awakening.

At dawn the guard patrols reported to the tribune and handed in the collected tablets. If a tablet was missing, the culprit on the respective watch would be identified and then forced to run the gauntlet, where he was either beaten or stoned. If he survived, he was expelled from the camp. A guard inspector who failed to make his rounds properly suffered the same punishment. Needless to say, night watches were scrupulously observed.

Dawn and dusk were a busy time for officers. The six tribunes were on duty in pairs. At dawn, while one tribune was receiving the guard duty reports, the other attended the commander's briefing and received the orders for the day. He then returned to his tent to brief the centurions and their subordinates. Cavalry patrols would then be despatched to reconnoitre the enemy's position. Their report would be considered at a council of war attended by the commander, officers, senators accompanying the legion at the commander's invitation, and senior centurions. If the commander decided to give battle, a red flag was run up outside his tent to alert the legionaries, who would stop the chores they had been assigned and assemble beneath the camp's ramparts.

the condensed idea
Roman field tactics were doggedly conservative and determinedly disciplined

07 Roman siegecraft
262 BC–AD 75

The siege is the set-piece that demonstrates the remorseless application of Roman method and technology to the demands posed in the ancient world by the extremes of military engineering.

We know little about Roman siege warfare before the third century BC, and the earliest siege for which we have any accurate details is the investment of Carthaginian Agrigentum (Agrigento) in Sicily during the First Punic War in 262 BC. In a system known as bicircumvallation, a twin line of fortifications, linking two camps, was built around the town, the inner line to confine the enemy to the town, and the outer to repel any relieving force. Between the two lines there was a broad thoroughfare up to several hundred metres wide, ensuring the rapid transfer of troops to any part of the bicircumvallation.

Forts and picket posts were positioned at intervals along the inner and outer rings. It was as important to hasten starvation within the beleaguered town as it was to prevent the intervention of a relief force. The Carthaginian relief force arrived and a double siege ensued before the defenders of Agrigentum gave battle and were defeated. Thereafter bicircumvallation became standard Roman siege practice, although the only surviving comprehensive description we have comes from Julius Caesar's siege of Alesia in central Gaul in 52 BC, which is extensively covered in his *Commentaries on the Gallic War*.

timeline
262 BC
Siege of Agrigentum

Siege of Alesia   Alesia (the modern town of Alise-Sainte-Reine, northwest of Dijon) was sited at the western end of a plateau between two rivers, which separated it from hills on either side, and was occupied by the Averni chieftain Vercingetorix, who had led a revolt against Rome. Caesar built inner and outer lines around Alesia, which were covered during their construction by 23 forts built on the forward slopes around the town. The inner line was fronted by a water-filled trench. Both the inner and outer lines were topped by a rampart and palisade with towers every 25 metres (82 ft).

To free the greater part of his army to forage and gather timber, Caesar seeded the ground in front of his inner line with dense thickets of booby traps, the ancient equivalent of mines. Trenches 1.5 metres (5 ft) deep bristled with sharpened branches and in front of them were eight rows of circular pits from which protruded pointed stakes, nicknamed 'lilies'.

Julius Caesar on the siege of Alesia

In front of them [the branch-filled pits] arranged in diagonal rows called quincunxes, pits three feet deep were dug, narrowing gradually towards the bottom; embedded into them were smoothed logs as thick as a man's thigh, with their top ends sharpened and charred, so that only four inches project above the ground. To keep these logs firmly and securely in position earth was thrown into the pits and stamped down hard to a depth of one foot, the rest of the pit being filled with twigs and brushwood to hide the trap . . .

Commentaries on the Gallic War, c.50–40 BC

There was one more line of booby traps ahead of the 'lilies': 30-centimetre (1-ft) long timbers fitted with iron hooks and sunk at random into the ground. These were known as 'goads'. When this was completed, the process was repeated on the outer line.

Attacks were made on the bicircumvallation from within and without Alesia but were poorly co-ordinated in spite of the Gauls' numerical superiority. Vercingetorix surrendered, was taken to Rome as a captive and imprisoned. In 46 BC he was paraded during Caesar's triumph and then executed.

Masada Masada, the palace complex created by Herod the Great (r. 37–4 BC) was the last stronghold of Jewish resistance at the end of the revolt against Rome (AD 66–70). It is perched on a column of rock that rises to 396 metres (1,300 ft), on the arid shores of the Dead Sea, and was seized by 1,000 members of the Jewish Sicarii sect early in the revolt.

Techniques of siege warfare

Roman engineering skill and dogged determination seldom failed in siege operations. An essential part of the Roman arsenal was the battering ram, a long iron-tipped beam suspended by ropes from a sturdy mobile housing known as a 'tortoise' (testudo). The men operating the testudo were protected by boards and layers of clay or hide mattressing. The Romans also used iron-, wicker- or hide-clad siege towers as platforms for missile attack by archers or artillery, often incorporating a battering ram at ground level. Each Roman legion had its own complement of artillery: arrow-shooting catapultae and stone-throwing ballistae. The most common catapulta was some 1.5 metres (5 ft) high and fired arrows about 60 centimetres (2 ft) long; stone-throwers stood about 4.5 metres (15 ft) high and could hurl missiles weighing 45 kilograms (100 lb).

The task of recapturing Masada was given to Flavius Silva, who was commanding the Roman legion X Fretensis. Silva duly surrounded the outcrop on which Masada perched with a thick wall fortified by towers at 30-metre (98-ft) intervals. His forces were dispersed around eight camps below Masada. However, Masada's huge water tanks and food stores meant that the Jewish occupiers within could not be starved into submission.

Silva was already under increasing pressure, as his own supplies of food and water had to be brought up. He decided to build a huge ramp up the west side of Masada, on top of which he would erect a siege tower. The Jewish historian Josephus recorded the details in *The Jewish Wars*. The ramp was constructed of earth and rubble held together by a timber framework. At the top a 30-metre (98-ft) iron-plated siege tower was built to command the wall and make ready for a ram assault into the palace complex. According to Josephus, the ramp was 114 metres (375 ft) high, but modern archaeologists have suggested that Silva had exploited a natural spur and that the ramp itself was only some 9.1 metres (30 ft) high.

Catapults housed within the tower cleared the battlements and a ram brought down the wall. However, the Romans then encountered a huge earth rampart, reinforced with timber, that the Jews had erected within the walls. Torches were summoned and the wooden cladding set on fire. As the Romans readied themselves for the final assault, the Jewish leader Eleazar urged his followers to commit mass suicide. The next day the Romans are said to have been met by a few survivors, women and children, although recent archaeology has failed to unearth any evidence of mass suicide.

the condensed idea
The Romans kept the besieged in and their rescuers out

08 Heavy cavalry and chain mail
378–1494

The characteristic figure in early and late medieval warfare is that of the knight, a heavily armed cavalry soldier who fought with lance and sword. From about 1100, the knight's armour became increasingly heavy and expensive, and by the end of the 15th century knights were covered from head to foot in steel plate. By then, however, their role on the battlefield was becoming less significant.

The supposed dominance of warfare by heavy cavalry can be seen as an arc rising and falling over some 1,100 years from the Battle of Adrianople in AD 378 to the French invasion of Italy in 1494. The Battle of Adrianople has often been cited as a victory of cavalry over infantry and a revolution in warfare. The truth is more complicated. The battle, fought on 9 August 378, was the 'Black Day of the Roman Army'. It was the result of the failure of the Eastern Roman Emperor Valens to contain the expansion of the Goths, an East Germanic tribe of Scandinavian origin, who had appeared on Rome's Lower Danube frontier in the third century. In the battle, some of the Roman cavalry units launched a premature attack on the Goths' wagon circle, were checked and thrown back. The Gothic cavalry, which had been out foraging, then fell on the exposed Roman infantry, scattering the rest of the Roman cavalry and pinning their infantry against the wagons. The battle descended into a bloody mêlée before the Romans broke and fled. Valens and two-thirds of his army were killed.

timeline

378	455	c.700	732
Battle of Adrianople, the 'Black Day of the Roman Army'	Collapse of the Roman empire in the West	Adoption of the stirrup in northern Europe	Battle of Tours

The square at Tours Another turning point in the rise of heavy cavalry has been placed some 400 years later, in the eighth century, when the Frankish leader Charles Martel defeated an Umayyad (Muslim) army at the Battle of Tours (732). Martel drew his infantry army into a square on high ground, anticipating Wellington's tactics at Waterloo (1815). In spite of repeated attacks by the Umayyad heavy cavalry, Martel's infantry square, bristling with spears, remained unbroken. The wall of infantry presented an obstacle against which the Umayyad horse pulled up short, as did Napoleon's cavalry at Waterloo. Having emerged victorious, Martel nevertheless decided to build up his own cavalry arm.

'Rigid as a wall . . . like a belt of ice frozen solidly together.'

A contemporary description of Martel's infantry square at Tours

Cavalry The one quality indisputably lent by the horseman to medieval armies was that of mobility. In an era where raiding rather than pitched battles was the most important element in campaigning, the horseman's ability to undertake rapid long-range movements in reconnaissance and punitive roles was invaluable.

Charlemagne (747–814), Frankish king and Emperor of the West, deployed a formidable heavy cavalry arm. It is nevertheless significant that in nearly 50 years of campaigning he fought only two pitched battles, both in 783. The Frankish cavalry were well disciplined, their usual tactic being a close-order charge, and they were prepared, on occasion, to dismount to fight. This discipline was maintained by the 'men of iron' in the heavy cavalry of the Saxon duke Henry the Fowler (876–936).

The stirrup

The introduction of the stirrup into northern Europe in the eighth century was a significant step in the development of heavy cavalry. It had long been in use in the Byzantine and Muslim worlds and was used by the Umayyad cavalry at Tours. It has often been argued that the arrival of the stirrup enabled mounted warriors to use the couched lance – a lance held rigidly under the armpit. Combined with the weight of horse and armour, this enabled the knight to crash through any infantry obstacle in his path by sheer force of impact. However, there is no evidence that this method of fighting was a feature of warfare in the years immediately following the introduction of the stirrup.

772	773–4	791	791–6	800	810
Charlemagne begins conquest of Saxony	Charlemagne conquers Lombardy	Charlemagne puts down Saxon revolt	Charlemagne campaigns against the Avars in modern Hungary and Austria	Charlemagne crowned Holy Roman Emperor. Institutes military reforms	Charlemagne repels Danish invasion in his last campaign

The couching of the lance (see box, page 33) can be seen in the Bayeux Tapestry (c.1080), which also provides the only medieval illustrated instance of cavalry charging infantry. It shows that repeated charges by the Norman cavalry in the Battle of Hastings (1066) were, for most of the battle, unable to break the Saxon shield wall. It was only in the final stage of the battle, when the English line had broken, that the Norman knights are shown taking a toll on the dispersed Saxon infantry.

Chain mail Around 800, Charlemagne systematized the equipment of his army. Infantrymen were to carry spear, shield and bow. Cavalry were armed with lance, shield, bow and long sword. The armoured knights of the Carolingian cavalry, the spearhead of the Frankish army, included in their equipment helmets, metal leg guards and mail shirts. These horsemen were the 'big ticket' component of Charlemagne's military expenditure. Between them, the cost of the war horse and the mail might be the equivalent of 30 cows. Thus the essentials of mobile warfare were necessarily limited to the wealthiest of Charlemagne's free men and royal vassals, and the companions to whom they supplied this equipment. Mail from the fallen was frequently looted and used by its new owner or sold on.

Mail had been around since about 300 BC, when it was invented by the Celts. It was adopted by the Romans and eventually became a feature of warfare worldwide, from North Africa to Japan. In the Dark Ages, mail was referred to as 'ring maille', meaning a mesh or a net. The term we use today, chain mail, is a Victorian invention of the Gothic revival. The mail itself is the armour material, not the garment made from it.

> ❛[Charlemagne] was heavily built, sturdy and of considerable stature, although not exceptionally so, as his height was seven times the length of his own foot.❜
>
> Charlemagne's biographer Erhard, *Vita Karoli Magni*

After the collapse of the western Roman empire in 455, the infrastructure needed to fashion plate armour was lost and it was replaced by mail armour. In Europe the method of manufacture had changed little since Celtic times. The rings composing a piece of mail were riveted closed to minimize the risk of their splitting open when they were hit by an arrow or received a thrusting attack from sword or spear. Until the 14th century, mail was made of alternate rows of riveted and solid rings of wrought iron. The German chronicler Thietmar of Merseburg (975–1018) noted that the Saxon king Aethelred II (r. 975–1016) had 24,000 coats of mail stored in London.

The limits of mail

Mail was an effective defence against slashing blows with an edged weapon and penetration by thrusting and piercing weapons. Nevertheless, a sword blow striking at an angle exactly perpendicular to the surface could slice through the chain-mail links. When the mail was not riveted, a well-placed thrust from a spear or thin sword might strike home. Nor was chain mail proof against a blow from a poleaxe or halberd – any blow might cause heavy bruising or fractures. Mail was not proof against head traumas caused by maces and war-hammers, prompting warriors to wear separate rigid helms over the mail coifs. Medieval surgeons were able to set and care for bone fractures, although their ignorance of hygiene meant that cuts were a more serious problem as the risk of infection was serious.

The Norman hauberk, a chain-mail tunic, required a substantial cloth shirt to be worn underneath it to prevent the metal chafing the skin, and would probably have had a surcoat over it to keep the iron dry in bad weather and also to carry the wearer's blazon or coat of arms. In front, the tunic would have been divided to allow the wearer to ride a horse whilst ensuring that he had some protection for his thighs. The latter would have been supplemented by mail leggings kept in place by a waist belt.

By the 14th century, plate armour was supplementing mail. In time it replaced it, providing increased protection against crossbow bolts, bludgeoning weapons and lance thrusts. However, during the 14th and 15th centuries, disciplined foot soldiers equipped with longbow and halberd were proving a match for the mounted knight.

the condensed idea
Chain mail secured the supremacy of the mounted warrior

09 Viking longship 785–1429

The Vikings lived in what are now the modern Scandinavian nations of Denmark, Norway and Sweden, and were principally farmers, shipbuilders and sailors. Agriculture in Scandinavia was restricted by topography – mountains in Norway, forests in Sweden, sandy soil in Denmark – and the Vikings turned to raiding in northwest Europe, Russia and the Mediterranean.

The Vikings from Sweden tended to look east into Russia while those from Denmark and Norway sailed west to establish colonies in England and France. The size of the 'Great Danish Army', which in the ninth century conquered and settled three of the four Anglo-Saxon kingdoms, has long been the subject of scholarly speculation, but it probably numbered no more than a few thousand and was a coalition of the small personal war bands that regularly conducted hit-and-run raids on the English coastline.

Viking warfare Until the end of the 11th century, Vikings fought principally on foot, dispersing after campaigns to resume their lives as farmers and shipbuilders, or joining other war-bands. The Anglo-Saxon Chronicle (871) mentions that while campaigning in England the Vikings sometimes over-wintered in specially built camps. This is evidenced by the many 10th-century ring forts found in Scandinavia, but only one English example has been found, in Repton, Derbyshire, where the Great Army spent the winter of 873–4.

timeline

785	839	865	866	873–4	948	954
Vikings destroy the abbey on Lindisfarne	Viking emissaries reach Byzantium	Great Danish Army arrives in England	Vikings take York (Jorvik)	Great Danish Army winters in Repton, Derbyshire	Eric Bloodaxe becomes king of York and claims all Northumbria	Bloodaxe murdered

The Vikings' principal weapons were the spear, sword and long-handled battleaxe. They were status symbols, and surviving examples are often exquisitely decorated. Early sword blades were pattern-welded, a technique in which strips of wrought iron and mild steel were twisted and forged together, with the addition of a hardened edge.

The Vikings carried circular shields made of wooden boards, with a central hole for an iron hand-grip that was riveted to the back of the board. Some Vikings also wore *byrnies* – mail armour tunics reaching below the waist. They were very expensive items and confined to the war-band leaders, as were helmets (the horned helmet of legend is just that: a myth). Most Vikings had to make do with caps made of animal hide.

The Vikings did not fight in regular formations, and battle tactics were rudimentary. Loyalty to the war-band leader provided cohesion. The Vikings used the 'shield wall' (see chapter 10) tactic favoured by the Anglo-Saxons, and battle began by throwing a spear over the enemy line, to dedicate it to Odin, closely followed by a shower of missiles.

Berserkers

The famous and feared Viking berserkers were dedicated to the cult of Odin, the god of war, and derived their name from the term *bare-sark* (bare of shirt). Swathed in bearskins but without armour, they fought in bands of about a dozen. These elite troops went into battle in a frenzy induced by alcohol or hallucinogenic mushrooms, and in Hrólf's saga are described thus:

On these giants fell sometimes such a fury that they could not control themselves, but killed men or cattle, whatever came in their way . . .

In the *Ynglinga Saga*, the poet Snorri Sturluson wrote:

His [Odin's] men rushed forward without armour, were as mad as dogs or wolves, bit their shields, and were strong as bears or wild oxen, and killed people at a blow, but neither fire nor iron told upon them. This was called Berserkergang.

The longship The longship, the most beautiful troop transport ever built, was the symbol of Viking naval power from the 9th to the 11th centuries. It represented the culmination of a tradition of Scandinavian boat-building that stretched back to the Stone Age.

991	998	c.1000	c.1042	10th–14th century	1429
Battle of Maldon between English and Viking raiders	Olaf Tryggvason orders the building of the *Long Serpent*	Short-lived Viking settlement in Newfoundland	Building of the *Sea Stallion* longship near Dublin	Vikings are recruited into the Byzantine emperor's Varangian Guard. Christianity takes root in Denmark and Norway	Last levy of Viking warships

> ❝I'll ask of the beserks,
>   you tasters of blood,
> Those intrepid heroes,
>   how are they treated,
> Those who wade out
>   into battle?
> Wolf-skinned they are
>   called. In battle
> They wear bloody shields.
> Red with blood are their
>   spears when they
>   come to fight.
> They form a closed group.
> The prince in his wisdom
>   puts trust in such men
> Who hack through enemy
>   shields.❞

A ninth-century saga describing the beserkers of King Harald

There were several different types of longship used in warfare, the smallest being the *snekkja* ('thin and projecting'), some 17 metres (56 ft) long and 2.5 metres (8.2 ft) wide, which was crewed by 41 men (40 rowers and one helmsman). William the Conqueror is said to have used some 600 in the invasion of England in 1066. Among the largest longships discovered by archaeologists is the *skei* ('that which cuts through water'), which was just under 30 metres (98 ft) long with a crew of up to 80. There were even bigger longships – that of the Norwegian king Olaf Tryggvason (r. 960–1000), the Christian hammer of Norway's pagans, was nearly 46 metres (150 ft) long. They all have one thing in common: a marriage of design, structure and material to create the perfect raiding machine, a rapier of a warship with inherent stability in a seaway and a shallow draught that enabled it to land on any beach and sail up waterways in Europe.

Longships were built without written diagrams or design patterns. The shipbuilder simply envisaged the finished boat before work began. The majority of longships were clinker built, with each hull plank overlapping the next. The hull was waterproofed with moss drenched in tar. After tarring, newly built longships were left in a boathouse over winter to enable the tar to dry. Wooden disks were fitted into the oar holes to prevent the longboat flooding.

Swedish gravestones depict longships with sails from about 700, although the earliest archaeological evidence dates from a ship buried in 835. The sails were made of wool and stiffened with strips of leather to help them keep their shape when wet. The arrival of sails opened a new era of shipbuilding – keels became deeper, hulls broader and sides higher. Oars were used when approaching a coastline or on a river. The oarsmen sat on sea chests containing their personal possessions. In favourable circumstances, longships could reach speeds of up to 11 knots.

Longship battles

Battles at sea were rare and invariably fought close to the shore. Ships were roped together in lines to face the enemy fleet and showers of spears and arrows would have been exchanged before the adversaries fell to hand-to-hand fighting as they attempted to board each other's ships from their prows. The aim was to capture rather than destroy the enemy ship, as it represented a huge investment in time, resources and labour.

The fearsome animals' heads on prow and stern were placed in position only when the longship was nearing land, thus avoiding damage in a heavy sea. Depictions of longships at sea with their sides lined with shields are anachronistic – shields were too valuable to be lost overboard. They were steered by a single oar mounted on the starboard side.

Viking navigation depended on keen observation of the sun, sea and wind direction. Historians have speculated that Vikings used a primitive astrolabe and made use of the stars to plot their course. It has also been suggested that the navigators used the 'sun stones' that are mentioned in some of the sagas. The stones might have been natural crystals of cordierite, which in Norway was nicknamed 'the Viking's compass' and which changes colour when exposed to sunlight, enabling the navigator to determine the sun's azimuth, even on an overcast and foggy day.

Time ran out for the longship with the development in the 12th and 13th centuries of the higher-boarded Hanseatic cog, the ancestor of the next generation of sailing ships. The longboat, designed for raiding, could not compete in a world of fortified port cities and developed naval warfare. The last levy of Viking warships was raised in 1429 and defeated by seven cogs.

the condensed idea
The longship was a triumph of form and function

10 The shield wall
577–1087

The Anglo-Saxons were descended from the Germanic tribes, who from the fourth century had arrived in England and carved out a patchwork of kingdoms of varying sizes, much as they had done in their European homeland. Their tactic of standing shoulder to shoulder holding up their shields was their principal defensive ploy.

From the sixth century, war had become endemic as rival warlords (*dryhtens*) strove to protect their own people from the depredations of neighbours and led them on armed expeditions (*fyrds*) of plunder and conquest. Peace was simply the aftermath of one war and the prelude to another. The system was based on a web of reciprocity in which the giving of gifts by the warlord (arms and armour and later land) was repaid by the counter-gift of military service.

Anglo-Saxon armies

Anglo-Saxon armies of this period were often very small. King Ine of Wessex's (r. 688–726) law code states that 'we use the term "thieves" if the number of men does not exceed seven, "band of marauders" [a war band] for a number between seven and thirty-five. Anything beyond this is an "army" . . .'

Alfred the Great By the time Alfred the Great succeeded to the throne of Wessex in 871, the military environment was undergoing a period of rapid change. The Kingdom of England was forged in the furnace of Viking invasions. The Anglo-Saxon Chronicle of 871 gives a clear picture of the military system Alfred inherited. There was a national host

timeline

c.520	793	865	871	871
Anglo-Saxons establish settlements in eastern and southern England	Vikings sack Lindisfarne	Viking Great Army lands in England	King Alfred fights eight battles with the Vikings	Anglo-Saxon Chronicle appears

(*folc*, led by the king), the shire forces led by individual noblemen and the war bands of individual *thegns* (noblemen). Each of these territorial units was a self-contained army.

In May 878, Alfred defeated Guthrum's Danish army at the Battle of Ethandun in the West Country and thereafter introduced a thoroughgoing reform of the Saxon military system. He created a system of fortified and garrisoned *burhs* (boroughs) throughout his realm and reorganized the *fyrd*, transforming it from a sporadic levy of the king's men and their retinues into a powerful standing army. It was divided into two components and, as the Anglo-Saxon Chronicle comments, '. . . always half of its men were at home, half on service, apart from the men who guarded the boroughs.'

The *fyrd* was still composed of noblemen and their less well-born followers, but the higher-ranking *fyrdman* was now a member of a semi-professional warrior class expected to face a well-equipped and professional enemy. Alfred's reforms involved huge numbers of men – it is estimated that the garrisoning of the *burhs* alone involved some 30,000 men, and this at a time when the population of England was about a million. Alfred's genius ensured that 20 years after his death the territory seized by the Danes in the West Country had been retaken by the West Saxon kings and their Mercian allies. By the middle of the 10th century, the last Danish king had been driven out of England.

The shield wall at Hastings In 1066 King Harold Godwinson, the Saxon king of England who had been crowned in January, faced war on two fronts. On 25 September he defeated an invading army led by his brother Tostig and the Norwegian king Harald Hardrada at the Battle of Stamford Bridge in the East Riding of Yorkshire. Godwinson then had to turn on his heels and march south to confront another claimant to his throne, Duke William of Normandy, who had landed with his army at Pevensey on 27/28 September. William pushed inland to Hastings, where he was met by Harold on the morning of 14 October.

1066	**1066**	**1066**	**1066**
JANUARY Harold Godwinson crowned king of England	**25 SEPTEMBER** Battle of Stamford Bridge	**27 SEPTEMBER** William of Normandy lands at Pevensey	**14 OCTOBER** Battle of Hastings

> **❝He truly reigned over England; and by his capacity so thoroughly surveyed it, that there was not a hide of land in England that he wist not who had it, or what it was worth and afterwards set it down in his book.❞**
>
> The Anglo-Saxon Chronicle on the Domesday Book

The Saxon army customarily fought on foot behind its shield wall. The shield wall was a tactic of ancient origin that had been used by the Greeks from the seventh century BC and later by the Romans. The legionaries called this formation a *testudo* (tortoise), in which the front row formed a vertical shield wall while those behind them held their shields over their heads, presenting an impenetrable barrier to missile weapons.

In northern Europe in the early Middle Ages, the shield wall remained a familiar defensive battle tactic, particularly when deploying semi-professional troops. The weakness of the tactic was that once breached or dispersed, the defending troops became vulnerable to attack by cavalry. Saxon shields were round and made of lime wood, making them light in the hand. Lime wood also had the advantage of being very durable and hard to split. The most common shields had a diameter of about 92 centimetres (36 in).

At Hastings, Harold chose a superb defensive position on a sharp ridge, Caldbec Hill, with well-defended flanks. If William was to win England, he had to attack. The battle began at about 9 a.m. Two lines of Norman infantry failed to break the English line before the Norman cavalry was ordered to charge uphill at the Saxon army. The Saxon infantry were drawn up in a dense line bristling with spears, ten men deep in places. The Norman cavalry were forced to ride shield side facing the wall, while they threw their javelins into the seething mass of Saxon warriors as they passed from left to right along their line. They then had to ride to the bottom of the hill to re-arm with more javelins.

Feigned retreat At this point a rumour spread in the Norman army that William was dead. The left flank fell back, threatening a rout. In the crisis of the battle William rallied his men and, crucially, changed his tactics. The Saxons, who were exhausted after the cavalry onslaught,

Bayeux Tapestry

The Bayeux Tapestry, an embroidered cloth almost 230 ft (70 m) long, records in strip cartoon fashion the events leading up to the Norman conquest of England which culminated in the Battle of Hastings, providing a unique wealth of material on the military practice of the day. It shows the arrival of Halley's Comet (April 1066), a bad omen for Harold, a Norman motte-and-bailey castle, the Saxon shield wall at Hastings and the Norman horse. Two fallen knights are named as Leofwine and Gyrth, Harold's brothers. The muscular Christian Bishop Odo wields his mace and rallies the Normans at a critical point in the battle. To reassure his knights that he is alive and well, William raises his helmet and shows his face. It is not possible to pinpoint exactly the fate of King Harold as his name appears above a number of knights. The arrow in the eye of one victim, over which appears the legend Harold Rex, is a later addition stitched in during repair. In the final scene we see unarmed Saxon troops quitting the field.

were lured into abandoning the shield wall by a feigned retreat. Now they were vulnerable, and Norman cavalry took their toll. Towards the end of the day King Harold, standing in the centre of the line with his 3,000-strong housecarl bodyguard, was struck in the face by an arrow and then cut down by a party of Norman knights. The housecarls fought to the last man but the day, and the crown of England, went to William of Normandy. It was four more years before Saxon resistance was finally quelled. Thereafter, William ruled a sullen and rebellious people with an iron hand.

the condensed idea
William the Conqueror
outmanoevred the shield wall

11 The castle

992–1487

In the years between 1000 and 1400, fortification, expressed in the form of the castle, was central to the conduct of war. After the death of the Emperor Charlemagne in 814, a number of factors, including the attacks of the Vikings, Muslims and Magyars and the decline of central, monarchical authority, meant that power in western Christian Europe gravitated to the local level. Any lord with a castle and following of knights was a force to be reckoned with and a 'player' to be wooed by princes.

Castle warfare often proved to be more important than the pitched battle. The absence of castles in Anglo-Saxon England eased the task of the Normans after the Battle of Hastings (1066). The Normans favoured 'motte-and-bailey' castles, which could be built quickly of timber and earth. The Bayeux Tapestry shows one such castle, built in a matter of days before the Battle of Hastings. The motte-and-bailey consisted of a mound (motte) topped with a wooden tower and an attached defended enclosure (bailey), which contained a chapel, storehouse and living quarters for the inhabitants.

Stone castles Stone-built castles, like the tower at Langeais, built by Foulques Nerra of Anjou in 992 in the Loire region of France, took much longer to construct, and it was not until the 12th century that in England the motte-and bailey was replaced by the stone castle. The White Tower in London, a massive statement in stone of Norman domination, was completed in 1100. Castle Rising in Norfolk, completed in 1138, is a fine example of a tower keep, with each floor reserved for a different function.

timeline

992	1031	1066	1099	1100
Building of the stone tower at Langeais	Building of Krak des Chevaliers begins	Normans build a motte-and-bailey castle before the Battle of Hastings	Krak des Chevaliers is taken by Raymond of Toulouse	White Tower in London is completed

Fortification now became more complex and led to the emergence of the concentric castle, essentially one castle nestled inside another, creating an inner and outer ward. Harlech Castle in Wales, perched on a crag above the estuary of the River Dwyryd and built between 1283 and 1290 by Edward I as part of his conquest of Wales, is a good example of the concentric castle.

Its outer walls were much lower and thinner than the colossal inner walls, with no towers to defend them beyond a small gatehouse. However, the square inner ward has a large round tower in each corner; the main gatehouse, which once overlooked the sea, is flanked by two massive towers and is defended by a series of doors, portcullises and murder-holes. The last were apertures in the gateway roof through which arrows could be aimed or boiling oil, quicklime or scalding water poured on attackers. Murder holes were also built in machicolations, projecting parapets hanging balcony-like over the castle walls.

Resupply of Harlech Castle by sea, which was dominated by English ships, was secured by a fortified stairway that hugs the rock and runs down almost 60 metres (200 ft) to the foot of the cliffs. In the Wars of the Roses (1455–87), Harlech was a Lancastrian stronghold that withstood a seven-year siege thanks to resupply by the sea.

The garrison at Harlech

Garrisoning a castle was an expensive business, and in times of peace castles were often held by a skeleton garrison. An inventory for Harlech Castle from 1404 records that the garrison had just three shields, eight helmets, six lances, ten pairs of gloves and four guns. In 1404 when the castle was seized by the Welsh prince Owain Glyndwr, the garrison had been reduced by starvation and sickness to just 21 men.

1150	1271	1283–90	1404	1455–87
Krak des Chevaliers becomes headquarters of the Knights Hospitallers	Krak des Chevaliers is taken by Sultan Baibars	Building of Harlech Castle	Harlech Castle captured by Owain Glyndwr	Harlech is a Lancastrian stronghold in the Wars of the Roses

Krak des Chevaliers Before the age of gunpowder artillery, castles functioned as bases for supplies, refuges in the event of a military defeat and launching pads for raids and expeditions. The building of a castle in, or on the borders of, enemy territory was a statement of hostile intent. Furthermore, the castle's garrison could threaten lines of communication. It ceased to become a threat only when it was taken and either razed or used against the enemy.

> **❛ . . . perhaps the best preserved and most wholly admirable castle in the world.❜**
>
> **T.E. Lawrence on Krak des Chevaliers, 1935**

Krak des Chevaliers in Syria, some 30 miles (48 km) west of the city of Homs, was built as a magnificent Crusader statement of intent and is one of the great medieval concentric castles. Squatting atop a hill some 659 metres (2,126 ft) high, it sat on the only route from Antioch to Beirut on the Mediterranean Sea and was a key part of the network of castles defending the borders of the old Crusader states. From Krak des Chevaliers, the garrison's Hospitaller knights could control the fishing industry on Lake Homs to the east and keep an eye out for Islamic armies concentrating in Syria.

The building of Krak des Chevaliers began in 1031 on the orders of the emir of Aleppo. It was captured by Raymond of Toulouse in 1099 during

Baibars (1223–77)

Baibars, sultan of Egypt from 1260 to 1277, was a product of the Mameluke system, a slave-soldier in the Bari regiment. He first achieved prominence for his role in the Battle of Ayn Jalut, fought in Syria in 1260. Afterwards he had Sultan Qutuz murdered and seized power. As a soldier-statesman he extended Mameluke power, campaigning in Frankish Syria and taking Caesarea, Haifa and Arsuf. In 1266 he captured the castle of Safad and in the following year he seized the port of Jaffa. In 1270, he dealt with the Crusaders led by Prince Edward of England by negotiation but went on to the offensive in 1271, taking Krak des Chevaliers and Safitha castles. In 1275 he came up against the Mongols in Anatolia and defeated them. Two years later he defeated them again. Baibars was celebrated for the excellence of his intelligence system and the secrecy with which he surrounded the conduct of his own affairs.

the First Crusade and then abandoned before being reoccupied by Tancred, prince of Galilee, in 1110. The headquarters of the Knights Hospitallers in the Crusades between 1150 and 1250, the castle was hugely expanded to house a garrison of 2,000 men, which included some 60 Hospitaller knights. Its two vast vaulted stables were capable of housing up to 1,000 horses.

Concentric castle The Hospitallers turned the Krak into a concentric castle by adding an outer wall and seven guard towers. Between the inner and outer wall on the southern side there is a large open cistern fed by an aqueduct from outside the castle. The covered entrance to the castle through the inner eastern wall makes two U-turns, exposing attackers to archers raining missiles down from hidden arrow-loops and from above. The inner walls of the castle are up to 30 metres (100 ft) thick on the vulnerable southern side, reinforced with a sloping talus at the base and overlooked by seven guard towers some 9 metres (30 ft) in diameter.

In April 1271 the Krak was captured by the Mameluke sultan Baibars, whose siege train included heavy trebuchets and mangonels (see chapter 12). However, subterfuge proved his most important weapon. Baibars was a past master in the world of military dirty tricks, and he gained access to Krak des Chevaliers by presenting a forged letter from the Crusader commander in Tripoli, ordering Krak's defenders to surrender the castle. Having secured the building, Baibars repaired the fortifications, added a tower on the southern wall, converted the Hospitaller chapel to a mosque and used it as a base against Tripoli.

> ❝The third bashuriya (barbican) was taken by the miners of Malik Sa'id . . . Then the troops stormed their way into the castle, massacred the Hospitallers, took prisoner the mountaineers, but let the villagers go, to keep up cultivation in the country.❞
>
> Contemporary Arab chronicler of the siege of the Krak

the condensed idea
Seemingly impregnable, easily taken

12 Medieval siege engines 1047–1521

The strength of medieval fortifications, and their importance in warfare, required careful attention to be paid to the art and science of reducing them. Initially the advantage lay with the defenders. In 1047 William, duke of Normandy (later William I of England), defeated an alliance of rival nobles at the Battle of Val-ès-Dunes before bottling up one of them, Gui of Burgundy, in the castle of Brionne, situated in a highly defensible position in the middle of a river. William laid siege to the castle but it took three years to force its surrender.

Twenty years later, in 1067, as William I, he took less time over the city of Exeter, which after the Battle of Hastings (1066) had become a centre of Anglo-Saxon resistance. At the city's east gate he was confronted with the townspeople atop the walls making obscene gestures at him. William's engineers swiftly went to work, digging tunnels under the gate and wall, which partially collapsed within 18 days. The citizens escaped further punishment after the city's bishop and his clergy presented holy relics to William, who later charged the Sheriff of Devon to build a castle at Exeter. Its gatehouse was the earliest Norman structure in England.

Siege of Rochester Confronted with a castle, a besieger had a choice between going under or over the walls, or combining both options. Mines were chosen by King John when, in October 1216, Rochester Castle was seized by a force of knights loyal to rebellious barons. John personally supervised the subsequent operation in which five large siege engines

timeline

1067	1099	1124	1147	1188	1216	1249
William I takes Exeter	Siege of Jerusalem	Siege of Tyre	Siege of Lisbon	Siege of Ashyun	Siege of Rochester	Siege of Dametta

initially failed to make any impression on the castle's outer walls. When they were finally breached, and the defenders retreated into the keep, John resorted to mining.

Forty pigs were slaughtered and piled up by the wooden props supporting the tunnel dug beneath the keep. They were then set alight to collapse the mine, this bringing down the wall above it. One corner of the keep collapsed, but the garrison clung on until hunger forced the remaining defenders to surrender. John spared the survivors. Of the siege, the contemporary Barnwell chronicler observed: 'Our age has not known a siege so hard pressed nor so strongly resisted . . . Afterwards few cared to put their trust in castles.'

Usually an all-out assault on the walls of a city or castle was preceded by a bombardment from artillery. Known as mangonels (derived from the Greco-Latin word *manganon*, 'engine of war'), these catapult siege engines were designed to lob projectiles into the enemy positions. Mangonels could shoot rocks, flammable materials or, in an early form of biological warfare,

> ❝. . . send to us with all speed by day and night forty of the fattest pigs of the sort least good eating to bring fire beneath the tower.❞
>
> **Letter from King John to his chief justiciar, Hubert de Burgh, 25 November 1216**

The siege of Jerusalem

At the siege of Jerusalem in July 1099 the Genoese, led by Guglielmo Embriaco, broke up the transport ships that had brought them to the Holy Land to construct siege towers, which were then trundled up to the city's walls before his men broke in and forced a rapid surrender by the Muslim garrison. A contemporary chronicler recorded, 'When the pagans had been overcome, our men seized great numbers, both men and women, either killing them, or keeping them captive, as they wished.'

1304
Siege of Stirling Castle

1521
Cortés uses trebuchet (unsuccessfully) in the siege of Tenochtitlán

> **❝Our leaders also ordered all the Saracen dead to be cast outside because of the great stench, since the whole city was filled with their corpses, and so the living Saracens dragged the dead before the exits of the gates and arranged them in heaps, as if they were houses.❞**
>
> **Aftermath of the siege of Jerusalem**

decomposed bodies or the decaying carcasses of animals. By the 12th century, as the result of contact with the Arabs, Crusaders had developed an even more formidable weapon: the trebuchet. In the 13th century the trebuchet was the foremost siege weapon.

The trebuchet The trebuchet's catapult works by using the energy of a raised counterweight to hurl a projectile. The structure consisted of two A-frames securely fixed to a wooden base. Between the tips of the A-frames the throwing arm was pivoted so that approximately one-eighth of its length was in front of the pivot and the remainder behind. A heavy counterweight – a box filled with large stones – was hung on the short end of the throwing arm. Attached to the other end was a rope-and-pulley arrangement, which allowed the end of the throwing arm to be pulled down by a windlass, raising the counterweight into the air. Sometimes the end of the throwing arm was spoon-shaped, enabling it to contain the missile. More often the sling principle was used. The tip of the arm was shaped to release one end of the sling as the arm swung up to the vertical. The sling could hurl large missiles, including dead horses and corpses, for considerable distances inside the walls of besieged castles and towns.

The trebuchet at Warwick

Modern trebuchets built by enthusiasts have established some remarkable feats of throwing. For example, the 22-ton trebuchet at Warwick Castle, which is 18 metres (59 ft) high, has hurled 36-kilogram (80-lb) missiles over a distance of 100 yards (91 metres).

Pet names The counterweight trebuchet is first mentioned in the writings of the 12th-century Byzantine historian Niketas Choniates. In the siege of Tyre in 1124, the Crusaders employed 'great trebuchets', and by the 1130s the siege engine had entered the inventories of the Normans of Sicily. King Richard II of England and King Philip II of France used trebuchets in the siege of Acre (1189–91). Philip named the two trebuchets under his command 'God's Stone Thrower' and 'Bad Neighbour'. During the siege of Stirling Castle in 1304, Edward I ordered his engineers to make a giant trebuchet, which was dubbed 'Warwulf'. The rate of fire of these mighty machines varied: at the siege of Ashyun in 1188, a trebuchet hurled rocks weighing up to 1,500 kg (3,300 lb), while at the siege of Lisbon in 1147 two trebuchets achieved a rate of fire of a stone every 15 seconds. The trebuchet could also throw 'Greek fire', an incendiary weapon consisting principally of saltpetre (potassium nitrate) or crude oil (naptha).

The principal drawbacks of the trebuchet were its sheer size and its immobility. At the siege of Damietta in 1249, Louis IX of France was able to build a stockade for the entire Crusader camp from 24 captured Egyptian trebuchets. Trebuchets had to be assembled and disassembled on the spot, and all within range of the enemy's engines of war. With the arrival of gunpowder, the trebuchet rapidly lost its status as the destroyer of cities. One of the last recorded instances of its use was by the conquistador Hernán Cortés during the siege of the Aztec capital Tenochtitlán in 1521. It was an inglorious swansong. The trebuchet self-destructed as the first projectile was launched.

❛By the which engine [the Turks] threw on us the Greek Fire, which was the most horrible thing I ever saw in my life.❜

Jean de Joinville, *Histoire de Saint Louys*, completed 1309

the condensed idea
Before gunpowder, the catapult was the main ballistic weapon

13 The sword
*c.*1500 BC–AD 2012

In November 1943 the British prime minister Winston Churchill presented Joseph Stalin with the Sword of Stalingrad, a ceremonial long sword forged as a token of appreciation from the British people to the defenders of that Soviet city. At a critical moment in the Second World War, the Sword of Stalingrad took its place as an emblem of military honour.

The sword was developed in the Bronze Age, having evolved from the dagger. In the first bronze swords – dating from *c.*1500 BC – the hilt and blade were two separate pieces riveted together. This created a weapon that was effective when thrusting but tended to shatter if used too vigorously as a slashing weapon. Some 500 years later, the characteristic shape of the Bronze Age sword, in which the blade and hilt were forged in one piece, had emerged. The tang – that part of the blade extending into and usually through the grip to which it is attached – broadened as it met the blade, which narrowed and then gradually grew wider to about two-thirds of its length before it swept to a point. This produced a weapon useful for cutting and thrusting.

Celtic swordsmen A pattern was set that was followed by iron swords, while smiths began to experiment with differing shapes and forms. Curved blades found favour in the Middle East while Roman legionaries used a short, wide sword, the *gladius*, which could be worn on the right side and drawn with the right hand, an advantage in close combat.

timeline

c.1500 BC	4th century BC	3rd century BC	2nd century AD
The first Bronze Age swords	Celtic swordsmen make their mark	Romans adopt the *gladius*, derived from the Celtic sword	Introduction of the *spatha*, the sword of the late-Roman army

Pattern welding

One of the problems of sword-making is that the difficulty of forging a piece of iron hard enough to serve as a weapon often meant that the sword could snap in battle. This was solved in the second century AD by Frankish smiths, who developed a technique known as pattern welding. This involved layering hard and soft iron rods and then twisting and hammering them into a homogeneous mass. Hardened rods were then laid along the edges and hammer-welded to the mass to achieve a hard cutting edge. After heating and water cooling, the blade was left to further cool naturally before shaping and sharpening.

Celtic heavy infantry, doughty foes of the Romans in the fourth century BC, were formidable swordsmen. The historian Dionysius of Halicarnassus, writing in the first century BC, describes the Celts whirling their swords above their heads, slashing the air from side to side and then striking downwards at their opponents as if they were chopping wood. Just over a hundred years earlier, Polybius noted that the Romans were trained to take the first blow of the sword on the reinforced rim of the shield. Polybius claimed that the effect was often to bend the sword double like a *strigil* (a half-moon-shaped skin scraper), forcing the Celt to straighten his sword with his foot and allowing his Roman adversary to attack him.

Mythic swords In succeeding centuries the sword acquired a mythic quality, doubtless the result of the high expense of fashioning a first-class example. The Vikings ascribed magical properties to their swords, longer versions of the late-Roman *spatha* with long, wide double-edged crucible steel blades and a heavy pommel on the end of the handle. The steel was

7th century	13th century	17th century	19th century
Vikings use variant of the *spatha*	Longer, heavier swords appear to deal with armoured opponents	Introduction of the basket-hilted sword	Swords, in the form of curved sabres, are retained by cavalry

> ❝It was in the first charge I took the eagle from the enemy; he and I had a very hard fight for it. He thrust for my groin; I turned him off and cut him through the head; after which I was attacked by one of their lancers, who threw his lance at me, but missed the mark by my throwing it off with my sword by my right side; then I cut him from the chin upwards, which went through his teeth.❞
>
> **Sergeant Ewart,** Scots Greys, Waterloo, 1815

often imported from Afghanistan or Iran, and such a sword might cost as much as a dozen milk cows. The Vikings gave the swords their own pet names, such as Fotbitr ('Leg-Biter') or Gramr ('Fierce').

Development of the sword From the 13th century the growth in armour led to a change in the sword. A single-handed slash would bounce off the metal, and swords took on a more slender and pointed shape with which to seek vulnerable spots in the armour. Swords became longer, with an extended hilt to allow a two-handed grip. A longer, heavier sword stood a greater chance of inflicting damage on an armoured opponent, possibly unbalancing him and exposing him to another form of attack.

When armour began to fall into disuse in the 16th century and swordsmen's hands were no longer protected by a gauntlet, the hilt and its *quillons* (protective wings below the hilt) necessarily became more complex to protect the hand. The art of fencing with the rapier (a civilian weapon) accelerated the process, bringing the hilt round on itself in a semi-circle to form a knuckle guard, while the *quillons* were extended to protect the swordsman's fingers and entrap his opponent's blade.

By the 17th century, the basket-hilted sword had become popular. Fencers, for whom the thrust was the scoring stroke, favoured a 'cup hilt' to prevent a thrust striking the hand.

Firearms replaced the sword as an infantry weapon, although it was retained by the cavalry. In the 19th century the lance and sword remained cavalry weapons of choice; the cavalry sword changed from a straight blade to the curved sabre introduced by Hungarian hussars. In the 20th century the Dutch armed forces were equipped with cutlasses during colonial conflicts in the East Indies.

Men of the Nepalese Gurkha Regiment still carry the feared kukri, a machete-like cutting and slashing weapon. The origins of the kukri can be traced back to the 17th century. Made by Nepalese blacksmiths, a kukri is usually about 14 to 16 inches (35.5–41 cm) long with a steel blade and a wooden, bone or metal curved handle. Because of its compact size, less metal is used in the manufacture of the kukri than in a conventional sword. It can be used as a slashing and stabbing weapon. A man skilled in its use can disembowel a horse or, in battle, cut off an arm or a head. Nepal is Britain's oldest ally in Asia, diplomatic relations having been established in 1815, and since then the kukri has stood the test of time. Troops fighting the Gurkhas know full well that the kukri will be used against them in close combat, a certainty that induced dread in the minds of the Argentine conscripts facing the Gurkhas deployed to the South Atlantic during the Falklands War in 1982.

Today swords are commonly worn as ceremonial items in many military and naval services around the world. The occasions on which they are worn include any event in dress uniform where the rank and file bear arms – parades, reviews, tattoos and changes of command.

the condensed idea
From essential weapon to ceremonial adornment

14 The longbow
1136–1545

The bow is a straightforward weapon of war, essentially a spring by which a missile – an arrow – can be launched at a much higher speed, and thus with greater range, velocity, accuracy and lethality, than can be achieved by the unaided arm. In one form or another it has been in use for at least 8,000 years. However, the era in which it established an unparalleled dominance on the battlefield covered the years between 1300 and 1500, when in the hands of English and Welsh archers, the longbow underwrote 200 years of English military dominance in northwest Europe.

The armies of Edward I (r. 1272–1307) employed large numbers of Welsh bowmen. The weapons they carried were approximately 1.8 metres (6 ft) long. The process of making the bow – drying the wood and bending it into shape – could take up to four years before it was coated with water-resistant wax, resin and fine tallow, and strung with a cord made of hemp, flax or silk.

By 1350 there was a serious shortage of bow staves in England, prompting Henry IV to order his royal bowyer to enter private land and cut yew and other woods. Yew remained in short supply and much of it was imported from southern Germany and Austria. Monopolies were established by Richard II (r. 1377–1400) to safeguard the continuity of supply. By the 17th century these sources were nearly exhausted, but by then the bow was being supplanted by the gun.

timeline

1138	1333	1340	1341–59	1346	1350	1356
First significant English archery victory at the Battle of the Standard	Battle of Halidon Hill	English archers wreak havoc on a French fleet at the naval Battle of Sluys	English crown is supplied with 1.2 million arrows	Battle of Crécy	Shortage of bow staves in England	English archers prevail over French knights at the Battle of Poitiers

Because of improvements to the armour used in medieval Europe, it required great strength to drive the longbow's arrows home. Lengthy practice was needed to sustain the effectiveness of combat shooting – Edward I banned all other sports at the butts on Sunday but archery – and the skeletons of archers examined by archaeologists exhibit notable deformities, among them enlarged left arms and bone spurs on the left wrist, left shoulder and right finger.

> **'A longbow should be of yew or boxwood, 70 inches between the points of attachment for the cord.'**
>
> **Gaston Phoebus, Comte de Foix, Livre de Chasse, 1387–38**

Precise medieval ranges are difficult to estimate with any degree of precision. However, it is known that by decree of Henry VIII, every practice range had to be at least 220 yards (200 m) long. Accurate fire could be maintained up to approximately 200 yards (183 m). But a ranged volley fired in the opening stages of a battle, as at Agincourt in 1415, would descend on the enemy at a range of some 250 yards (228 m).

Machine gun of the Middle Ages A medieval archer went into battle with about 70 arrows, and might be resupplied by young boys (the equivalent of the 'powder monkeys' of the 19th-century Royal Navy) throughout the battle. In favourable circumstances the longbow was the machine gun of the Middle Ages, subjecting the enemy to a storm of fire that was as psychologically damaging as it was physically painful. An expert archer could loose off 6 to 12 shafts a minute.

The first significant English archery victory was at the Battle of the Standard (1138), fought against a Scottish army in Yorkshire. At the Battle of Halidon Hill (1333) another Scottish army, attempting an uphill charge against English positions launched from boggy ground, was again very roughly handled by English archers.

During the Hundred Years War (1337–1453), outstanding victories were won by English and Welsh archers at Crécy (1346) and Agincourt (1415). These victories earned the English a deserved reputation and made their archers sought-after mercenaries and increasingly significant in an army's composition.

1403	**1415**	**1450**	**1545**	**1545**
Battle of Shrewsbury	Battle of Agincourt	Much yew for bows is imported from Germany and Austria	The first book on the longbow, *Toxophilus* by Roger Ascham, is published	Henry VIII's warship *Mary Rose* sinks in the Solent, providing 20th-century archaeologists with a treasure trove of late-medieval longbows

Wounds

The only way to remove an arrow cleanly was to tie a piece of cloth, soaked in boiling water or some or other sterilizing substance, to the end of it, and then push it through the victim's wound and out the other side – a very painful procedure. Sometimes specialized tools were used when bones prevented extraction. One such, a pair of smooth tongs, was employed by the royal physician John Bradmore to extract an arrowhead from Prince Henry (later Henry V) after he had been wounded in the face at the Battle of Shrewsbury (1403). The wound had been widened and sterilized by the insertion of dowels coated with honey; after the extraction a poultice of barley honey mixed with turpentine was applied. The prince recovered within three weeks.

Archers at Agincourt In the Middle Ages, archers became the dominant element in English armies. In 1350 there were twice as many archers as 'lances' (men-at-arms and their body-servants); by the end of the 15th century, the ratio had risen to ten archers to every one lance.

In Henry V's invasion of France in August 1415 the ratio was approximately five to one – 5,000 archers to 1,000 men-at-arms. Having established a base at Harfleur, he planned to demonstrate to the French that he could lead his army to Calais with impunity. Marching through enemy territory, often sacking and burning along the way, was known as a *chevauchée*. It was a way of humiliating the enemy and provoking a battle. On 8 October, he led his army out.

Eve of battle The French moved to block his passage. On 24 October Henry was informed that a French force of some 25,000 men-at-arms, plus large numbers of unengaged foot under the joint control of French nobility, was deploying ahead of the English. Henry encamped for the night at the village of Maisoncelles and the next day gave battle. His army was wet, tired and hungry, and many of them were suffering from dysentery.

Confronted by vastly superior French forces, principally composed of mounted and dismounted men-at-arms, Henry skilfully placed them at a disadvantage on a cramped battlefield of recently ploughed and rain-sodden fields squeezed between two woods. French numerical superiority was thus severely reduced. Henry's archers were deployed on his left and right flanks and distributed among the men-at-arms in the centre.

Archers advance The French chose not to attack, so Henry seized the initiative and advanced to just within bowshot – some 300 yards (274 m). The archers stabbed their arrows upright in the ground at their feet, reducing the time it took to notch, draw and loose them. Protected by a thicket of pointed stakes, they loosed off their first flights of arrows, provoking the French into launching a charge by their mounted and fully armoured men-at-arms, aimed at the archers in the flanks of the English line. The sound of thousands of English arrow volleys clattering down on their armour must have raised a fearsome cacophony.

The French charge was driven off. Heading back towards their own line, many riders and horses crashed into the advancing body of dismounted men-at-arms who, ignoring the English archers on their left and right flanks, aimed for the English centre. As they laboured over the heavy ground and the gap between the two lines narrowed, they would have been subjected to repeated sheets of up to 5,000 arrows fired on a flat trajectory, many of which would have found weak spots in their armour.

> **❝The Scots who marched to the front were so wounded in the face and blinded by the multitude of English arrows that they could not help themselves, and soon began to turn away their faces from the bows of the arrows and fall.❞**
>
> *The Lanercost Chronicle* **(1839) on the Battle of Halidon Hill**

Men-at-arms The dismounted men-at-arms dented the British centre, but were confined on a narrow front and so tightly packed that they could not use their weapons to widen the breach. In turn they were driven back by the English men-at-arms and archers, the latter having temporarily cast aside their bows. The dismounted men-at-arms were now at a grave disadvantage. Their armour weighed up to 32 kilograms (70 lb), and if they lost their footing and fell they could be swiftly despatched by the nimbler English archers and men-at-arms. Threatened with an enveloping attack by the English, the French broke and ran.

the condensed idea
The key weapon of the Hundred Years War

15 Early cannon
1265–1540

Gunpowder, whose principal use is that of a propellant, was invented by the Chinese in the ninth century. The first written reference to the black powder in the West was made by the scientist and philosopher Roger Bacon in his *Opus maius* and *Opus tertius*, published in the 1260s, in which he refers to 'the powder, known in divers places, composed of saltpetre, charcoal and sulphur'.

The earliest depiction of a firearm occurs in a manuscript of 1326, *De officiis regum* (On the Duties of Kings), which shows a man firing a primitive cannon, mounted on little more than a trestle table, at the walls of La Rochelle. The gun has a bulbous rear section tapering to a flared muzzle and the charge appears to be ignited through a vent by a red-hot iron. The projectile emerging from the muzzle is an arrow.

In the same year an Italian manuscript mentions the manufacture of brass cannon and iron balls for the defence of Florence. They appear for the first time in an English context in a contract drawn up in 1338 for the delivery of several cannon to the keeper of the king's ships. A French document of the same year refers to the fitting out of the French fleet at Harfleur and the provision of an iron cannon fitted with 48 iron bolts and supplied with saltpetre and sulphur for making the powder.

> **'The besieged did great harm among the Christians with iron bullets they shot.'**
>
> Spanish historian Juan de Mariana **on the siege of Algeciras (1342)**

Effect on morale It is clear that earliest guns were fired from baulks of timber – the table in *De officiis regum* seems to be an example of artistic licence – which were pointed towards the enemy and discharged. At this

timeline

1260s	1326	1326	1346	1346	1415	1453
Roger Bacon publishes *Opus maius* and *Opus tertius*	Earliest European depiction of a firearm	Italian manuscript mentions the manufacture of brass cannon	Edward III uses brass cannon in siege of Calais	Edward III uses cannon at the Battle of Crécy	Henry V employs siege train at the siege of Harfleur	Cannon play important part in the Battle of Castillon

stage the morale effect of cannon counted for more than the material damage they could inflict. Edward III used cannon at the siege of Calais (1346), although it was starvation rather than cannon shot that forced that city's surrender.

A dangerous profession The nascent artillery arm was initially stigmatized by the church as something akin to witchcraft. On a more practical level, cannon were often as dangerous to those who fired them as they were to their targets. There were frequent frightful accidents. During their training, gunners were warned not to trample on powder that had been spilled around the gun, because the unstable compound might ignite and cause an explosion. Rather than bear the heavy financial burden of setting up their own artillery parks, monarchs contemplating a campaign would hire their guns and gunners from contractors.

By the 15th century, the arrows fired from the earliest cannon had long since been replaced, first by iron balls and then by lighter stone balls. The latter were cheaper, could smash down light structures and, when they shattered on impact, proved effective anti-personnel weapons. Gunpowder, known as 'serpentine powder', had also been vastly improved by the early 15th century. Previously, carriage in jolting barrels tended to leave the saltpetre and sulphur in the bottom while the lighter charcoal sat on the top. Thus the gunner had to remix the powder before he could use it.

'Corned powder' The answer came from France in the form of 'corned powder', in which the three

Casting cannon

The early cannon were probably cast from bronze or bell metal and were known as *pots-de-fer*. However, this method of manufacture was expensive and limited the size of the cannon. Simpler and cheaper methods were developed based on the cooper's trade. By the end of the 14th century, cannon were built up by laying strips of iron lengthways before they were welded together by hammering. They were then bound by iron hoops, which led to the adoption of the word 'barrel'. Rope or hide binding added extra strength and also reduced the threat of rust.

1449–53	1451	1453	1455	1483	1512	1544	c.1550
Mons Meg is cast	Mons Meg is presented to King James II of Scotland	Ottomans employ cannon at the siege of Constantinople	Siege of Thrieve Castle	Siege of Rhodes	Mons Meg is said to have been deployed in the warship *Great Michael*	Queen Elizabeth's Pocket Pistol is presented to Henry VIII by the Emperor Maximilian	Introduction of cast-iron guns

The Great Michael

The four-masted *Great Michael* warship was 73 metres (240 ft) long and 10.5 metres (35 ft) in the beam. It is said that her oak sides were 3 metres (10 ft) thick. She displaced 1,000 tons and, in addition to the possibly apocryphal Mons Meg, carried 24 guns purchased from Flanders on her broadside, 1 basilisk gun forward and 2 aft, and 30 smaller guns. A basilisk gun derived its name from the mythological fire-breathing serpent. It was a very heavy bronze cannon with a calibre of up to 25.5 centimetres (5 in) and usually about 3 metres (10 ft) long. The so-called Queen Elizabeth's Pocket Pistol, presented to Henry VIII in 1544 by the Emperor Maximilian, was 7.3 metres (24 ft) long and of 12-centimetre (4.75-in) calibre, and could fire a 4.5-kilogram (10-lb) ball some 2,000 yards (1,828 m). *Great Michael* had a crew of 300 sailors and could also carry up to 1,000 soldiers.

constituents were ground, wetted and then mixed together. This produced a 'cake', which was dried and then broken up before being sieved to ensure a consistent size of grain. In the gun the charge ignited almost instantaneously, making corned powder three times as powerful as serpentine. It left no residue after firing, was less susceptible to damp or jolting and was easier to handle. However, it proved too powerful for the built-up guns of the time; artillerymen had to wait for the introduction of cast guns in the mid-16th century before it enjoyed universal use.

Cast guns and corned powder gave a new lease of life to iron projectiles. Stone had to be painstakingly shaped, but it was simple and relatively cheap to cast iron. The corned powder and stronger guns combined to increase the destructive power of iron balls. Chaining two shots together produced a useful anti-personnel device.

Siege trains Henry V used 12 guns at the siege of Harfleur in 1415. The French king Charles VII had a formidable siege train – oxen and horses which hauled cannon and mortars along primitive roads – under the command of his master gunner, Jean Bureau. In 1453 artillery played a significant part in the defeat of the English at the Battle of Castillon, where the English commander, John Talbot, earl of Shrewsbury, died after his horse was shot from under him by a cannonball. The Ottomans employed European experts to develop their own siege trains, which they employed in the sieges of Constantinople in 1453 and Rhodes in 1480. At Constantinople, the Ottomans deployed 69 different guns in 15 separate batteries. Their barrage lasted 55 days.

Mons Meg Mons Meg is a massive bombard, the 'supergun' of its day, which now stands on the walls of Edinburgh Castle. She was cast in Wallonia for Philip the Good, the duke of Burgundy, around 1449–53, under the direction of his master of artillery, Jehan Cambier. She was tested at Mons, and this may be the origin of her name. Mons Meg was later presented by Philip to King James II of Scotland to make mischief with their mutual enemy, the English.

State of the art The bombard was made from longitudinal iron bars bound with rings and fused into one mass. In her day she represented state-of-the-art technology, 4.5 metres (15 ft) long, weighing 6,967 kilograms (15,366 lb) and with a 50-centimetre (20-in) calibre. Her shot weighed some 180 kilograms (400 lb), but the enormous heat generated by the huge charge meant that Mons Meg could only be fired about ten times a day. There are conflicting theories about the bombard's service with James II. One states that Mons Meg was used during the siege in 1455 of Threave Castle, the island home of the 'Black' earls of Douglas. The siege lasted two months and was ended not by Mons Meg but by the bribing of the castle's garrison with an offer of safe conduct. A second speculative theory places the bombard aboard James IV's warship *Great Michael*, built in Newhaven and completed in 1512. The *Great Michael* was another remarkable weapon of war – at her launching she was the biggest warship in Europe with twice the displacement of her English equivalent, *Mary Rose*. It was said that her construction had consumed 'all the woods of Fife'.

the condensed idea
A significant but not decisive addition to the medieval inventory

16 Naval warfare
1509–1697

At the end of the 15th century the major Mediterranean naval powers – the Ottomans, the Venetians and the Habsburgs – all relied on the galley, a warship with a low-boarded design that had changed little in 2,000 years. Galleys were fitted with lateen sails for cruising, and for action were propelled by banks of oars manned by criminals or prisoners of war.

By the 16th century, galleys were armed with forward-mounted cannon, which meant that the entire ship had to be turned against its target. However, galley tactics relied primarily on the large numbers of soldiers on board, whose role was to board their opponents' ships after an exchange of missiles, many of which contained incendiary devices. The last great major fleet action fought exclusively by galleys was at Lepanto in 1571, when a

War at sea

Men like Sir Walter Raleigh, Sir John Hawkins and Sir Francis Drake adopted an alternative approach to war at sea. They saw the warship as a self-contained weapons system, capable of disabling and sinking its enemy by gunfire alone. They favoured slimmer vessels with more effective sail plans, which enabled them to fight at ranges of their own choosing. The debate over the respective merits of the floating fortress and the nimble warship was settled by the English defeat of the Spanish Armada in 1588.

timeline

1509–10	1512	1545	1588
Mary Rose built	English warship *Regent* is destroyed off Brest when a French ship's magazine explodes	**JULY** *Mary Rose* sinks in the Solent	Defeat of the Spanish Armada

fleet of Christian galleys commanded by Don John of Austria inflicted a crushing defeat on a Turkish galley fleet on the northern edge of the Gulf of Patras off western Greece.

Floating fortress The future lay not with the galley, but with the carrack, a high-sided merchant ship adapted for war and much more suitable as a gun platform than the low-sided galley, particularly after the introduction of the hinged gun-port at the beginning of the 16th century. In one form, the carrack became a floating fortress, employing its guns as a preliminary to boarding. From this evolved the galleon, with its towering forecastle, like Henry VIII's great ship *Mary Rose*, built in 1509–10 and specifically designed to batter her enemies before despatching soldiers to board.

> **❝The noblest ship of sayle [of any] gret ship at this howr, that I trow [believe] be in Christendom.❞**
>
> **Admiral Edward Howard**
> **on the sinking of the *Mary Rose***

Mary Rose, one of the earliest examples of a purpose-built sailing warship, was a four-masted carrack with orlop, main and upper decks, fore- and sterncastles and fighting tops on each mast. She was square-rigged on the fore and main masts with lateens on the mizzen and bonaventure. Her 700-ton displacement was given in 'tuns burthen', a contemporary measure of cubic capacity. On launching, her armament comprised 43 guns and 37 anti-personnel weapons.

In 1536 this veteran of the French wars underwent an extensive and ultimately fatal refit. In all probability her fore- and sterncastles were raised and her armament was increased, making her centre of gravity dangerously high. In July 1545, shortly before she sailed to engage French galleys off the Isle of Wight, she took on 300 more soldiers, many of whom were placed on the upper decks, above her centre of gravity. On 19 July, *Mary Rose* left harbour in a light breeze, with some 700 men on board.

A stronger wind was blowing as she entered the Solent to engage the French. She had fired all of her guns on one side and was turning to present her guns on the other side when she heeled over to starboard,

1637	1649	1651	1652–4	1660	1665–7	1672–4
Sovereign of the Seas is launched	*Sovereign of the Seas* renamed *Commonwealth*	*Commonwealth* is refitted	First Anglo-Dutch War	On the accession of Charles II, *Commonwealth* is renamed *Royal Sovereign*	Second Anglo-Dutch War	Third Anglo-Dutch War

Salvaging the Mary Rose

An attempt to salvage the *Mary Rose* was made immediately after the sinking in 1545, but it failed. It was not until 1982 that she was salvaged by an international archaeological team led by Margaret Rule. The recovery of *Mary Rose* marked a milestone in maritime archaeology, and revealed a wealth of material, providing insights in areas ranging from 16th-century naval warfare to barber-surgeon's tools, navigation instruments and the history of musical instruments, many of which were recovered from the wreck of the great ship.

taking in huge amounts of water through her open lower gunports, and went straight to the bottom. A similar fate overtook the Swedish warship *Vasa* in Stockholm harbour in 1629.

Sovereign of the Seas *Mary Rose* represented an intermediate stage of naval warfare. In the 17th century the key warship was the ship of the line, built specifically to fight in a line of battle in which two columns of opposing warships manoeuvred to bring the greatest weight of broadsides to bear.

Sovereign of the Seas, designed by Phineas Pett, built by his son Peter and launched in 1637, was the pride of Charles I's fleet. She was a colossal status symbol, ordered on the king's initiative amid much opposition, not least to the special tax, 'Ship Money', which he levied to pay for her. The cost of *Sovereign of the Seas*, some £66,000, was ten times that of an average warship. The gilded carvings, designed by Anthony van Dyck, that decorated her from stem to stern and were known as 'gingerbread-work', cost that much alone. Her primary weapons were 102 bronze cannon (later reduced to 90 and then increased to 100), making her the most powerfully armed warship of her day, displacing 1,700 tons. She was to serve as the prototype for every ship of the line until 1860.

> ❦**Too much folly . . . for she was laden with much ordinaunce, and the portes left open, which were low, and the great ordinaunce unbreached, so that when the ship should turne, the water entered, and sodainly she sanke.**❧
>
> **Lord High Admiral John Russell on the *Mary Rose***

Sovereign of the Seas had three gun decks flush throughout the hull, with extra guns on the beak forecastle, half- and quarterdeck; gun crews on the upper decks were shielded from falling debris by heavy gratings. Her unique sail plan included royal sails above the fore and main topgallants, and a topgallant on the mizzen.

In the time of the Commonwealth, which ruled first England and then Ireland and Scotland between 1649 and 1660, she was renamed *Commonwealth*, and then reverted to *Sovereign*. In 1651 she was refitted by Peter Pett, and her forecastle and after superstructure were lowered to improve her weatherliness. She served throughout the wars of the Commonwealth and became the flagship of General at Sea Robert Blake. During the first Anglo-Dutch War (1652–4) a reward of 3,000 guilders was offered by the Dutch States General for her destruction by fireship. She ran aground in the Battle of the Kentish Knock (1652) and, during fierce fighting between the Dutch and English, *Sovereign* changed hands several times.

In 1660, after the English Restoration, she was renamed *Royal Sovereign*, underwent a major refit in 1685 and subsequently served in the War of the Grand Alliance (1688–97) against Louis XIV. She was eventually laid up at Chatham and was destroyed by fire, possibly the result of an overturned candle, on 27 January 1697. Fire, coupled with the volatility of gunpowder, was always the greatest hazard in wooden ships. In 1512, off Brest, the English *Regent*, fighting at close quarters with the French *Marie la Cordelière*, was burnt out when the French ship's magazine exploded.

> **❝There is no port in the Kingdom that can harbour this shipp. The wild sea must be her port, her anchors and cables her safety; if either fayle, the shipp must perish, the King lose his jewel, four or five hundred man must die, and perhaps some great and noble peer.❞**
>
> **The Brethren of Trinity House**

the condensed idea
Navies were expensive and fragile

17 The Vauban revolution
1539–1808

Unless they were sited in inaccessible positions – on a rocky outcrop or in the middle of a lake – medieval castles were unlikely to survive a siege mounted with modern artillery, though in the English Civil War (1642–51) a number of castles achieved this singular feat. By the same token, guns defending a castle could deal relatively easily with towers and battering rams, the paraphernalia of medieval siegecraft. Gunpowder had sparked an escalating race between an irresistible force – siegecraft – and an immovable object – fortifications. Vauban had the answer.

Fortress-builders favoured sinking most of their defences into the earth, ensuring that only fighting parapets and gun embrasures, positioned to sweep the approaches with fire, were visible above ground. In 1539 Henry VIII, fearful of invasion by France or Spain, built a series of artillery forts along the southern coast of England, the largest defence programme since the days of Alfred the Great and one in which the king took a personal interest, approving and amending the designs himself.

Henry's so-called 'Device Forts' were sited so that they were, to an extent, mutually supporting, and their circular bastions were less vulnerable to cannon fire than square towers. But the dead ground on the forts' landward approaches could be exploited by an attacking force.

timeline

1539	1646	1655	1657	1665
Henry VIII begins construction of forts along southern coast of England	St Mawes Castle surrenders without a fight in the English Civil War	Vauban becomes an engineer	Vauban conducts his first siege	Vauban publishes *Treatise on the Attack of Places* (revised in 1703)

Henry's fortifications: St Mawes

St Mawes Castle in Cornwall is a fine example of the method of Henry VIII's architects, consisting of a central tower overlooking three huge circular bastions, which appear like a clover leaf when seen from above and provide a platform for tiers of guns covering the approaches to the important anchorage of Carrick Roads. However, St Mawes's seaward defences were not matched by provision against a landward attack, and in 1646, during the Civil War, the fort surrendered without a fight.

The answer to this conundrum was found in Europe in a new type of fortress design: wedge-shaped bastions, which were positioned to provide mutual support covering every angle of approach.

From this evolved the so-called 'star system', which took its name from a design in which bastions were linked by curtain walls making a star shape. From their outer edge, the permanent defences consisted of a sloped glacis, counterscarp, ditch, scarp and ramparts. To protect gateways and vulnerable sections of the curtain, ravelins and other outworks were added, each with its own counterscarp, ditch and scarp, producing an effect of great complexity, although much of it was invisible to an attacker. The parapets were cloaked in a thick layer of earth to soak up the impact of cannonballs and reduce the shrapnel effect of flying splinters.

The fortifications revolution presented enormous problems to an attacker. If the ditch was dry, mining could be attempted, although this was a formidable task. The attacker would have to tunnel through the foundations of the counterscarp, then under the ditch before tackling

1668	**1673**	**1674**	**1678**	**1692**	**1703**	**1703**
Vauban appointed governor of Lille	Vauban's siege of Maastricht, which is taken in 13 days	Vauban supervises his only defensive operation, at Oudenaarde	Becomes commissionnaire des fortifications	Vauban perfects ricochet firing	Vauban's last siege, at Breisach	Vauban appointed marshal of France

The language of the siege

The new era of siege warfare generated a fresh vocabulary of technical terms. A *banquette* was the fire step behind a protecting parapet. A *bastion* was a work with two faces and two sides forming part of the main defences. A *casemate* was a vaulted chamber within a rampart, containing an artillery port. A *counterscarp* was the exterior wall of a defensive ditch. A *curtain* was a section of rampart connecting bastions. A *ditch* was a wet or dry excavation in front of the ramparts. An *embrasure* was an opening in the parapet through which artillery fired. A *glacis* was a clear slope on the enemy side of the ditch, covered by fire from the parapets. A *parados* was an embankment behind a defensive position, protecting it against fire from the rear. A *rampart* was a thick wall of earth and/or stone forming the main defence. A *ravelin* was a work beyond the curtain consisting of two faces meeting in a salient, closed at the rear by the counterscarp. It was used to protect gates and the flanks of bastions. A *scarp* was the inner wall of the ditch, leading towards the rampart.

the scarp. Even if this was achieved and a charge laid and fired, the stone-clad earth rampart would absorb the effects of the explosion. The best hope of success was to concentrate artillery fire from a range of about 600 yards (550 m) on what was judged to be the weakest link in the defences and then dig a sap towards it. The attacker's batteries were connected by a trench, the so-called First Parallel, from which zig-zag saps would snake out to establish a Second Parallel 300 yards (275 m) closer to the defences. This manoeuvre would be repeated once more to establish a Third Parallel within musket range of the defenders. If the defences were now sufficiently cowed and a breach had been made in the walls, a surrender might be accepted or an assault mounted.

Vauban Sébastien Le Prestre de Vauban (1633–1707), commonly referred to as Vauban, was a marshal of France and the leading military engineer of his age, as famous for designing fortifications as he was for reducing them. The son of minor nobility, he was left an orphan at ten and educated under the supervision of the Carmelite prior of Semur, who ensured that Vauban had an education grounded in science, mathematics and geometry. This was to stand the future marshal in good stead in his career as a military engineer.

Vauban was appointed an engineer in 1655 and directed his first siege, at Montmédy, in 1657. He made his name in 1667 in the war against Spain, besieging and taking Douai, Tournai and Lille. Appointed the governor of Lille in 1668, Vauban had within three years turned the city into the cornerstone of the defence of northern France.

By the end of the 1670s, Vauban had systematized his doctrine of siegecraft. The introduction of a deliberate approach by a series of parallel trenches dates from Vauban's siege of Maastricht in 1673. The well-garrisoned city fell in 13 days and the siege established an orthodoxy that lasted until the end of the 19th century. Vauban's masterwork was the Pré Carré, his double line of fortresses guarding France's northern frontier. In 1692, at the siege of Namur, Vauban perfected the science of ricochet firing in which cannon, howitzers and, on occasion, mortars were fired to just clear the outer parapet of a fortress, causing maximum mayhem among defenders as their shots ricocheted around inside the walls.

Vauban's last siege was in 1703 at Breisach, which he reduced in two weeks. His appointment as a marshal of France in January 1703 effectively brought his active career to an end. He had built over 100 fortresses and conducted some 40 sieges, many of them against strongholds of his own design. His systems of both defence and attack were so precise that, given the number and type of guns employed, and the construction of the fortress under siege, it was possible to predict with a fair degree of accuracy how long resistance would last.

the condensed idea
Vauban is the father of military engineering

18 The age of artillery 1500–1699

In 1500 the infantry component of most armies consisted of pikemen, archers and halberdiers, the last armed with a 1.8-metre (6-ft) spear incorporating an axe-blade below its head and, occasionally, a hook for dragging a man out of the enemy's ranks. The arrival of cannon had not yet transformed the battlefield, but another weapon, the arquebus, was making an impact.

Arquebus and musket Developed from a light anti-personnel gun often mounted on the walls of fortifications, the arquebus was initially tucked under the infantryman's right arm and fired from a rest rammed into the ground. Smaller versions were subsequently produced that could be held against the chest and gripped with both hands. Arquebusiers, positioned in trenches or behind barricades and protected by units of pikemen and halberdiers, proved effective at Cerignola (1503), the first battle to be won by gunpowder-based firearms.

> **❛The Lord God is my armour!❜**
>
> **Gustavus Adolphus, 1630**

Halberdiers and archers were becoming an irrelevance. A Royal Ordinance of 1595 decreed that henceforth the English trained bands (militia) were to replace the longbow with firearms. The accuracy of the arquebus was very limited but at short range it could penetrate plate armour. Firing small shot rather than a single ball, it could cause multiple wounds. Its rate of fire was greater than that of archers armed with crossbow; and the training of an arquebusier took a fraction of the time required to produce a skilled longbowman. The arrival of the arquebusier set in train the development of the lightly armoured, low-skilled infantryman who would make the archer redundant.

timeline

1503	1539	1613	1617	1627
Battle of Cerignola, the first to be won by gunpowder-based firearms	Introduction of wheel-lock musket	Gustavus concludes war with Denmark	Gustavus concludes war with Russia	Gustavus takes a bullet in the shoulder near Dirschau in Prussia. It cannot be removed and he can no longer wear armour. Two fingers of his right hand are also paralysed

> 'The said Master of the Ordnance, his office is, that if there be any Captain that lacketh ammunition for his soldiers, the said captain shall come to the Master of the Ordnance and he must command the clerk to deliver such ammunition as he lacketh.'
>
> **Military manuscript of 1578**

The arquebus had many drawbacks. Heavy rain could render its gunpowder useless, and misfires were frequent. In the confusion of battle, the arquebus could prove as dangerous to the men who carried it, and those around them, as it was to the enemy. They tended to overheat and explode and had a violent recoil. The arquebusier's lit match prevented concealment and could set off the gunpowder packed in little cartouches of tin and leather carried in a bandolier over his shoulder.

The musket evolved from the arquebus. It could be fired from the shoulder, although it was initially so heavy, weighing some 11.5 kilograms (25 lb), that a rest was required. Arquebusiers and musketeers fought in ranks ten deep. The musket's rate of fire was painfully slow; the reloading drill required 18 separate steps, and it probably took about seven minutes to fire two shots. The men in the front rank fired their weapons and then filed to the rear to reload before making their way back to the front rank in rotation, thus maintaining a desultory stream of fire on a narrow front.

The musket's first firing mechanism was the matchlock, which required the insertion of a burning slow match into the priming pan. The wheel-lock, introduced in 1539, was the first self-contained ignition mechanism. Now the weapon could be carried cocked and ready to fire at any time without the intervention of a cumbersome match. By the end of the 17th century, the wheel-lock had been replaced by a third firing mechanism, the flintlock. The flintlock used a spring-loaded hammer

1629	1630	1631	1632	1633	1648	1699
Gustavus concludes war with Poland	Gustavus brings Sweden into the Thirty Years War	Superiority of Swedish army demonstrated at the Battle of Breitenfeld	**NOVEMBER** Gustavus killed while leading a charge at Lützen	Gustavus is proclaimed 'The Great'	Thirty Years War is ended by Treaty of Westphalia	Flintlock firing mechanism predominates

containing a flint, which was activated by the weapon's trigger and struck sparks in the priming pan. The flintlock was to serve the British soldier for over 150 years.

By now the weight of the musket had been reduced to 5 kilograms (11 lb), enabling the musketeer to fire it from the shoulder without a rest. Gustavus Adolphus introduced a 'fixed' cartridge, increasing the rate of fire and thereby slimming down the ranks of musketeers from ten to six. A three-deep formation, achieved by doubling the files, could

Gustavus Adolphus

In the 1630s, during the Thirty Years War (1618–48), the art of warfare was revolutionized by the Swedish king Gustavus Adolphus. He multiplied the fire of his infantry and artillery with flexible new tactics, and paid great attention to the care of his troops, introducing regular pay and standardized uniforms to encourage better health and morale. The army had its own chaplains and every man was issued with a prayer book. There were no floggings, but punishments like the *gatlopp*, the origin of running the gauntlet, were harsh.

The Swedish king's innovative integration of infantry, cavalry, logistics and, above all, artillery earned him the title of 'the father of modern warfare'. He refused to allow himself to be encumbered by heavy cannon, but rather embarked on a series of experiments that enabled him to settle on smaller, more manoeuvrable weapons, which were the first light field artillery in the history of warfare.

Twelve regimental guns were attached to each brigade. In an attempt to achieve a lighter gun that would bridge the gap between muskets and heavy stationary cannon, Gustavus developed the 'leather gun'. A thin copper tube was reinforced by heavy ropes and finally clad in leather, or alternatively clad in leather straps first and then rope.

The leather gun was light and extremely mobile but had a serious design flaw. The reinforcing material acted as an insulator and did not allow heat to dissipate fast enough. After only a few shots the gun became red hot. The leather gun was abandoned, but it was succeeded by the more successful three-pounder regimental cannon, firing fixed grape or canister ammunition that could be towed by a single horse or three men, and had a range and rate of fire three times greater than the muskets of the period. Sweden had arrived as a major military power.

> **❝What kind of thing is neutrality?**
> **It surpasses by understanding.❞**
>
> Gustavus Adolphus, **1630**

deliver concerted volleys, the front rank kneeling, the second crouching and the third standing upright. After delivering their volleys, the musketeers then withdrew into the shelter of the pikemen, who charged home. Gustavus reorganized each infantry company into 72 musketeers and 54 pikemen. A battalion comprised four companies; eight battalions made up a regiment; two to four regiments formed a brigade.

Cavalry tactics were also radically overhauled. For over a hundred years, cavalry had been denied its traditional role of shock action against infantry, deterred by dense masses of 5.5-metre (18-ft) pikes and the fire of arquebusiers and musketeers. Cavalry actions had been reduced to wheel-lock pistol engagements conducted at walking pace or at most a trot. In what was dubbed the *caracole*, the leading cavalry would fire their weapons before riding to the rear to reload and in rotation rejoin the fray. The same tactic was used against hostile cavalry. Gustavus trained his cavalry to charge home knee to knee and engage with the sword. In anticipation of what would become known as 'all-arms' warfare, each cavalry regiment enjoyed the support of a company of musketeers and light artillery.

the condensed idea
Firepower now dominated the battlefield

19 Firepower and shock action
1642–1918

It was in the lifetime of another great soldier, John Churchill, the duke of Marlborough (1650–1722), that the long and painful transition from medieval to un-mechanized modern warfare was consolidated. For infantry and artillery the key to battlefield mastery was firepower. For cavalry the restoration of shock action, pioneered by Gustavus Adolphus, became a vital breakthrough weapon.

The flexible military environment that Marlborough moulded enabled commanders to deploy infantry, artillery and cavalry according to the terrain and the commander's intentions. A pattern was established that would last for another 150 years. It has been said that an infantryman veteran of the War of the Spanish Succession (1701–14), transported suddenly to the Battle of the Alma (1854) in the Crimean War, would have understood everything that was going on around him, with the exception of the mobility of 19th-century artillery. He would have been able to take his place in the firing line, bearing a musket that had changed little since those used by Marlborough's forces at the Battle of Blenheim (1704).

On the outbreak of the War of the Spanish Succession in 1701, Churchill was appointed supreme commander of the British and Dutch forces by King William III. When Queen Anne succeeded to the throne in 1702, she added the appointment of captain-general to that of master-

timeline

1642–51	1660s	1685	1701–14	1701
Grenade appears in army inventories during the English Civil War	Grenadiers become recognized infantrymen in the army of Louis XIV	John Churchill defeats Monmouth's rebellion	War of Spanish Succession	Marlborough appointed supreme commander of British and Dutch forces

> **❝He never fought a battle that he did not win, nor besiege a fortress that he did not take . . . He quitted war invincible.❞**
>
> **Winston Churchill on his ancestor the duke of Marlborough,**
> ***Marlborough, His Life and Times* (vol. 1, 1933)**

general of the ordnance, which he already held, and created Churchill duke of Marlborough. Marlborough was a superb strategist and master tactician. He increased the pace of a cavalry charge from a good round trot to a canter, which was remarkably effective against the French, who were still wedded to the *caracole*. He took immense pains over the deployment of artillery, concentrating his guns against critical sectors or sending them forward to provide close-quarter support during a general advance. Recognizing that most of the troops in his service were there because they had no alternative, he made officers responsible for the welfare of their men. He had an eagle eye for any weakness in his enemy, and it was this quality that lay behind his great victories at Blenheim (1704), Ramillies (1706) and Oudenarde (1708) and enabled him to force his way through the formidable Ne Plus Ultra lines in 1711.

The Lines were a series of massive fieldworks in northern France stretching from the Channel coast to Namur in the Ardennes which severely hampered Marlborough's freedom to manoeuvre. His first move was to seize the minor fortress of Arleux, at the northern end of the Lines, but he was initially surprised by a rapid French sally from the Ne Plus Ultra Lines which retook Arleux. Marlborough responded with a feint attack on the Lines near Arras before passing through them to lay siege to Bouchain with 30,000 men. Repeated French attempts to raise the siege were thwarted and Bouchain fell on 13 September. It was Marlborough's last campaign. Under his leadership the British army gained a prestige unequalled since Agincourt.

> **❝The most shameful, humiliating and disastrous of routs.❞**
>
> **Marshal Villars on his defeat by Marlborough at Ramillies in 1706**

1702	1704	1706	1708	1815	1904–5	1914–18
Churchill created duke of Marlborough	Battle of Blenheim	Battle of Ramillies	Battle of Oudenarde	1st Foot Guards renamed Grenadier Guards	Grenade enjoys revival in Russo-Japanese War	Grenade becomes staple trench weapon in the First World War

Grenadiers Marlborough began his military career at a time when a new type of infantryman, the grenadier, was appearing on the battlefield. Grenades – small bombs thrown by hand – have their origins in the Chinese Ming dynasty (1368–1644) but their first appearance on English inventories came during the English Civil War (1642–51). In the 1660s grenadiers became a recognized class of infantryman in the army of the French king Louis XIV.

> **❝The human world could not produce a man of more humanity.❞**
>
> **Corporal Matthew Bishop**

The grenades were originally hollow iron balls, approximately the size of cricket balls, packed with gunpowder and ignited by a length of slow match. Grenadiers had to be tall and strong, capable of hurling the grenade far enough so as not to hurt themselves or their comrades. They also had to possess sufficient discipline to remain at the forefront of the fight, light the fuse and throw at the appropriate moment, not giving the enemy enough time to return

The grenade 1900-45

The grenade was often used by the defenders in sieges. Although its use had virtually died out by the end of the 19th century, the grenade enjoyed a revival in the Russo-Japanese War of 1904–5, in which the siege of Port Arthur by the Japanese was a harbinger of the trench warfare that was to grip the Western Front in 1914–18. This was, in many ways, another form of siege warfare. At first neither the Allies nor the Germans had effective grenades. The British Grenade No.1 – a cast-iron canister on a 46-centimetre (18-in) stick – frequently failed to clear the trench when thrown, usually killing the thrower. Three models stood the test of battle: the British Mills bomb, the French 'pineapple' and the German 'potato masher'. The Mills bomb, another pineapple-shaped percussion bomb, was an ovoid cast-iron bomb with a central spring-loaded firing pin and a spring-loaded lever locked by a pin. The fingers were held over the lever, the pin was removed and the bomb thrown. When it exploded, it produced a shower of incapacitating metal fragments. A later version could be fired from a rifle. The German 'potato masher', or stick grenade, had a wooden handle about 25 centimetres (10 in) long carrying a metal canister at its head. Pulling a string inside the wooden handle lit a friction igniter and time fuse. The potato masher stayed in service virtually unchanged until 1945.

❝I can conceive nothing greater than Marlborough at the head of an English army.❞

The duke of Wellington

the missile with interest. Fuses were notoriously unreliable, and as late as the 1860s army manuals cautioned against holding the grenade too long after igniting the fuse.

Because the wide-brimmed and tricorn hats characteristic of the late-17th-century infantryman interfered with the swing of his arm, the grenadier initially adopted brimless headgear. By 1700, standard attire was a cap in the shape of a bishop's mitre, often bearing the regimental insignia or royal cipher in embroidered cloth.

During the 18th century, linear infantry tactics and the effectiveness of flintlock technology ensured that the use of grenades declined. Nevertheless, because size and courage had been the determining factors in choosing the original grenadiers, they remained important in the establishment of elite infantry formations. One of the eight companies in a British infantry regiment was always a grenadier company. Following their role in the routing of Napoleon's Imperial Guard at Waterloo (1815), the 1st Foot Guards was renamed the Grenadier Guards, and it remains to this day the most senior of Foot Guards.

the condensed idea
Marlborough was the master of the all-arms battle

20 Brown Bess
1647–1853

Just over a hundred years passed between the Battle of Malplaquet (1709) in the War of the Spanish Succession, and the Battle of Waterloo (1815), the culminating battle of the Napoleonic Wars, but the armaments employed by the European powers changed very little. In this period the principal infantry weapon remained the smooth-bore infantry musket or 'firelock'; in English hands, the 'Brown Bess'.

This period saw a rapid expansion of the British empire. By the late 18th century, the British had become the dominant power in North America and India. After the loss of the American colonies in 1780, the British turned their attentions towards Africa, Asia and the Pacific. Following the defeat of Napoleon in 1815, the British enjoyed global dominance for the best part of a century. The transformation of a small island off the coast of Europe into a world power was underwritten by a combination of factors both large and small, among them Britain's industrial and agrarian revolutions; the global outreach of the Royal Navy; and the robustness of the British army, which was symbolized by its principal infantry weapon, the smooth-bore Land Pattern Musket flintlock or 'Brown Bess'.

Flintlock musket The origins of the name 'Brown Bess' remain unclear, but the musket was designed in 1722 and remained in production for over 100 years. It was loaded via the muzzle, with a lead ball and gunpowder in a cartridge, and ignited by the flintlock mechanism. When the trigger was depressed, it struck a spark that was sent to the propellant charge via a touch hole in the barrel.

timeline

1647	1722	1787	1800
Introduction in France of the bayonet	Brown Bess designed	Arthur Wellesley enters the British army	Establishment of the Rifle Corps (originally established in North America in 1756 as the 62nd Royal American Regiment)

At the Battle of Waterloo (1815) the Brown Bess was the standard British infantry weapon, firing up to four 28-gram (1-oz) balls a minute over a range of about 250 yards (229 m), although for accurate shooting not more than 100 yards (91 m) was attempted. The battlefields of the 18th and early 19th centuries did not demand lethal marksmanship, as troops manoeuvred in dense formations, presenting a huge general target for the enemy's musket volleys. It was necessary to fire in volleys to ensure that the shower of sparks from

❛In the days of lace ruffles, perukes and brocade
Brown Bess was a partner whom none could despise –
An outspoken, flinty-lipped, brazen-faced jade,
With a habit of looking men straight in the eyes –
At Blenheim and Ramillies fops would confess
They were pierced to the heart by the charms of Brown Bess.❜

Rudyard Kipling, 'Brown Bess' (1911)

The 'Iron Duke'

The greatest commander of British infantry in the musket era was Arthur Wellesley, duke of Wellington, the 'Iron Duke' (1769–1852). Wellesley entered the British army in 1787 and won his reputation in India during the Second Anglo–Maratha War (1803–5) prompting Napoleon to dismiss him as a 'sepoy general'. Between 1809 and 1814 Wellington out-generalled Napoleon's marshals in Portugal and Spain, bringing the Peninsular War to a victorious conclusion. In Spain, whenever possible, he always placed his infantry on reverse slopes to minimize casualties in the opening phase of a battle. He had the great commander's instinctive eye for ground, and at Waterloo (1815), commanding a coalition army, the 'sepoy general' fought a superb defensive battle to end Napoleon's military career. Wellington affected disdain for the men under his command, famously observing that they were 'the scum of the earth . . . fellows who have enlisted for drink'. But his regard for 'that article', the British soldier, was immense.

1807	1809	1815	1840	1842	1853
Introduction of the percussion cap	Rifleman Plunkett's marksmanship kills French general in Spain	Battle of Waterloo	Last flintlock produced for the US army	Last flintlocks supplied to the British army	British army flintlocks replaced by the P53 Enfield and the Minié rifle

> **I'll be hanged if I know anything about the matter, for I was all day trodden in the mud and ridden over by every scoundrel who ever had a horse.**

British infantryman recalling the Battle of Waterloo

one infantryman's muzzle did not ignite his neighbour's powder as he was in the act of loading.

Because of the low velocity of musket balls, men could sustain serious wounds and remain on their feet, the wound spurting horribly as they talked to comrades. At Waterloo, a lieutenant of the Scots Greys saw a Royal Dragoon 'whose cheek, just as I looked at it, opened, while I felt a ball pass close to my lips'.

Light infantry carried the Baker rifle, a rifled musket, whose rate of fire was one round a minute. The Baker rifle was used by the Rifle Corps (established in 1800) in a skirmishing role, sniping at the enemy either in front of the main lines or from concealed positions in heights overlooking a battlefield. Its accuracy in expert hands was demonstrated in 1809 by

The bayonet

Rifle regiments in the early 1800s were equipped with a sword-type bayonet. The bayonet derives its name from the town of its supposed origin, Bayonne in France. It was introduced into the French army in 1647, in the form of the plug bayonet, which was rammed into the musket muzzle, with obvious disadvantages. The later socket bayonet had a cranked blade attached to a hollow sleeve that was slipped over the musket muzzle, allowing the weapon to be loaded and fired with fixed bayonet. An infantry square standing firm with fixed bayonets could see off a cavalry charge, as was demonstrated at Waterloo. Horses do not wish to be disembowelled any more than men. Old soldiers may have boasted about the bayonet charge, but in truth few men relished hand-to-hand combat with the bayonet. When ammunition ran out in Egypt in 1801, English and French troops threw stones at each other rather than close with the bayonet.

Rifleman Thomas Plunkett of the 95th Rifles, who shot the French general Colbert-Chabanais and one of his subordinates at long range (over 328 yards/300 metres) at Villafranca during the Peninsular War.

Percussion cap The flintlock mechanism remained in military and civilian use for over 200 years. It gradually fell out of fashion after the invention of the percussion cap system by the Reverend Alexander John Forsyth in 1807, which replaced the flintlock's flint and flashpan with a waterproof copper cap that created a spark when struck. The percussion cap proved more reliable than the flintlock, which was always prone to misfires, particularly in wet weather, and accidental firings.

The flintlock's legacy

The flintlock's long military career has bequeathed the English language many familiar expressions: 'lock, stock and barrel', 'flash in the pan' and 'going off at half cock', the last referring to an accidental discharge.

The Model 1840 musket was the last flintlock firearm produced for the US military, although obsolete muskets were used in the American Civil War. The last British flintlocks, manufactured in 1842, remained in service until the outbreak of the Crimean War in 1853, when they were replaced by the P53 Enfield rifled musket and the Minié rifle.

the condensed idea
The first
mass-produced rifle

21 Mobile artillery
1499–1763

By the end of the 15th century, artillery pieces had acquired a degree of mobility with the addition of wheeled gun carriages. However, this innovation had little impact on the speed of manoeuvre, which was limited to that of the gunners marching alongside. Artillery moved no faster than walking pace.

Gustavus Adolphus had tackled the issue in the early 17th century with the introduction of the battalion gun, a light piece hauled by his infantry. This was not a complete solution, as the relative lightness of the weapon limited its effectiveness on the battlefield. It was left to an 18th-century master of war, Frederick the Great, to solve the problem.

Frederick the great

Frederick II of Prussia (r. 1740–86) survived a wretched youth at the hands of a brutal and boorish father to become the military genius of his age and an enlightened autocrat who corresponded with Goethe and Voltaire. His early military career was characterized by swift offensive manoeuvre, an emphasis that hastened the demise of the fortress warfare practised in an earlier era. Infantry was the mainstay of the Prussian army and became the model for contemporary armies in Europe. Frederick had a genius for logistics and wrote two military treatises one of which is *General Principles of War (Military Instructions for the Generals)* (1748). Both remained important works of reference well into the era of Napoleon.

timeline

1740	1740	1742	1744	1748	1748	1754
Frederick II succeeds to the throne of Prussia	Frederick precipitates First Silesian War	Frederick wins Battle of Chotusitz	Start of Second Silesian War	Treaty of Aix-la-Chapelle concludes War of the Austrian Succession	Frederick completes *Military Instructions for the Generals*	Beginning of Seven Years War

Frederick's solution stemmed from his decision to restore manoeuvrability to Prussian cavalry, previously trained to halt and engage the enemy with their firearms. He reinstated swords and lances as their primary weapons and provided them with added firepower in the form of horse artillery. The gunners in Frederick's horse artillery were mounted, giving the arm a new coherence and speed. His guns were necessarily light but sufficiently powerful to inflict serious damage. During the Seven Years War (1754–63) the light carts in which the ammunition was carried were replaced by specialist two-wheeled limbers (gun carriages).

Oblique order Frederick's other crucial development was the use of the 'oblique order', a device designed to counterbalance the numerical inferiority that he often faced in long years of campaigning and to maximize the effectiveness of his superbly drilled and disciplined infantry. Rather than engage the enemy along the entire length of his line, the oblique order involved Prussian units moving forward in echelon against the enemy's flank while an advanced guard frontally engaged the centre. Whenever possible, Frederick skilfully exploited natural features of terrain to disguise this manoeuvre. Successive units were brought to bear on the enemy's flank, stepping up the pressure until it buckled. Frederick's cavalry, which up to this point had been screening the flank attack, was then thrown in to exploit any collapse in the enemy's line with shock action, a concentrated charge with the sword. This was a task given to Frederick's heavy cavalry. His light cavalry, notably his hussars, were principally tasked with skirmishing, reconnaissance and raiding.

> **❝. . . when we looked towards the north, from there shone Frederick, the Pole Star, around whom Germany, Europe, even the world seemed to turn.❞**
>
> **A letter by Johann Wolfgang von Goethe**

Battle of Leuthen Frederick's masterpiece was the Battle of Leuthen (1757), in which he achieved a victory over an Austrian army twice the size of his own, thus ensuring Prussian control of Silesia during the Seven Years War.

1756	**1757**	**1758**	**1760**	**1762**	**1763**
AUGUST Frederick invades Saxony	**DECEMBER** Frederick's greatest victory at Leuthen	Frederick secures pyrrhic victories at Zorndorf and Hochkirk	Frederick prevails over the Austrians at Leignitz	Death of the Empress Elizabeth of Russia saves Frederick from defeat at the hands of the alliance against him	Seven Years War brought to a conclusion

> **When the King of Prussia speaks on problems connected with the art of war . . . then everything is taut, solid and uncommonly instructive. There are no circumlocutions . . . for he is well versed in history . . . a genius and a man who talks admirably. But everything he says betrays the knave.**
>
> The Austrian emperor Joseph II in a letter to his mother, Maria Theresa

The Austrian commander, Prince Charles of Lorraine, anticipated a Prussian outflanking movement and this proved his undoing. His army, pivoted around the town of Leuthen, was extended on a front of 4 miles (6.5 km), precisely to prevent it being outflanked. Frederick engaged the Austrian right with a feint attack by his cavalry, while simultaneously making for the Austrian left in four columns that were largely concealed by a line of low hills and a bank of fog.

As the Prussian columns had passed the Austrian left flank, the latter now lay at a right angle to Frederick's army, which advanced in two

The growth of light infantry

An 18th-century development not influenced by Frederick the Great was the arrival on the battlefield of light infantry: troops skilled in skirmishing in 'open order', that is not in a rigid line of battle. The Austrians made extensive use of such troops, often recruited from the wild country on the Hungarian border and imbued with scouting and woodcraft skills. Frederick maintained similar units in the Prussian army but never wholly trusted them. Such troops also made their presence felt in the American War of Independence (1775–82).

Service in the light infantry demanded a degree of initiative, marksmanship and ability to exploit natural cover that was completely at odds with the rigid infantry formations favoured by Frederick. The British Volunteer Manual of 1803 noted:

Vigilance, activity, and intelligence are particularly requisite . . . a light infantryman . . . should know how to take advantage of every circumstance of ground which can enable him to harass and annoy an enemy.

lines of battle to roll up the enemy's exposed flank. The Austrian army's position was further weakened by the fact that the troops on its left flank were Protestant Württembergers whose natural sympathies lay with the Prussians closing with them. They broke and ran, forcing Charles to transfer troops from his right to shore up the centre of his line around Leuthen.

An artillery duel followed before Leuthen was taken by the Prussians, whose cavalry then drove off a determined counterattack by the Austrian horse. In three hours of fighting the Austrian army was routed. Frederick's execution had been perfect. He had successfully concealed his intentions, achieved total surprise and struck the critical blow (the *Schwerpunkt*) at his enemy's weakest point. It was a victory in which his reformed cavalry, horse artillery and ultra-disciplined infantry each played a complementary part.

The key to Frederick's victory lay in his operational mastery before battle was joined. He was able to conceal his intentions from the hapless Charles of Lorraine, thus achieving complete surprise when he delivered the crucial blow against the most fragile sector of the Austrian line. This anticipated the essential elements of Blitzkrieg, employed some 180 years later by the German generals who plotted the destruction of the British Expeditionary Force (BEF) and the French army in May 1940. In 1757 victory at Leuthen secured Silesia for Prussia and ended the ill-starred military career of Prince Charles. Above all, it was the vindication of Frederick's magnificent infantry, whose elite regiments wore the metal-fronted mitre cap signifying their status as grenadiers.

> **❛Terminate every business prudently and quickly.❜**
> **Frederick the Great** in *Military Instructions*, 1748

the condensed idea
Frederick's legacy was indomitable infantry and unbeatable artillery

22 Napoleonic corps d'armée
1754–1815

Napoleon Bonaparte (1769–1821) was a unique historical figure, relentlessly hardworking and ambitious, the template for many a modern dictator. Until his powers began to wane, he was an undoubted strategic genius, but he was certainly not an innovator.

Napoleon breathed life into the military reforms he inherited at the beginning of his career. He was an artilleryman, and in his hands French artillery became one of his most effective battlefield weapons. This was not his work alone. In the years before 1765, French artillery had been modernized by Jean-Baptiste de Gribeauval (1715–89), whose reforms led to the abandonment of lighter field pieces that supplied fire support at battalion level and the assembly of massed batteries. Their concentrated fire could blast holes in an enemy line, which might then be exploited by cavalry or infantry. In similar fashion, Napoleon created a formidable cavalry arm, but the tactics it employed had been established well before his arrival on the scene.

Speed and flexibility Among the distinguishing characteristics of the Napoleonic method of waging war were speed and flexibility. In this Bonaparte was influenced by the comte de Guibert (1743–90), an advocate of mobility over positional warfare. Guibert also urged the organization of armies into self-supporting divisions, a practice adopted by Marshal de Broglie (1750–94) during the Seven Years War (1754–63) but later abandoned by the French

timeline

1754–63	1765	1772	1799	1800	1804
Seven Years War	Gribeauval completes work on modernizing French artillery	Guibert's *Essai générale de tactique*	Napoleon becomes France's first consul	Napoleon reorganizes Grande Armée into autonomous all-arms corps	Napoleon is crowned emperor

military establishment. Guibert, whose *Essai générale de tactique* (1772) was among Bonaparte's favourite reading, also favoured the formation of citizen armies, the French Revolution's legacy to Napoleon.

Napoleon was also influenced by Pierre-Joseph de Bourcet (1700–80), French chief of staff during the War of the Austrian Succession (1740–8) and Seven Years War, and an expert in mountain warfare, who advocated the dispersal of forces to oblige the enemy to cover many different points and also for marching in order of battle. The dispersal of forces during the march was to be followed by their speedy concentration at the decisive point, before the enemy had time to regain his balance.

> **❝The standing armies, while a burden on the people, are inadequate for the achievement of grand and decisive results in war and the hegemony over Europe will fall to the nation which . . . creates a citizen army.❞**
>
> **Comte de Guibert,** *Essai générale de tactique* **(1772)**

Bataillon carré In 1800 Napoleon reorganized his army into autonomous all-arms *corps d'armée*, self-sustaining formations that could fight on their own for up to 36 hours until they were joined by other corps. In effect the corps was an army in miniature, with its own staff, infantry, cavalry, artillery train and headquarters. Its commander's general line of advance was determined by Napoleon, but thereafter the latter was allowed a degree of flexibility on the march. On engaging the enemy, the corps commander could use his own initiative while other corps commanders in his vicinity would march towards the sound of guns.

The *corps d'armée* concept was fully expressed by the *bataillon carré* (battalion square) in which separate corps marched along parallel roads, each within one or two days' march of each other. With an advance guard, screening cavalry force and reserve corps, and cover on its left and right flanks, Napoleon's army enjoyed an all-round defence and could concentrate in any direction once one of its elements made contact with the enemy.

1805	**1805**	**1806**	**1807**	**1813**	**1815**
OCTOBER Manoeuvre of Ulm	DECEMBER Napoleon smashes the Russo-Austrian army at Austerlitz	Battle of Jena-Auerstadt	Treaty of Tilsit makes Napoleon master of almost all western and central Europe	Battle of Leipzig, after which the defeated Napoleon lost control of Germany	Battle of Waterloo brings Napoleon's career to an end with exile to St Helena

The operational dispersal of his forces enabled Napoleon to find and then fix the enemy with part of his army while other corps converged on him. It was all but impossible to manoeuvre out of the path of the oncoming juggernaut. At his peak this gave Napoleon the prize he most craved: the destruction of one or more enemy forces in the field as the climax to a series of rapid manoeuvres.

Jena-Auerstädt Napoleon's method is strikingly illustrated by the campaign that preceded the double Battle of Jena-Auerstädt, fought against the Prussian army in October 1806, west of the River Saale in modern Germany. On 8 October Napoleon began his advance through the Thuringian Forest to force the Prussian army to give battle. His army adopted the *bataillon carré* formation of some 180,000 men in three columns, each comprising two corps. His cavalry corps and the Imperial Guard followed the middle column and a division of Bavarians followed the right column.

Napoleon was unsure of the location of the Prussian army, but remained confident that the *bataillon carré* would allow him to find and fix the enemy. Initially he advanced on a front of 125 miles (200 km), which

The manoeuvre of Ulm

One of Napoleon's masterstrokes was the so-called manoeuvre of Ulm (1805). He used one *corps d'armée* to absorb the attention of the Austrian army, while the latter was enveloped by another six *corps d'armée* sweeping round the Austrian right in a manoeuvre that anticipated the Schlieffen Plan of 1914, a flank march by almost an entire army. Obligingly, the Austrian army remained motionless, like a tethered goat awaiting the sudden arrival of a tiger. The Austrians were outmanoeuvred and enveloped on the same ground across which Marlborough's army marched at the Battle of Blenheim in 1704. On 20 October 1805, the Austrian commander General Mack, seeing no way out, capitulated in Bonaparte's presence.

Napoleon's pattern of attack

A Napoleonic all-arms attack followed an unvarying pattern. After a heavy bombardment from massed batteries of artillery, light infantry advanced to skirmish and reconnoitre the enemy position. Cavalry was then thrown in to defeat the enemy's horse and force his infantry to form squares, which were ideal targets for the horse-artillery batteries that were attached to the French cavalry.

Then infantry was moved up to deploy into line for fire action, or into columns – 50 men wide and 12 deep – to crash into the enemy position and achieve a local victory with the bayonet, which in turn would be exploited by the hussars and dragoons of Napoleon's light cavalry. When this sequence was not followed, as at the Battle of Waterloo (1815), disaster loomed.

shrank to 28 miles (45 km) for the passage through the forest and widened out to 37 miles (60 km) when he emerged. At this point his enemy had no clear idea of where Napoleon's main blow would fall. In 1806 the Prussians were the heirs of Frederick the Great in name only. In Corelli Barnett's words, the Prussian army was like 'an antique weapon lovingly preserved in a glass case, worm-eaten and brittle'.

On 13 October Napoleon discovered that the withdrawing and dispersed Prussians were on his left flank, and wheeled the *bataillon carré* to trap them. He was able to concentrate overwhelming force (75,000 French to 47,000 Prussians) against part of the Prussian army at Jena and destroy it, while one of his corps, under Marshal Davout, engaged and defeated a numerically superior Prussian force (45,000 to 26,000) at Auerstädt. In a single day's fighting he had precipitated the collapse of the leading military monarchy of the ancien régime.

the condensed idea
The *corps d'armée* provided a template for 19th-century armies

23 Naval firepower
1588–1805

From the 16th century, warships evolved from being made-over merchantmen into specialized fighting machines. This significant change was underlined in 1588 when the Spanish Armada, scorning cannon and relying on infantry to board enemy ships, was roundly defeated by smaller, nimbler, cannon-armed English ships, which kept their distance and relied on shot and seamanship to disable their opponents.

However, the light guns of the day could not sink ships. Heavier ordnance was needed to send a ball through 90–120 centimetres (3–4 ft) of oak below the waterline. In the mid-17th century, warships were built with guns of one calibre on each deck; *Royal Sovereign* (see chapter 16) was a striking example of that era. In turn this produced the broadside, the enduring feature of naval warfare for the next 200 years.

Tactics now changed to accommodate this development. Warships no longer fired from a distance to keep the enemy away, but closed to point-blank range to pound the opponent with a full broadside. At a range of 250 yards (229 m), a warship's shot could smash the timbers of its target and kill or injure the crew with flying splinters. Ships in parallel 'lines of battle' would slug it out at these short ranges. When the ships were locked together, boarding parties would cross to enemy ships, the crews fighting hand-to-hand.

timeline

1779	1781	1794	1794
John Clerk propounds the theory of breaking the line	Carronade equips 429 Royal Navy ships	Glorious First of June fought in the Bay of Biscay	Nelson loses the sight in one eye in Corsica

This simplistic approach to war at sea was superseded by a new method, reputedly devised by John Clerk (1728–1812), who in the privately published *Essay on Naval Tactics* (1779) advocated breaking the line of battle. If attacked from the bow or stern, a ship could not bring its guns to bear. Clerk suggested that the Royal Navy should aim to break the enemy's line, overwhelming the ships behind the break before the rest of the enemy fleet could change course and rejoin the fight.

Ships of the line

In the 18th century the Royal Navy's warships fell into six categories. Larger ships were 'ships of the line' ('of the line of battle'), had two or three decks and were essentially floating gun platforms designed to pound the enemy with their heavy armament. The number of guns they carried determined their classification. As a rule of thumb, 'first-raters' carried 110 guns or more, 'second-raters' 98, 'third-raters' 64–80 and 'fourth-raters' 50–64. The Royal Navy's smallest ships were 'fifth-rater' frigates (32–44 guns) and 'sixth-rater' sloops (up to 28 guns).

At the Battle of Trafalgar (21 October 1805) Admiral Horatio Nelson refined Clerk's doctrine, breaking the Franco-Spanish line at right angles and at two points, with two columns of ships led respectively by his own flagship *Victory* and his second-in-command Sir Cuthbert Collingwood's *Royal Sovereign*. This bold plan overwhelmed Franco-Spanish commander Vice-Admiral Villeneuve's centre and rear, precipitating a close-quarter 'pell-mell' battle in which superior British gunnery and ship-handling prevailed. Seventeen of Villeneuve's ships were captured, including the French and Spanish flagships, and one was destroyed. Nelson was mortally wounded by a French marksman aboard the French *Redoutable*.

❛Your mission is of the greatest importance. Whether I [eventually] choose to march on London or to make peace . . . the whole thrust of my strategy is against Britain.❜

Napoleon writing to General Brune, his envoy in Constantinople, January 1804

1797	1797	1798	1801	1805
Nelson is largely responsible for victory in the Battle of Cape St Vincent, fought in the Atlantic off Spain. Loses an arm in Tenerife	Battle of Camperdown against the Dutch	Battle of the Nile, Nelson's victory over the French on the coast of Egypt	Battle of Copenhagen, another of Nelson's victories over the French	Battle of Trafalgar

❝Something must be left to chance; nothing is sure in a sea fight, beyond all others. Shot will carry away the masts and yards of friends as well as foes; but I look with confidence to a victory before the van of the enemy could succour their rear, and then that the British fleet would most of them be ready to receive their twenty sail of the line or to pursue them should they endeavour to make off.❞

Nelson's formal order to his captains, 9 October 1805

The Royal Navy lost no ships at Trafalgar. When *Victory* returned to Dover, 80 shot holes 'between wind and water' were counted at places at which the sea came in. All of them had been plugged by *Victory*'s carpenters during and immediately after the battle. Her spars had sustained some damage, reducing her sailing qualities, but her primary function, as a gun platform, remained intact. The survivability of England's 'wooden walls' was quite exceptional. They absorbed solid shot and then elastically regained their shape. They splintered but with nothing like the lethality inflicted on the defenders of Vauban's stone fortresses. They rarely exploded or sank, even after a heavy pounding and, given good weather, the survivors of battle could sail home.

Naval artillery

Naval artillery was usually heavier than that used on land. The standard gun was a cannon firing a 14.5-kg (32-lb) shot. In 1747 a new type of gun, developed by Benjamin Robins, was offered to the Royal Navy. It was the same weight as existing types but was of larger calibre and threw a heavier ball. The project languished until it was taken up again in 1778 after a short, light, large-calibre cannon had been manufactured by the Carron ironworks in Scotland to arm merchantmen. The carronade, as it was called, was adopted by the Royal Navy and by 1781 it equipped 429 of its ships. It was dubbed 'the smasher'.

English gunnery

At Trafalgar, Nelson's fleet of 27 ships mounted 2,232 guns, of which the lightest missile was 5.4 kilograms (12 lb) and the heaviest 31 kilograms (68 lb). Some 14,000 men serviced a fleet broadside and their daily food and water rations amounted to 3.6 kilograms (8 lb). Motive power – the wind and tide – was free. In contrast, at Waterloo, Napoleon's army deployed 366 guns firing between 2.7 kilograms (6 lb) and 5.4 kilograms (12 lb). His artillerymen numbered 9,000 plus some 5,000 horses in the artillery train. The horses required around 50 tons of fodder a day, all of which had to be collected. It can be seen that the gun power of Nelson's fleet exceeded that of Napoleon's army by a factor of six. To campaign with an equivalent amount of artillery, Napoleon would have needed over 50,000 artillerymen, 30,000 horses, 300 tons of fodder and 75 tons of food daily, all of which would have moved at a speed five times slower than that of the Royal Navy and at one-fifth of the logistic cost.

The French and Royal navies differed in another significant tactical respect. In battle the French aimed to destroy the enemy's masts and rigging, thus rendering them incapable of pursuit. It was a French priority only to seek combat when they perceived a definite outcome. In contrast, the British, who were often at a numerical disadvantage, considered the destruction of enemy ships an end in itself. Their gunnery focused on targeting the enemy's hulls, to destroy the guns and kill or maim the crews, rendering the enemy vessels incapable of further operations.

the condensed idea
Trafalgar was the last great encounter of wooden warships

24 Mass production
1801–1918

The leitmotif of 19th-century Europe was industrialization. It revolutionized society and the waging of war. Previously, the pace of change had been slow. The 'Brown Bess' musket carried by Wellington's infantry at Waterloo in 1815 was not dissimilar to those used by their grandfathers at Blenheim in 1704.

Infantry, the most numerous arm, delivered massive short-range firepower from dense formations. Under optimum conditions, a soldier might hit a man-size target at 80 yards (73 m), but conditions were rarely so favourable. The dense smoke that shrouded the battlefield reduced visibility, the fouling of burnt powder clogged musket barrels and locks, and the unreliability of the flintlock mechanism meant that up to a quarter of all shots were misfires.

Nor had artillery undergone a radical change, remaining a direct-fire weapon that did most of its killing at a range well below 1,000 yards (914 m). Round shot or multiple rounds like grape or canister were still favoured over bursting shells. Cavalry would also have been recognizable to a veteran of Blenheim. Light cavalry was tasked with scouting and reconnaissance, and joined in the pursuit of a beaten enemy; heavy cavalry, usually armoured in cuirass and helmet, relied on shock action to scatter the enemy.

timeline

1801–1900	1801–1900	1840–70	1853
Population of Germany (within the borders of 1871) increases from 24 million in 1801 to 57 million in 1900	Size of German conscript increases by 50 per cent	German rail network increases from 291 miles (469 km) to 10,700 miles (17,215 km)	German census established

But significant changes in civilian technology, underway since the 18th century, were harbingers of a dramatic change in the military environment. James Watt's introduction of viable steam engines in the last quarter of the 18th century had improved coal production and iron founding. In Germany iron production rose from 85,000 tons in 1823 to over 1 million tons in 1867. Just under 50 years later, on the eve of the First World War, it had reached 15 million tons, and Germany had overtaken Britain as the world's leading industrial power.

Manpower In Europe, industrial muscle and healthier, expanding populations produced deep pools of manpower that could be mobilized as an act of policy to achieve national ends. Much of the modern state's increasing revenue was devoted to military equipment, particularly the 'big ticket' items – artillery and warships – but uniforms, preserved foods and modern barracks were also significant in conferring a new status on the armed forces of the modern state.

Steam and steel were the leitmotifs of European and North American warfare in the 19th century. The rapid deployment by rail of ever-larger numbers of troops to the front had became commonplace after 1859, when France went to war with Austria in northern Italy. In 1866 and 1870 it underlay Prussia's victories over Austria and France. Railways also played an important part in the American Civil War (1861–5) in which the industrialized North, with its developed railway network, enjoyed an inherent advantage over the agrarian South. In the 19th century, technology revolutionized communications (railways, steamships, the electric telegraph); strengthened military defences, from the armoured turret to the concrete fortress carapace; and vastly increased the range and lethality of weapons.

The breech-loading bolt-action rifle In the 18th century, the production of small arms had changed little since the Middle Ages. By the 19th century, precision tools and the beginnings of industrial automation enabled government arsenals and private manufacturers to move to the rapid production of standardized weapons with interchangeable parts.

1863	**1864**	**1866**	**1867**	**1870–1**
British Enfield armoury, equipped with automatic milling machines, produces 100,370 rifles	Needle gun is combat-tested in the Second Schleswig War	French Puteaux armoury, re-equipped for mass production, produces 300,000 chassepot rifles a year	Universal conscription introduced in Austria-Hungary	Needle gun and chassepot are used in the Franco-Prussian War

> **❝I could see only infantry there [at about] 1,600 paces distant. But the moment the head of the Brigade was about to cross the bridge we suddenly received . . . such a hail of chassepot bullets that one officer, the trumpet-major, three men and six horses were hit.❞**
>
> Prince Kraft zu Hohenlohe Ingelfingen, *Letters on Artillery*, 1887

In the first 30 years of the century, musketry was vastly improved by the replacement of flintlocks with percussion locks. The rifling of barrels – the cutting of grooves in a weapon's barrel to impart spin, and greater accuracy, to a bullet – had introduced the rifleman to the battlefield in the American War of Independence (1775–81) and the Peninsular War (1808–14).

Minié bullet Rifling demanded a bullet that was tight-fitting on firing but could be loaded easily. The problem was finally overcome by the development in France of the Minié bullet, named after its inventor. This was a conical bullet with a hollow base and flanged rim. It slipped easily down even a heavily fouled barrel and, on firing, the gases of the explosion drove into the hollow base, forcing the flanges to bite into the rifling. The Minié bullet was widely used in the American Civil War.

The next step was the replacement of muzzle-loaders by breech-loaders. One of the principal problems with the muzzle-loader was that reloading while lying down was immensely difficult.

Needle gun The breech-loading rifle did not come into its own as a military weapon until 1848. It was the brainchild of a Prussian gunsmith, Johann Nikolaus von Dreyse, and was known as the 'needle gun'. Adopted by the Prussian army in 1848, it was the first to feature the bolt system of closure and thus became the ancestor of every bolt-action rifle. The needle gun gave Prussian infantry a rate of fire of eight rounds a minute and demonstrated its effectiveness in the Second Schleswig War of 1864 and the Austro-Prussian War of 1866.

Chassepot The needle gun had been developed in conditions of great secrecy, but when the French first got wind of it they launched their own version, the chassepot bolt-action rifle, which appeared in 1863 and, with its shorter firing pin, was a marked improvement on the needle gun.

The Franco-Prussian War of 1870–1 saw the needle gun and the chassepot put to the acid test. The chassepot, with its longer range of 600 yards (550 m), emerged the winner of this contest, although the French lost the war. At the Battle of St Privat in August 1870, the Prussian Guard launched a massed frontal attack on the French 6th Corps, in which they lost some 8,000 men, mainly to chassepot fire, in less than half an hour. By the same token, the Krupp breech-loading artillery pieces deployed by the Prussians, the equivalents on a larger scale of the needle gun and the chassepot, were to prove decisive.

> **❝The rifle made all men tall.❞**
>
> **Thomas Carlyle**

The bolt-action rifle, with a box magazine at the breech or a tubular magazine below the barrel, was to become the standard infantry weapon of armies across the world. The introduction of smokeless powder after 1885 completed the process, and by 1900 the infantry rifle had assumed the shape it was to retain through the First World War and well into the Second World War. Mass-produced, accurate and reliable, it had a range of up to 1,000 yards (914 m) against a mass target, and its magazine held 5 to 10 rounds. A well-trained infantryman could achieve a rate of fire of 15 rounds a minute.

the condensed idea
The Industrial Revolution transformed the range and lethality of small arms and artillery

25 The machine gun 1718–1918

From the early years of firearms, inventors sought the ultimate prize: a weapon that could maintain a continuous stream of fire. However, while ammunition remained powder and ball ignited by a spark, there was little prospect of a feasible mechanical solution.

Early attempts to overcome the problem concentrated on revolvers. James Puckle's 'Defence' of 1718 was a large six-cylinder revolver firing through a single barrel that had to be unlocked and turned manually. Nevertheless, the Defence achieved the respectable rate of fire of 63 shots a minute.

The advent of the percussion cap saw the development of a number of volley guns – a collection of rifle barrels mounted on a wheeled frame, which, after loading, could be fired in succession. The result was an impressive volley followed by a less impressive hiatus while the barrels were all reloaded.

The American Civil War (1861–5) prompted further developments. In 1861 the Union army purchased a small number of Ager machine guns. They were dubbed 'Coffee Mills' because of the hopper that surmounted the Ager. Into the hopper were fed steel tubes, each loaded with powder and ball and a nipple with a percussion cap. The turn of a crank forced a tube from the hopper into the chamber, dropped a hammer onto the cap, extracted the tube and loaded the next one. When the supply of tubes was exhausted there was a pause for reloading.

timeline

1718	1861	1865	1870–1	1882
James Puckle produces his Defence revolver	Invention of the Gatling gun	Gatling gun adopted by the US army	*Mitrailleuse* battle-tested in Franco-Prussian War	Hiram Maxim acquires the patent for a machine gun, which appears in 1884

Gatling gun and *mitrailleuse* The best-known mechanical machine gun of the period was the carriage-mounted Gatling gun, invented in 1861 by the Chicago dentist Richard Jordan Gatling. The gun consisted of six barrels mounted in a revolving frame. As the barrels were rotated, each in succession came level with the magazine, where a cartridge dropped into its loading tray. The cartridge was then forced into the chamber by a rammer, was fired and had its spent case extracted as the barrels turned. The Gatling gun proved its worth in the Civil War, but because Gatling came from the South, and was suspected of Confederate sympathies, it was not until 1865 that the Gatling gun was officially adopted by the US army.

In 1869 the *mitrailleuse*, developed from a Belgian design in the artillery workshop in Meudon, was adopted by the French army. The *mitrailleuse* was mounted on a wheeled carriage, and had 25 rifle barrels in a cylindrical casing, behind which was a breech block that slid back to allow a plate carrying 25 cartridges to be dropped into the weapon. The block was then closed, chambering the cartridges. The turn of a crank deposited 25 firing pins in succession. Reloading involved opening the breech, removing the plate with spent cases and dropping in a freshly loaded plate. The *mitrailleuse* was an efficient weapon, but on its operational debut in the Franco-Prussian War (1870–1) it was tactically mishandled. The *mitrailleuse* batteries were often held back with the artillery, where they were at the mercy of superior Prussian guns. And because the weapon had been developed in conditions of great secrecy, few battery commanders had received adequate training in its effective use.

The Maxim gun While machine guns relied on gravity feed and black-powder cartridges they were dogged by unreliability. Metallic cartridges and smokeless powder released their potential. The American Hiram Maxim, an all-round inventor who worked in many fields, decided to use the

> **❛Hang your electricity! If you want to make your fortune, invent something which will allow those fool Europeans to kill each other more quickly.❜**
>
> **A fellow countryman of Hiram Maxim**

1885	1886	1891	1895	1897	1912
Hiram Maxim demonstrates the Maxim gun to the British army	Maxim travels Europe to demonstrate his gun	Maxim gun is in service with the British, Austrian, German, Italian, Swiss and Russian armies	Browning machine gun adopted by the Royal Navy	The French adopt the Hotchkiss gun	The British adopt the Vickers .303 machine gun; the Germans adopt the Parabellum

The Maxim gun in action

Sir Francis de Winton had the machine gun ready and, working it himself, poured a tremendous volley into the nearest tower. The bullets rained in through the portholes and between the planks, killing numbers of the enemy . . . and in a few minutes it was seen that the garrison was issuing from the fort and flying for their lives. Such was the consternation created by the rapid and accurate shooting of the gun that the chief war town was evacuated, as well as the other villages of the same nature, and the chiefs surrendered.

Report of the use of the Maxim gun in the Gambia, November 1887

recoil of one round to load and fire the next. Cartridges were contained in a fabric belt that was cranked automatically into action. Here was a genuine machine gun, which freed its firer from operating its mechanism. He merely had to keep his finger pressed.

Maxim made his home in London and in the mid-1880s toured Europe demonstrating the superiority of his gun, then went into partnership with Vickers. By 1891 the British army had adopted the Maxim gun. Many others followed suit. Basic machine-gun design had been established and was to last for the next 30 years.

There were a number of modifications. The American John M. Browning used some of the gas that fired the bullet to assist the loading process, an addition incorporated by the water-cooled Vickers machine gun, which was adopted by the British army in 1912. In 1914 a British battalion usually had two Vickers guns, although few in the high command foresaw the importance it would rapidly assume. The Germans fielded between 6 and 12 belt-fed, water-cooled 7.92-millimetre (0.3-in) Parabellums per three-battalion regiment, forming a machine-gun company that placed formidable centralized firepower into the hands of its commanding officer. The onset of trench warfare during the First World War, in the late summer and autumn of 1914, led to a rapid rise in the number of machine guns deployed by both sides. In 1914 a British division fielded 24; by 1916 the number had risen almost tenfold to 204.

Vickers .303 machine gun By 1915 on the Western Front, platoon and battalion tactics were dominated by the machine gun. The majority were based on the reliable Maxim design, but they were costly to manufacture, complex to operate – it took two and a half months to train a Vickers gunner – and very cumbersome. A loaded Vickers weighed almost 45 kilograms (100 lb) and devoured colossal quantities of ammunition.

In a long-range barrage a single Vickers was capable of firing 100,000 rounds; some companies consumed nearly a million rounds over a 24-hour period.

The key fact about the Vickers and its counterparts was that it placed in the hands of one man the firepower formerly wielded by 40 fellow soldiers. A good rifleman could fire some 40 shots a minute; a machine-gunner could fire 600. Moreover, riflemen, however well trained, were less reliable agents of wounding and death. Their dispersal on the modern battlefield, in contrast to their musket-bearing predecessors in squares, inevitably meant a loss of overall control. The machine gun restored to a commander the ability to inflict multiple and simultaneous destruction by the issuing of a single word of command.

> **❝I could see, away to my left and right, long lines of men. Then I heard the "patter patter" of the machine guns in the distance. By the time I'd gone another ten yards there seemed to be only a few men left around me; by the time I had gone twenty yards, I seemed to be on my own. Then I was hit myself.❞**
>
> **Sergeant with the 26th Northumberland Fusiliers,** 1 July 1916, the first day of the **Battle of the Somme**

Above all, a machine gun is, in essence, an item of precision engineering, a machine operating within strictly defined limits. On the Vickers, and all its contemporaries, this involved adjusting the angle of the barrel relative to its fixed firing platform and tightening or loosening its traversing screw. Then, like a lathe or automatic press, it was activated by the pressing of a button. Thus the machine-gunner was largely reduced to the role of machine minder, feeding ammunition belts into the breech, topping up the water in the cooling jacket and traversing the gun from left to right and back again. The last was achieved by a simple procedure known by the British as the 'two-inch tap', nudging the side of the breech with the palm of the hand first one way and then the other to maintain a dense and fatal stream of bullets.

the condensed idea
By 1915 the machine gun dominated the Western Front

26 The all-big-gun battleship
1807–1945

From the Battle of Trafalgar (1805) to the 1840s, little changed in the design of ships of the line. They remained three-decked, full-rigged wooden sailing vessels armed with muzzle-loading cannon firing through ports. However, technology was about to render them obsolete.

The design revolution was felt in three key fields – propulsion, protection and firepower. As early as 1807, two years after Trafalgar, the American engineer Robert Fulton demonstrated the commercial viability of steam-powered vessels, but the vulnerability of the paddle wheel limited the application of the steam engine to the warship. However, 1843 saw the launch of the first screw-driven warship, the USS *Princeton*.

Ironclads The French were responsible for developments in firepower. Traditionally, naval guns, housed at 3-metre (10-ft) intervals in unobstructed open spaces running the length of the ship, had fired solid shot at hostile ships, supplemented with grape- or case-shot for fighting at close range against enemy personnel and their ships' rigging. In 1837 the French began to arm their warships with exploding shells and in 1859 launched the steam-driven, shell-firing *La Gloire*, whose wooden hull had been sheathed in iron armour 121 millimetres (4.8 in) thick at the belt. In 1860 the British responded with *Warrior*, the first battleship of the modern era, steam-propelled, shell-firing, iron in construction from keel to bulwarks and more heavily armoured than *La Gloire*.

timeline

1807	1843	1849	1862	1906
Fuller demonstrates steam-powered vessels can be commercially viable	Launch of USS *Princeton*	French navy launches *La Gloire*	Union gunboat *Monitor* pioneers turret warfare against Confederate warship *Virginia*	HMS *Dreadnought* enters service

Although *La Gloire* and *Warrior* enjoyed armour protection, were screw-powered and were armed with mounted guns firing exploding shells, they nevertheless fired broadsides like the ships at the Battle of Trafalgar. In March 1862, in the American Civil War (1861–5), there was a naval encounter of great significance. The Union gunboat *Monitor*, armed with two smooth-bore 11-inch guns housed in a rotating turret clad in eight inches of iron, fought a furious close-range battle in Hampton Roads with the Confederate warship *Virginia*. The duel was indecisive but of the greatest significance, as the *Monitor*'s turret, crude though it was, pointed the way to the future of the warship.

However, the sheer weight of these turrets meant that warships armed with them rode very close to the waterline and were thus confined to inshore operations. Moreover, the victory of a technically inferior Austrian fleet over a technically superior Italian fleet in the Battle of Lissa (1866) drove designers down the dead-end of fitting warships with armoured rams. Nevertheless, in the latter half of the 19th century, any navy with pretensions to modernity deployed iron ships that were driven by steam, mounted with shell-firing guns, and protected over their engine rooms, magazines and gun batteries by plates of metal armour.

By the turn of the century, the dizzying pace of change in the technology of naval warfare prompted Admiral Fisher, appointed Britain's First Sea Lord in 1904, to establish a committee to design an 'all-big-gun' battleship. Urgency was added to his deliberations by the Japanese victory over the Russians in the naval battle of Tsushima in May 1905, a dramatic demonstration of the power of modern naval gunnery.

Dreadnought In 1905, Admiral Fisher inaugurated a new programme of battleship construction that would consign all other existing types to obsolescence. The aim was to concentrate in a single hull the many advances in propulsion, protection and armament now available – among them rotary turbine engines, armour protection, range-finding optics, fire control systems and detonation-retarding fuses.

❛A snake among rabbits.❜

Prime Minister Palmerston
on seeing *Warrior* beside the wooden walls of the Channel Fleet

1914	**1914**	**1915**	**1915**	**1922**	**1945**
Royal Navy has 20 *Dreadnought*-class battleships and 9 cruisers to the German High Seas Fleet's 13 and 5	**8 DECEMBER** Battlecruisers *Inflexible* and *Revenge* defeat German squadron in Battle of the Falklands	**16 JANUARY** German battleships bombard Britain's east coast	**24 JANUARY** Battle-cruisers clash at the Battle of the Dogger Bank	*Dreadnought* scrapped	Sinking of Japanese super-battleship *Yamato* by US carrier-borne aircraft

The 18,000-ton battleship *Dreadnought* was constructed and launched in record-breaking time between October 1905 and February 1906. *Dreadnought* was driven by 13,000-horsepower Parsons steam turbines giving her, at 21 knots, the speed of a cruiser rather than a battleship. She was better armoured than any battleship afloat, with ten 30.5-centimetre (12-in) guns housed in five turrets. Twenty-seven 7.6-centimetre (3-in) quick-firers provided protection against torpedo-boat attacks, keeping them beyond the 3,000-yard (2,743-m) range of existing torpedoes. However, her vulnerability to hidden threats in the shallow waters of the North Sea – 'contact' mines and torpedo-firing submarines – was well understood by the Royal Navy's high command.

> ‘The Admiralty had demanded six ships; the economists offered four; and we have finally compromised on eight.’
>
> **Winston Churchill, home secretary 1909**

Dreadnought's technological leap into the future was intended to forestall the ambitions of all or any of Britain's naval rivals – France, Russia, Japan, the United States and Germany. The last, spurred by the maritime ambitions of Kaiser Wilhelm II, launched its own *Dreadnought*–building programme, which began to eat away at the Royal Navy's lead in the 'naval race'. In the summer of 1914, Britain remained the pre-eminent naval power, its capital ships the guardians of the biggest empire the world had ever seen. The Royal Navy's order of battle included 20 *Dreadnought*-class battleships and 9 *Dreadnought*-class battlecruisers, the latter being

Improving armaments

Dreadnought's absolute claim to omnipotence lay in the technology and technique devoted to her centralized direction of salvoes from the main armament. Developed principally by the British Admiral Percy Scott and the American Admiral William Sims, the fire control system combined range-finding devices, plotting machinery and electric communications, coupled with the precise calibration of guns and ammunition with regard to spotting and interpreting fall of shot. Here the improvement was dramatic. The trials of 1904 registered only 42.86 per cent hits; two years later, the new methods boosted performance to 71.12 per cent.

warships of the same weight as the original *Dreadnought* but faster and less heavily armoured. The German High Seas Fleet had 13 *Dreadnought*-class battleships and 5 battlecruisers.

The latter were smaller and more lightly armed than their British opposite numbers. Crucially, however, they possessed a number of significant advantages. They were more strongly armoured. The belts along their waterlines, which protected machinery and magazines against shells, were markedly thicker. They were broader in the beam, making them more stable gun platforms. They were also internally subdivided into numerous watertight compartments, the sine qua non of survival in action. The Royal Navy's ships adopted the same 'honeycomb' system but, with fewer cells, were less battleworthy. If they were hit, they would have to pull out of the line to repair the damage.

The weakness of the British battlecruisers' thin armour was compounded by inferior magazine protection, carelessness in the handling of ammunition and insufficient awareness of the dangers of flash being transmitted from the turrets to the magazines below. These vulnerabilities were exposed when the British Grand Fleet and the German High Seas Fleet clashed at Jutland (1916). The British lost three battlecruisers to the Germans' one. The High Seas Fleet could claim tactical success, but the strategic advantage still lay with the Royal Navy. Within a week it was ready to sail back into the North Sea. Germany was never able to risk a major encounter again.

> **❛It is quite within the bounds of possibility that half our battle fleet might be disabled by underwater attack before the guns opened fire at all, if a false move is made.❜**
>
> **Admiral Sir John Jellicoe, commander of the Grand Fleet, October 1914**

the condensed idea
Within 30 years the battleship was obsolete

27 Trench warfare 1914–18

The First World War began as a war of movement, but with the arrival of fixed trench systems on the Western Front it took on many aspects of a gigantic siege, requiring colossal quantities of all types of guns and ammunition.

Neither the British nor their French allies were initially prepared for this eventuality. In 1914 the backbone of the French artillery was the quick-firing 75-millimetre (3-in) field gun introduced in 1897. The 75's hydro-pneumatic recoil system made it exceptionally stable when fired, and its quick-acting breech mechanism gave it a firing rate of up to ten rounds a minute. It could throw a 5.4-kilogram (12-lb) high-explosive or 7.2-kilogram (16-lb) shrapnel shell up to 10,000 yards (9 km). However, the French belief in all-out attack meant that the 75 was far from suited to trench warfare and its shells were too light to pose a threat to a heavily defended position.

At the outbreak of war the British Expeditionary Force (BEF) had no heavy artillery, but deployed the rapid-firing 18-pounder field gun which, like the 75, did not have the weight of shell or the angle of fire to be effective against well-dug trenches. Nevertheless, when deployed 2–3 miles (3–5 km) behind the battle line, the 18-pounder could play its part in barrages.

German superiority In the latter half of the 19th century, the Germans had developed weapons to tackle the hardened fortress complexes built along their borders by the French in the west and the Russians in the east. Thus the German army had a far higher proportion of howitzers

timeline

1904–5	1914	1915	1915
Russo-Japanese War provides pointers to the role of artillery in any future conflict	BEF arrives in France with no heavy artillery. Germany is the only combatant to use trench mortars	The British launch trench mortar programme	**MAY** The French employ 300 guns in the Artois offensive. Within months, in Champagne, the number has risen sevenfold

– which had short barrels and fired heavier shells on a high trajectory – in its field artillery batteries than did its enemies, and this gave it a crucial advantage. Of the super-heavy guns, howitzers and mortars that the Germans developed in the pre-war years, the most impressive was the formidable 75-ton Krupp 42-centimetre (16.5-in) howitzer capable of lobbing a 918-kilogram (2,052-lb) projectile a distance of 15,530 yards (14.2 km).

Indirect fire Another artillery technique perfected before 1914 was that of indirect fire, enabling gunners to fire on targets they could not see. A concealed spotter sent instructions to the gunners by telephone and, after observing the first shot, would talk them on to the target. In conditions of trench warfare this was to prove invaluable, but in the summer of 1914 the combatants anticipated a war of movement in which indirect fire would be irrelevant.

By the spring of 1915 this fond hope had been shattered. In May the French employed some 300 heavy guns in their offensive in Artois. When autumn came around, and with it a new offensive in Champagne, the French deployed no fewer than 2,000 guns and three railway lines had to be built to get them and their ammunition into position. The intensity of the French bombardment destroyed three German infantry regiments before heavy rain turned the battlefield into a quagmire and destroyed any chance of a breakthrough. The lesson that the French and the British drew from the failed offensives of 1915 was that an even greater weight of artillery was needed.

In August 1914 the BEF had landed in France with 486 guns. By November 1918 the number of British guns of all types in France

Breaking through

Breaking through the enemy's lines is largely a question of the expenditure of high explosive ammunition. If sufficient ammunition is forthcoming, a way can be blasted through the line.

Sir John French, commander of the BEF 1914–15, January 1915

1916	1916	1917	1917	1918
FEBRUARY For the preliminary bombardment at Verdun the Germans concentrate over 1,200 artillery pieces on an 8-mile (13-km) front	**JUNE** The preliminary British bombardment on the Somme expends over 1.5 million shells	**JUNE** At Messines, the British concentrate 2,388 guns on a 9-mile (14.5-km) front	**JULY** At Passchendaele the preliminary British bombardment destroys the fragile drainage system and, when it rains, produces seas of mud	The British deploy 3,000 trench mortars on the Western Front

had risen to 6,432. During the war the British had fired off over 170 million rounds, representing over 5 million tons. In June 1916 the bombardment that preceded the offensive on the Somme expended over 1.5 million shells, intending to break up the German barbed wire, bludgeon their batteries into silence and entomb the defenders in their dugouts.

They were wrong on all counts. At 7.30 a.m. on the broiling hot morning of 1 July, the bombardment moved on to the German second line. The German machine-gunners emerged from their dugouts, shaken but unscathed, to pour a withering hail of machine-gun fire into the 13 British divisions advancing at a walking pace across no-man's land.

> **❝Literally the ground quaked with the impact of each shell. They came at intervals of about 10 or 15 seconds; inexorable, closer overhead every time . . .❞**
>
> Gunner Aubrey Wade,
> *The War of the Guns* (1936)

At Messines in June 1917, the British concentrated 2,388 guns (808 of them heavy) and 304 large smooth-bore trench mortars on a 9-mile (14.5-km) front, a ratio of 1 gun to every 7 yards or 240 to the mile. In the 17-day preliminary bombardment, 5.5 tons of ammunition were delivered to each yard of enemy front. Artillery accounted for up to 70 per cent of the casualties on the Western Front between 1914 and 1918.

Even under the heaviest bombardment, sufficient soldiers survived to break up an infantry attack. The 4.3 million shells fired in the 14-day bombardment of July 1917 that opened the Battle of Passchendaele failed to destroy the German defence and shattered the battle zone's fragile drainage system. Then it rained. When the British infantry went over the top they advanced through a quagmire and into a hail of German bullets.

Trench mortar In 1914 only the Germans fielded mortars, having been impressed by the use the Japanese made of improvised mortars during the siege of Port Arthur in 1904–5 during the Russo-Japanese War. In addition to their large stocks of machine guns and heavy artillery, they possessed 180 trench mortars, or *Minenwerfers* (bomb throwers), dubbed 'moaning minnies' by the British, a corruption of the German word and a reference to the peculiar noise made by their wobbling flight.

At the start of the First World War the Germans fielded three purpose-built mortars: the 7.6-centimetre (3-in) light mortar that threw a

4.5-kilogram (10-lb) bomb up to 1,150 yards (1 km); the medium 17-centimetre (6.5-in) mortar that delivered a 49-kilogram (109-lb) bomb over a range of 600 yards (548 m); and the heavy 21-centimetre (8.3-in) mortar that fired a 100-kilogram (220-lb) bomb over 600 yards. The latter was one of the deadliest weapons on the Western Front. Its very high trajectory and heavy charges could devastate entire sections of trench. The German mortars were distributed among independent mortar detachments. Each infantry regiment had one *Minenwerfer-Abteilung*, consisting of twelve 7.6-centimetre (3-in) mortars and 24 grenade launchers.

From early 1915, the British strove hard to catch the Germans. In the first quarter of the year British factories produced 75 mortars and 8,000 shells. By the last quarter output had risen to 424 mortars and 189,000 shells. By the opening of the Somme offensive in July 1916, British infantry divisions had three batteries of light mortars and three of medium mortars, each consisting of four weapons. Single batteries of heavy mortars were introduced later. By 1918 the British deployed some 3,000 mortars on the Western Front.

In 1916 the standard weapon was the light 7.6-centimetre (3-in) Stokes Mortar, initially employed to fire only smoke rounds, whose rate of fire was 30 rounds a minute. In the spring of that year the British introduced a medium mortar firing a 27-kilogram (60-lb) projectile from prepared positions within 150 yards (137 m) of the enemy line. The heavy mortar was introduced late in 1916, firing a 68-kilogram (150-lb) projectile to a maximum range of 1,000 yards (914 m). Fired from 25 feet (7.6 m) below the surface, it could gouge out a trench to a similar depth.

the condensed idea
Machine guns and artillery imposed trench warfare from 1914 to 1918

28 Chemical warfare 431 BC–2012

The history of chemical warfare – the employment of the toxic qualities of chemical substances as weapons of war – has a history as old as warfare itself. Stone Age hunters and the Ancient Greeks used poisoned arrows. 'The Laws of Manu', a fourth-century BC Hindu treatise on statecraft, forbids the use of poisoned arrows but recommends poisoning food and water. In the sixth century BC, Sun Tzu's *The Art of War* urged the use of 'fire weapons', a method with which the Athenians and Spartans were familiar.

When besieging the city state of Athens in the Peloponnesian War (431–404 BC), the Spartans resorted to an early form of gas warfare, placing a mixture of wood, pitch and sulphur under the walls, hoping its fumes would incapacitate the defenders. In the Middle Ages the English navy is said to have thwarted a French invasion fleet by blinding its sailors with quicklime (calcium oxide).

In the sieges of the 17th century, armies attempted to start fires in beleaguered cities by bombarding them with incendiary shells packed with sulphur, tallow, turpentine and saltpetre. In 1854, during the Crimean War, a British chemist, Lyon Playfair, proposed a cacodyl cyanide shell for use against Russian warships. The British Ordnance Department considered the proposal as mean-spirited as the ancient practice of poisoning the wells of the enemy. Playfair's response is illuminating: 'It is considered a legitimate mode of warfare to fill shells with molten metal which scatters among the enemy, and produces the most frightful modes of death. Why

timeline

431–421 BC	1854	1899	1914
Sulphur used in siege of Athens	Proposal to use cyanide shells against Russian troops in the Crimea is rejected	Hague Convention outlaws the use of gas shells	**OCTOBER** Germans use gas for the first time against British troops in France

a poisonous vapour which would kill men without suffering is to be considered illegitimate warfare is incomprehensible.' In 1899 the Hague Peace Conference prohibited the use of shells filled with asphyxiating gas, a decision confirmed by the Hague Convention of 1907.

> **❝Throw poison in the form of powder upon galleys. Chalk, fine sulfide of arsenic, and powdered verdigris may be thrown upon enemy ships by means of mangonels, and all those who, as they breathe, inhale the powder into their lungs will become asphyxiated.❞**
>
> **Leonardo da Vinci**

The First World War In the First World War the 'new weapon' took on a life of its own as the Western Front congealed and the stalemate of trench warfare set in. The Germans made the first move in October 1914, replacing the resin packing around the lead balls in shrapnel shells with an irritant chemical. They were used against the British but had no noticeable effect.

The Germans then used shells filled with xylyl bromide on the Eastern Front. In January 1915, they were used against the Russians near the town of Bolimów in Poland. In the severe cold the liquid froze in the shells and did not vaporize. Similar shells were used against the British at Nieuport on the Western Front in March 1915, but once more had little effect.

The Germans persisted. At 5 p.m. on 22 April 1915, two sinister greenish-yellow clouds crept across no-man's land towards the Allied lines at Ypres. The clouds were pressurized chlorine gas released from more than 500 cylinders in the German trenches as the preliminary to an offensive.

German prisoners and a deserter had warned of this new weapon, but no countermeasures had been taken. The two French colonial divisions in the north flank of the Ypres salient were engulfed by the cloud and fled in panic, leaving a 4-mile (6.5-km) gap in the front peopled only by the dead and those who lay suffocating in agony from chlorine poisoning.

1915	1915	1918		1936	1944
22 APRIL Germans use gas, released from cylinders, at Ypres	**26 NOVEMBER** Phosgene gas introduced	**OCTOBER** Adolf Hitler, a runner with the 16th Bavarian Reserve Regiment on the Western Front, is gassed during the closing weeks of the war		Italians use gas, delivered by shells and aircraft, in Abyssinia	Red Army discovers quantities of tabun nerve gas manufactured by German scientists

> ❝The effects of the successful gas attack were horrible. I am not pleased with the idea of poisoning men. Of course the entire world will rage about it at first and then imitate us.❞
>
> German writer Rudolf Binding, *A Fatalist at War* (1929)

Chlorine gas Chlorine gas poisoning led to a slow and agonizing death by asphyxiation. On 25 September 1915, the British released chlorine gas on the German lines at Loos, but little of it reached the enemy trenches. Thereafter increasing use was made of gas shells, and by 1918 no fewer than 63 different types of gas were in use, each with its own smell and grisly effects on the human body. Chlorine smelled of a mixture of pepper and pineapple; phosgene reeked of rotting fish; mustard gas was reminiscent of soap and sweets. Its effects were delayed for up to 12 hours before it began to blister the skin, close the eyes, attack the bronchial tubes by stripping off the mucous membrane and cause violent vomiting. It was also known to destroy the testicles of those who took shelter in

Geneva Protocol

In 1925 the League of Nations issued the Geneva Protocol, which condemned the use of gas and bacteriological weapons. However, they were used in the interwar years by the Italians in Abyssinia and by the Japanese against the Chinese. In the 1930s German scientists developed and manufactured tabun nerve gas. It was never used, but some 15,000 tons fell into the hands of the advancing Red Army in 1944. The Germans also discovered sarin in 1938 and soman in 1944 but never used them, possibly because Hitler feared that the Allies might reply with something even more terrible. The British contemplated using gas in the summer of 1940 when they faced a German invasion. In 1943 the Americans prepared to use mustard gas in Italy if the Germans deployed it there. A US ship, the SS *John Harvey*, carrying mustard gas, was sunk by a Ju 88 bomber in Bari harbour. Sixty-nine men died in the incident, which for many years was hushed up. In the post-war years the British developed the VX nerve agent, which they traded with the Americans for information on thermonuclear weapons.

shell craters where it lingered. One mustard gas victim was Adolf Hitler, serving with the 16th Bavarian Reserve Regiment, who was caught in a British attack in the Ypres salient in October 1918.

First World War countermeasures

Gas was an imperfect weapon: a change of wind could blow it back into the faces of the troops who had released it. Protective measures were quickly developed. The first countermeasures against gas were primitive, among them pads of cotton waste soaked in urine, which partially neutralized chlorine. By the early summer of 1915, the British had introduced flannel 'helmets', which were pulled over the head and tucked under the uniform collar. From 1917 these stopgap measures had been replaced by box respirators, which used filters containing chemicals to neutralize the gas.

Present danger

The danger of chemical weapons falling into the hands of terrorists has remained a constant threat since their first use by an apocalyptic group in Japan in June 1994, when sarin gas released in Matsumoto killed eight and injured 200. In October 2002 Russian special forces used a chemical agent in an assault on Chechen terrorists who were holding hostages in a Moscow theatre. In 2001 al-Qaeda announced that it was attempting to acquire radiological, biological and chemical weapons. In 2007 chlorine bombs were used in Iraq by terrorists affiliated with al-Qaeda.

By August 1915 the French had introduced an impregnated fabric design that covered the face but not the top of the head and was secured by metal strips and tapes. However, it was useless against phosgene, introduced on 26 November 1915 near Verdun. From January 1916, a new mask was introduced, consisting of a conical mask with elasticated straps and a separate pair of goggles. This provided four hours' protection against phosgene. A modified version, the M2, with integral goggles, was introduced in the autumn of 1916 and remained standard issue until 1918.

the condensed idea
Not a war-winner, but all sides used it to the end

29 Air warfare
1914–18

The simple statement on the outbreak of war in 1914 that 'the squadrons flew to France' marked the end of secure British isolation from Continental Europe and was the harbinger of a new form of warfare.

Sixty-three fragile but inherently stable aircraft of the Royal Flying Corps (RFC) accompanied the BEF. Their role, that of reconnaissance, was to remain the principal operational activity of the combatant air forces throughout the war. Nevertheless, air fighting began when bolder souls went aloft armed with carbines, darts and even bricks, to ensure that their duties went uninterrupted.

Forward-firing machine gun

In February 1915 two Frenchmen, Roland Garros and Raymond Saulnier, experimented with a forward-firing machine gun, fixing steel plates to the propeller of their aircraft to deflect the small percentage of bullets they calculated would hit it. In April, Garros came down behind German lines, and his captured Morane-Saulnier Type N aircraft enabled the Dutch-born engineer Anthony Fokker to produce a mechanical interrupter gear that allowed the gun to fire only when

Fokker's invention

The technical problem was to shoot between the propeller blades, which passed a given point 2,400 times a minute, because the two-bladed propeller revolved 1,200 times a minute. This meant that the pilot must not pull the trigger or fire the gun as long as one of the blades was directly in front of the muzzle. Once the problem was stated, its solution came to me in a flash.

Anthony Fokker, *Flying Dutchman* (1938)

timeline

1915	1915	1915	1916
APRIL Germans capture French aircraft equipped with a forward-firing machine gun	Dutch engineer Anthony Fokker designs an interrupter gear which is fitted to an Eindecker monoplane	**1 AUGUST** First combat victory scored in an E.III of Fl. Abt. 62. **AUGUST 1915–JANUARY 1916** The 'Fokker Scourge' on the Western Front	**18 JUNE** Immelmann dies during an air combat

no propeller blade was in the way. It was fitted to the Fokker E.I monoplane, the Eindecker, which thus became the first true fighter aircraft.

The first Eindecker victory came on 1 July 1915, when Leutnant Kurt Wintgens shot down a French Morane two-seater. In the hands of brilliant pilots such as Max Immelmann and Oswald Boelcke, the Eindecker, in its E.III version, established such an ascendancy over Allied aircraft on the Western Front that the mauling received by the British and French air services between August 1915 and January 1916 became known as the 'Fokker Scourge' and the hapless Allied pilots as 'Fokker Fodder'.

Air aces Oswald Boelcke drew on his experiences in the fierce aerial fighting over Verdun in February–June 1916 to form specialized fighting squadrons, the *Jagdstaffeln* (hunting flights), known as 'Jastas'. An early recruit to Jasta 2, commanded by Boelcke, was Manfred Freiherr von Richthofen, the top-scoring ace of the war with 80 victories.

Dicta Boelcke

Oswald Boelcke died on 28 October 1916, after scoring 40 victories, when his Fokker D.III collided with the aircraft flown by his patrol commander. The pithy set of rules he devised for air fighting, the 'Dicta Boelcke', were still relevant in the Second World War. They include:

1. The best position in aerial combat is that where one can shoot at the enemy from close range without him being able to reply. Thus . . .
2. Climb before the attack and dive from the rear. Altitude imparts speed in a dive and widens the patrol area.
3. Use natural cover – clouds and the glare of the sun.
4. Attack when the enemy is unsuspecting and preoccupied with other tasks.

With the introduction by both sides of new types of aircraft, the Allies began to produce their own air aces. Major Lanoe Hawker of No. 6 Squadron, who flew the 'pusher' DH.2 (armed with a Lewis gun in the pilot's forward-protruding cockpit), became the first RFC pilot to win the Victoria Cross (VC) in aerial combat. On 23 November 1916, at the close of the Battle of the Somme, Hawker became the 11th victim of von Richthofen, flying an Albatros D.II biplane, at the conclusion of a tense, circling dogfight.

1916
Immelmann's former colleague Oswald Boelcke forms specialist fighter units, 'Jastas'

1916
28 OCTOBER Boelcke dies in a mid-air collision

1916
23 NOVEMBER Boelcke's protégé Manfred von Richthofen scores his 11th victory by shooting down RFC ace Major Lanoe Hawker

1917
11 JANUARY Von Richthofen takes command of Jasta 11 which, combined with other Jastas, becomes his 'Flying Circus'

1918
21 APRIL Von Richthofen, the highest-scoring ace of the First World War, is shot down by ground fire

Physical pressures

Flying and fighting at altitudes up to 6,096 metres (20,000 ft) exacted a heavy physical toll, as No. 56 Squadron pilot Capt. James McCudden recalled:

We were now down to 10,000 feet, west of Cambrai . . . I turned away. I felt very ill indeed. This was not because of the height or the rapidity of my descent, but because of the intense cold which I experienced up high. The result was that when I got down to a lower altitude, and could breathe more oxygen, my heart beat more strongly and tried to force my sluggish and cold blood around my veins too quickly . . . My word, I did feel ill . . . and when the blood returned to my veins I can only describe it as agony.

Von Richthofen's younger brother Lothar is sometimes wrongly credited with shooting down another highly decorated British ace, Capt. Albert Ball of No. 56 Squadron, on 7 May 1917. Ball was found dead at the controls of his S.E.5a, his body badly mutilated and with only isolated bullet holes in his aircraft. Two weeks later King George V presented his parents with a posthumous VC.

Von Richthofen, dubbed the 'Red Baron' after his all-red Albatros fighter, seemed indestructible. He was awarded the Pour le Mérite (popularly called the 'Blue Max' after Max Immelmann) in January 1917 and then given his first command, Jasta 11, packed with some of the finest fighter aces on the Western Front. Jasta 11 then combined with Jastas 4, 6 and 10 to form an independent fighter wing, the so-called 'Flying Circus', which from 26 June was known as Jagdgeschwader 1 or JG 1. The Red Baron was shot down and killed, probably by ground fire from Anzac troops, on 21 April 1918. By then the day of the 'lone wolf' fighter ace was long gone and the sentimental code of chivalry in the air – if it had ever existed – had been replaced by the grim pragmatism of attrition.

Fokker Eindecker Before 1914, Anthony Fokker had built several rotary-engined monoplanes, two of which, the M5K and the M5L, achieved some success in the first year of the war. When Garros's Morane-Saulnier, with its crude forward-firing device, was captured in April 1915, an M5K airframe was used to ground test Fokker's interrupter gear. The result was that a fragile and under-powered monoplane of 1913 vintage became the most famous of the first generation of dedicated fighters – an aircraft designed solely to destroy other aircraft.

❝In the twilight . . . our machines returned singly or in pairs; names were checked and the pilots gathered together by the hangar, looking out for those not yet in . . . as long as light permitted them . . . they stood there, cap, goggles and gloves in hand, just as they had climbed out of the cockpit.❞

Lt. F. Suckling, No. 65 Squadron, RFC

Interrupter gear At the business end was Fokker's interrupter gear. A camshaft was fitted to the propeller and, by synchronizing the command lever with the trigger through an actuating connector, the gun was prevented from firing when the propeller blade was in front of the gun muzzle. The pilot had only to press the button mounted on his joystick to enable the gun to fire when clear of the blades.

The first E.III was delivered to Feldflieger Abteilung 62 (Fl. Abt. 62) in July 1915 and was flown by Boelcke and Max Immelmann, the latter scoring his first victory on this machine on 1 August. With the RFC flying virtually defenceless BE2 craft, the E.III enjoyed complete air supremacy. Immelmann pioneered offensive patrols rather than flying close escort. Between October 1915 and January 1916, he earned the title of the 'Eagle of Lille', flying over the important communications centre, becoming an ace when he gained his fifth victory and reputedly developing the celebrated manoeuvre dubbed the 'Immelmann turn'.

the condensed idea
Air combat added a new dimension to conflict

30 The arrival of the bomber
1900–1918

In *The World Crisis*, Winston Churchill wrote that from the beginning of the First World War there was a widespread belief that 'at any moment half a dozen Zeppelins might arrive to bomb London, or what was more serious, Chatham, Woolwich or Portsmouth'.

In 1914 the German armed forces fielded 30 rigid airships, all of them of the Zeppelin type, named after their designer, Count Ferdinand von Zeppelin. Although their most effective role throughout the war was that of maritime reconnaissance, it was not long before the Zeppelins were employed on bombing operations, first on the Western Front and then against mainland Britain.

The first effective Zeppelin raid on London was launched by the German navy's Airship Division on the night of 8/9 September 1915, when the L13 penetrated London's primitive air defences to drop its bombs in a line running from Euston to Liverpool Street, killing 26 people. Following this and later Zeppelin raids on London, much damage to property was done in anti-German riots. By the end of the war, 51 bombing raids had been carried out by airships, killing 557 people.

Fragile instruments of war In spite of their size – the 'super-Zeppelins' introduced in 1916 were 198 metres (650 ft) long – the airships proved fragile instruments of war, difficult to navigate with any accuracy

timeline

1900	1909	1915	1916
JULY Maiden flight of Count Zeppelin's first airship, LZ1	German army takes delivery of first airship	**8/9 SEPTEMBER** German navy launches first Zeppelin raid on London, killing 26	**NOVEMBER** RNAS takes delivery of the Handley Page O/100, Britain's first dedicated bomber

> **❝I am not in favour of frightfulness . . . single bombs from flying machines are odious when they hit and kill an old woman . . . If one could set fire to London in 30 places, then what in a small way is odious would retire before something fine and powerful. All that flies and creeps should be concentrated on that city.❞**
>
> **Grand Admiral Alfred von Tirpitz,** commander of the German High Seas Fleet, 1914

and vulnerable both to the elements and to RFC fighters armed with incendiary bullets. By the end of the war, more than 60 of the German armed forces' 88 Zeppelins had been lost, 34 to accidents caused by bad weather and the rest to Allied aircraft and ground fire. Nevertheless, they exerted a powerful psychological effect and diverted significant resources to the air defence of Britain that would otherwise have been employed in France.

The Gothas The German navy never lost faith in their airships, but by May 1917 the German army had become disillusioned with them and had developed a heavier-than-air bomber capable of raiding targets in Britain: the Gotha G.IV. The twin-engined Gotha was flown by a three-man crew, commanded by the observer, who was also the navigator and bombardier, occupying the 'pulpit' position in the Gotha's bulbous nose. It had a maximum bomb load of 500 kilograms (1,100 lb), which could be carried either externally or internally. An attack on the port of Folkestone on 25 May 1917 was followed by two dramatic daylight raids on London on 13 June and 7 July.

The raids caused a huge furore about the state of Britain's air defences, the rapid improvement of which soon forced the Gothas to bomb by night. By the end of the war, some 60 Gothas had been lost in operations against the British mainland, 24 of them being shot down or disappearing over the sea. The Gotha's successor was the four-engined Staaken R-type (R for *Riesenflugzeugen*, meaning 'giant aeroplanes'), none of which were lost to defensive action over England.

1917	**1917**	**1918**	**1918**
German navy introduces new 'height-climbing' Zeppelins	**SEPTEMBER** Gothas begin bombing Britain by night and are joined by the giant R-type bombers	**APRIL** Formation of the Royal Air Force (RAF) with merging of the Royal Flying Corps (RFC) and RNAS (Royal Naval Air Service)	**MAY** Last aircraft raids on London

'In the pale glimmer coming through the hatchway, I saw the bombs hanging in their release mechanisms like rows of pears.'

Oberleutnant Ernst Lehmann, commander of Zeppelin LZ12

The German raids on London had prompted the British to establish their own strategic bombing force, which emerged in the spring of 1918 as the Independent Force of the fledgling Royal Air Force in France, tasked with attacking German war industry. The force's main weapon was the Handley Page O/400, which could carry a maximum bomb load of 907 kilograms (2,000 lb). Maximum speed was 95 miles per hour (152 kph) and the operational ceiling was 2,590 metres (8,500 ft). Bad weather and demands for their use in a tactical role meant that the O/400s flew only a fraction of their missions against German war factories.

As the war drew to a close, frantic efforts were made by the British to bring the massive Handley Page V/1500 into service to launch 'terror raids' on Berlin, but the four-engined bomber, with a wingspan of 38.5 metres (126 ft) and a maximum bomb load over short distances of 2,994 kilograms (6,600 lb), never flew in anger against Germany.

L33 Super-Zeppelin L33 was the fourth of the R-type super-Zeppelins, commissioned on 2 September 1916. Powered by six 240-horsepower Maybach engines, it had a maximum speed of 63 miles per hour (101 kph) and a cruising range of 2,300 miles (3,700 km). Its massive streamlined hull was some 700 metres (645 ft) long and contained 19 gas cells, which were separated by the Zeppelin's main traverse rings (the largest spanning 23.9 metres/78 ft 6 in), firmly braced and installed at 10-metre (33-ft) intervals. The light weight and tightness of the cells were achieved by lining them with goldbeater's skin, the delicate membrane covering cattle gut. Each of L33's gas cells required 50,000 of them.

L33's bomb capacity was almost five tons, but the standard load was four 272-kilogram (600-lb) bombs, 40 of the 58-kilogram (128-lb) and 60 of the 11-kilogram (25-lb) incendiaries. The bombs were suspended vertically from racks amidships. The bombsight, made by the firm Carl Zeiss of Jena, was located in the control gondola. On the icy, windswept reaches of the R-type's streamlined upper hull were two gun platforms. The main platform was located at the bow 18 metres (60 ft) above the

Zeppelins under fire

I had just returned to my station after dispatching a radiogram reporting the success of the raid . . . when a bright light flooded our gondola . . . Almost instantly our 600 feet of hydrogen was ablaze. The quickest death would be the best; to be burned alive would be horrible . . . Just at that moment a frightful shudder shot through the burning skeleton and then the ship gave a convulsion like the bound of a horse when shot. The gondola struts broke with a snap, and the skeleton collapsed with a series of crashes like the smashing of a huge window . . . I remember a thrill of horror as I opened my eyes and saw myself surrounded by a sea of flames.

Executive Officer Otto Mieth, one of only three survivors of the destruction of L48, 16/17 June 1917

control gondola and housed three 8-millimetre (0.3-in) Maxim-Nordenfelt machine guns firing a mixture of armour-piercing and explosive shell. When not in use, the guns were swathed in cloth to prevent the cooling water freezing solid at the operational ceiling of 5,181 metres (17,000 ft). More machine guns were installed in the control and rear-engine gondolas.

The 22 crew members learned to live with the agonies of altitude sickness and the intense cold. The temperature in the control gondola rarely rose above freezing point and layers of fur-lined clothing were often supplemented by wads of newspaper stuffed inside the crewmen's overalls. Good hot food from tins heated by a chemical process provided some relief.

Nevertheless, the Zeppelins' immense size belied their vulnerability. L33 went down north of the Blackwater estuary in the small hours of 24 September 1916 after being damaged by anti-aircraft fire over London.

the condensed idea
The First World War saw the streaky dawn of strategic bombing

31 The tank
1914–18

By 1916, the devastating defensive firepower that both sides could bring to bear on the deadlocked Western Front added terrible urgency to the search for an armoured breakthrough weapon that could crush barbed wire, negotiate broken ground and bring direct and accurately aimed fire on the enemy.

The answer had been lying around since October 1914. Just two months after the outbreak of war, Major (later Colonel) Ernest Swinton had approached the British General Headquarters (GHQ) with a proposal to turn the pre-war Holt agricultural tractor, which ran on steel tracks, into an armoured box armed with cannon and machine guns and capable of traversing no-man's land, crossing opposing trenches and penetrating to the enemy's artillery positions, while employing its firepower to dominate the battlefield.

Teething problems GHQ was not interested, but Swinton's scheme eventually found a backer in Winston Churchill, First Lord of the Admiralty. In the autumn of 1914, the armoured cars operated in northern France by the Royal Naval Air Service (RNAS) had enjoyed some success, but had been hampered by the trenches that the Germans had dug across the roads. The Admiralty's work on a solution to this problem coincided with Swinton's proposal and led to the establishment, in February 1915, of an Admiralty Landships Committee.

timeline

1914	1914	1915	1916
Major Ernest Swinton approaches the British army with a proposal for an armoured vehicle based on the Holt tractor	During the Race to the Sea, the Royal Naval Air Service (RNAS) uses armoured cars in northern France	**FEBRUARY** Admiralty Landships Committee established	**15 SEPTEMBER** Mk I tanks make their combat debut at the Battle of the Somme

Little willie and Big willie

The two men credited with designing and building the first tank were William Tritton, managing director of the Fosters factory in Lincoln, and Lt. Walter Wilson of the Royal Naval Reserve. Before 1914, Wilson had been a motor engineer who specialized in gearing. The two men worked on a number of experimental designs. Tritton had produced a giant trench-crossing vehicle with huge wheels. He and Wilson worked on the Lincoln No. 1 machine, known as 'Little Willie', which ran on American-made Bullock 'Creeping Grip' tracks. When these proved impractical, Tritton devised a more reliable replacement. Little Willie's successor, the rhomboid-shaped 'Big Willie', was largely the work of Wilson, and was the first viable tank of the war.

The tank prototype, 'Big Willie', was successfully tested at Hatfield Park at the beginning of 1916. Some in the British high command remained sceptical, but General Sir Douglas Haig, commander of the BEF from December 1915, was keen for the speediest possible use of the machines, which were codenamed 'Tanks' because without their guns they looked like vehicles for carrying water.

Committed to battle In February 1916, Colonel Swinton submitted a report to the War Committee urging that tanks should not be used in 'driblets', but in one great 'combined operation' on a 5-mile (8-km) front with infantry, gas and smoke. However, when they first went into action on the Somme on 15 September, the 32 Mk I tanks that made it to the start line were as much the victims of their own mechanical fragility and short range as any shortcomings in their tactical deployment. Nevertheless, nine tanks forged ahead of their supporting infantry, straddled trench lines and engaged the enemy's infantry and machine guns. However, 13 either broke down or were stranded and 10 were badly damaged by enemy fire.

1917	**1917**	**1917**	**1917**	**1918**	**1918**
APRIL Tanks used again at Arras but most of them break down	**JUNE** Mk IV tank introduced at Messines Ridge	**JULY–NOVEMBER** Tanks swallowed by the mud at Passchendaele (Third Ypres)	**NOVEMBER** Tanks used successfully for the first time at Cambrai	Introduction of the Whippet light tank with all-round turret	**APRIL 24** First tank-on-tank encounter on the battlefield

At Arras in April 1917, only 60 tanks were sent into the attack in appalling weather, and almost all of them were stranded, broke down or were disabled by enemy fire. The French launched their first tank attack in the same month and suffered a similar setback. The Mk IV's introduction to combat came in June 1917 at Messines Ridge, where it outran the infantry on broken but dry terrain, but at Passchendaele (Third Ypres) in the sodden autumn of 1917, the Mk IVs of the newly formed Tank Corps were swallowed by seas of mud. It was not until November 1917 that they were effectively used at Cambrai, when numbers, conditions and tactics were in their favour, and opened a tantalizingly brief window of opportunity pointing to the future.

> **A pretty mechanical toy.**
>
> Lord Kitchener, Secretary of State for War 1914–16, on 'Big Willie'

Mk IV tank The Mk IV had the same semi-rhomboidal shape, with tracks running round the hull, as the Mk I, but was fitted with an improved radiator, silencer and pressed steel track with a better grip, although the last was still only good for about 20 miles (32 km). Its 12-millimetre (0.5-in) armour protection represented another improvement and was effective against armour-piercing bullets. Nevertheless, the Mk IV remained vulnerable to German artillery, which accounted for the destruction of the majority of tanks.

The Mk IV's six-cylinder Daimler engine gave it a maximum speed of 4 miles per hour (6.4 kph). So-called 'male' tanks carried a primary armament of two six-pounder guns housed in sponsons and secondary armament of four .303 Lewis guns. So-called 'female' tanks were armed with six .303 Lewis guns. At 29 tons, males were 2 tons heavier than the females.

The tank had a crew of eight, four of whom were required to drive. In action the interior of the Mk IV was an inferno of noise and heat. With no suspension, any slight bump or jar was magnified many times, and the crew were constantly at risk of being thrown against the hot engine. If the tank was hit, slivers of hot steel flew about, and bullets striking the tank's armoured plates exposed the crew to splash similar to that experienced in steel factories. To protect their eyes, they wore face masks.

On its front the Mk IV carried a fascine, a wood-and-chain bundle some 3 metres (10 ft) long and 1.4 metres (4.5 ft) in diameter, which was dropped into trenches to ease the tank's crossing. Trench-crossing

> ❝ . . . terribly noisy, oily, hot, airless and bumpy! Without any sort of cushions, as we had no springs and had thirty tons' weight, any slight bump and crash was magnified and many a burn was caused by a jerk throwing the crew about. Instinctively one caught a handhold and got a burn on the hot engine. ❞

Lt. Gordon Hassell, a veteran of Cambrai, Imperial War Museum archives

was also improved by the fitting of a 'tadpole tail', a mild steel extension, which increased the span that could be traversed from 10 feet (3 m) to 14 feet (4.3 m).

It was in the attack on the Hindenburg Line at Cambrai, in November 1917, that the Mk IVs enjoyed their first taste of tactical success. Three hundred and seventy-eight fighting tanks were concentrated in nine battalions, plus 54 supply tanks fitted with sledges, 32 fitted with grapnels for dragging wire to make gaps for the cavalry, 2 carrying bridging equipment and 5 wireless tanks. New tactics had been devised for the fighting tanks. They would advance in sections of three, rumbling forward in equilateral triangles with the two rear tanks followed by a 'snake' of infantry.

The attack dispensed with a lengthy preliminary bombardment and took the Germans by surprise, tearing a 6-mile (10-km) gap in the Hindenburg Line. The next day church bells rang out in London for the first time to mark a land victory. But the breakthrough was not successfully exploited and most of the ground gained was lost to a German counterattack.

the condensed idea
Initially ineffective, the tank pointed the way to the future

32 **Blitzkrieg**
1918–45

Great commanders from Alexander of Macedon to Gustavus Adolphus and Otto von Bismarck possessed the priceless ability to deliver swift and shattering blows to a slow-thinking, slow-moving enemy. In the mid-20th century the introduction of two well-integrated elements to the battlefield – armour and aircraft – provided a fresh opportunity to demonstrate the effectiveness of one of the enduring elements of the art of warfare.

In the aftermath of the First World War, military theorists grappled with the developing doctrine of mechanized warfare; the aim was to avoid the deadlock of trench warfare and restore the art of movement and manoeuvre to the battlefield. Progress was initially slow, partly due to the mechanical unreliability of the armoured fighting vehicles (AFVs) of the 1920s, and also because of the continued esteem accorded by military establishments to horse-mounted cavalry.

Blitzkrieg In Germany, following Adolf Hitler's repudiation of the Treaty of Versailles and adoption of a policy of rearmament – announced to the world in March 1935 – a new approach to mechanized warfare emerged. It bore a close superficial resemblance to the theories of Marshal Tukhachevsky (see box opposite) while also drawing on the writings of British military commentator and First World War tank expert J.F.C. Fuller. It is generally referred to as Blitzkrieg ('lightning war'), although the term seems to have its origins in the pre-war Western press, notably an article in the *Times* newspaper of 14 June 1939.

timeline

1936	1937	1937	1939	1940	1940
PzKpfw III prototypes appear	Ju 87 dive-bomber makes its combat debut in the Spanish Civil War	Guderian publishes *Achtung-Panzer!*	**SEPTEMBER** Mk III Panzer enters service with German army	**MAY** Germany deploys all its armoured and mechanized divisions in the campaign in the west. Some 350 Mk III Panzers take part. MK III's gun proves ineffective against British and French heavy tanks	**AUGUST** Ju 87 is withdrawn from the Battle of Britain

The doctrine had many begetters, but the man who received the greatest credit for the application of modern technology to ancient insight was Col. (later Gen.) Heinz Guderian, a signals and motor transport expert, who in 1937 published an influential book, *Achtung-Panzer!*, in which he outlined his ideas.

Guderian's object was not the frontal engagement of the enemy and his destruction by sheer weight of fire, but rather the rapid dislocation of his command and control system. The critical point on the battlefield, the *Schwerpunkt*, was to be smashed open by fast-moving and independent armoured formations co-ordinated by radio. These would penetrate the enemy's defences, drive deep into the rear and then, using the following-up infantry, slice up the isolated survivors in a series of pockets. A vital element in the initial breakthrough phase was the use of level- and dive-bombers of the Luftwaffe (German air force) as airborne artillery.

Soviet mechanized forces

In the 1930s the Soviet Union had been a leader in the development of large armoured formations, forming a number of mechanized corps. These owed much to the operational radicalism of Marshal M.N. Tukhachevsky, Joseph Stalin's chief of staff, who developed infantry-support heavy tanks and fast 'cavalry' tanks designed to cut through the enemy's frontal defences and penetrate to the rear. However, Tukhachevsky fell out of favour and was executed in Stalin's 1937 purge of the Red Army. His mechanized corps were broken up.

All these elements were features of Germany's six-week defeat of the French army and British Expeditionary Force (BEF) in the early summer of 1940. Speed and surprise were the keys. The French and British anticipated a repeat of the 1914 Schlieffen Plan, a German drive through Holland and Belgium into northern France. This had been the original German intention, but in the six months following Germany's invasion and defeat of Poland the plan had been radically changed. Maximum pressure – the *Schwerpunkt* – was to be applied not in the north but to

1940	1941	1941	1941	1943
SEPTEMBER Ju 87s fly first anti-shipping mission in Mediterranean	Nearly 1,500 Mk IIIs in service	**JUNE–OCTOBER** Red Army is almost destroyed in a series of massive 'cauldron' battles. Mk III proves vulnerable to Soviet T-34 and is replaced by the Mk IV	**DECEMBER** Guderian, commanding 2nd Panzer Group, is dismissed by Hitler after making a tactical withdrawal in Russia	**JULY** German armour is stopped dead in its tracks at the Battle of Kursk. Thereafter the story of the Eastern Front is one of Russian advance and German retreat

> **❝Everything lies in the hands of the military leaders. With the German soldier I can do anything, provided he is well led.❞**
>
> **Adolf Hitler, 23 November 1939**

the south through the heavily wooded and hilly Ardennes, which the British and French considered 'untankable'. France's supposedly impassable Maginot Line of fixed border fortifications would not be directly attacked but simply bypassed and isolated.

On 10 May 1940, Germany attacked Holland and Belgium, catching the British and French deployed in three army groups behind the French frontier. This feint drew their gaze northwards while German tanks broke through in the Ardennes. On 13 May some 700 German aircraft were operating over Sedan on the River Meuse, some 200 of them gull-winged Ju 87 Stuka dive-bombers. They saturated the French defences and carved out a bridgehead for the German infantry forces to cross the Meuse. By the end of the day, the German armour was over the river and racing past hordes of demoralized French troops who abandoned their guns and threw down their rifles whenever Stukas appeared in the sky. The Germans swept north to trap huge numbers of British and French troops in a pocket around the port of Dunkirk, from which some 340,000 (225,000 of them British) were evacuated by 4 June. Fighting ceased on 25 June, but the Battle of France had been won in mid-May when German tanks crossed the Meuse.

Tanks on the battlefield

In the spring of 1940, all ten of Germany's armoured divisions, and all six of its motorized divisions were deployed in the west along with 118 infantry divisions. This was in marked contrast to the British and French, whose tanks were technically and numerically superior but were principally confined to the role of supporting the infantry formations.

PzKpfw III battle tank

Some 350 five-man Mk IIIs fought in the Battle of France. Developed from the mid-1930s as Germany's main battle tank (PzKpfw), the Mk III was initially fitted with a 37-millimetre (1.5-in) gun, which was already in quantity production, with the proviso that the turret ring be made wide enough to accommodate the 50-millimetre (1.96-in) if the need arose. Following encounters with heavily armoured French and British tanks in 1940, the Mk III was fitted with the 50-millimetre L/42 gun but still struggled against the Soviet T-34 in 1941. By 1942, the MK III had grown considerably heavier and had reached the limit of its potential. Production ceased in 1943, by which time more than 5,500 Mk IIIs had been built.

In the summer of 1941, in the German invasion of the Soviet Union, known as Operation Barbarossa, the Red Army suffered the same fate, coming close to annihilation in a series of massive encirclements dubbed 'cauldron' battles. In three separate 'cauldrons' a million Russian soldiers were taken prisoner. Nevertheless, conditions on the Eastern Front conspired against the ultimate triumph of Blitzkrieg. The sheer size of Soviet Russia, its extremes of climate – sub-zero winters and mud-clogged springs and autumns – and the seemingly limitless supply of Soviet manpower sapped the strength of the German army in the east. After the United States entered the war in December 1941, it played a crucial role in arming and feeding the Soviet military and civilians, while a revitalized Red Army learned how to trade space for time, drawing Hitler into battles of attrition, notably at Stalingrad (August 1942–February 1943) and Kursk (July–August 1943), in which the underlying principles of Blitzkrieg – surprise, shock, movement – were blown away like the dust of a Soviet summer.

the condensed idea
From 1939 to 1942 the Germans combined aircraft and armour to devastating effect

33 Radar 1935–41

The fall of France in June 1940 had brought the seemingly invincible German army to the coast of northern France. Adolf Hitler brooded over the invasion of southern England, codenamed Sealion, an operation for which neither he nor his high command had any real enthusiasm.

The success of Sealion depended on the destruction by the Luftwaffe of RAF Fighter Command. Alone among Hitler's commanders, Hermann Göring, the commander of the Luftwaffe, was brimming with confidence. He estimated that it would take a mere four days to eliminate the RAF from southern England.

However, both sides were licking the wounds sustained in the Battle of France. In six weeks of fighting the RAF had lost 944 aircraft, including 386 Hawker Hurricanes and 67 Supermarine Spitfires. Excluding losses sustained in the Dunkirk evacuation, the RAF had lost 350 pilots killed, missing, wounded or taken prisoner. Nor had the Luftwaffe escaped lightly. In the fighting of May–June 1940 it had lost some 1,100 aircraft on operations. By 20 July, ten days into the Battle of Britain, RAF Fighter Command fielded 531 operational aircraft compared with 725 operational fighters and 1,289 combat-ready bombers of the three air fleets under Göring's command in the theatre.

Chain Home The British nevertheless enjoyed a significant advantage with the 'Chain Home' system of 30 radar stations established on the British coastline from Land's End in the southwest to Newcastle in the northeast. Radar, an American acronym for radio direction and ranging, was originally known by the British as radio direction finding (RDF). Radar works by sending out a pulse of radio energy to strike a target and then detecting the energy reflected back. As the speed of the pulse is known, measuring

timeline

1935	**1939**	**1940**	**1940**
British government sets up Committee for Scientific Survey of Air Defence	**SEPTEMBER** Chain Home radar stations are in place around the British coast	**10 JULY** Air fighting over Britain begins in earnest as Luftwaffe attacks Channel convoys	**JULY–AUGUST** Luftwaffe attacks ports, airfields and radar stations on the south coast

the time between transmission and reception enables radar operators to calculate the target range.

In the 1930s the system was developed independently by Britain, France, Germany and the United States. The British alone concentrated on the use of radar for air defence. Reports from the Chain Home stations were fed back to Fighter Command HQ at Bentley Priory. Along with information from coastal and inland observation posts, the reports were cross-checked and the 'filtered' results transmitted to Fighter Command's Group and Sector Stations (principal air bases). Allowing for the six-minute time lag between the radar observations and the plot of enemy formations on the map, group controllers allocated interceptor squadrons, which were then scrambled to meet the incoming aircraft. During the first ten months of the war, regular Luftwaffe reconnaissance flights and attacks on coastal shipping had enabled the RAF to develop the system to a high degree of effectiveness.

From early July 1940, the Luftwaffe had fatally switched back and forth between targets – Britain's aircraft factories, Fighter Command's Sector Stations and the RAF's coastal radar chain. The Germans underestimated the critical importance of the last. The Ventnor station was put out of action for 11 days, but those at Dover, Rye and Pevensey, which also came under attack, were soon back in action while Ventnor's disappearance from the chain was effectively concealed from Luftwaffe intelligence. The Luftwaffe decided not to press home the attacks on the radar chain.

Operations at Bentley Priory

In the Operations Room at Bentley Priory there was large table on which a map of the UK had been drawn on a grid system. Each of us who were plotting was plugged into a particular sector. From Group Operations Rooms we received through headphones the information, which we then plotted on the table. On receiving the first intimation of a raid through our headphones, we would stand up and say 'X Raid!' loudly, bringing everyone to alert.

Aircraftswoman Ursula Robertson, Bentley Priory plotter, *Daily Telegraph Battle of Britain*, 1990

1940	**1940**	**1940**	**1940**	**1941**
15 AUGUST Luftwaffe launches its main attack (codenamed Eagle)	**7 SEPTEMBER** London Blitz begins	**30 SEPTEMBER** Last large daylight raid on Britain	**OCTOBER** Nearly 200,000 civilians shelter in London Underground as Blitz continues. Battle of Britain comes to an end	**JULY** Blitz on Britain's major cities ends

Black Thursday On 15 August, the Battle of Britain was stepped up a gear as the Luftwaffe launched its heaviest attack, codenamed Eagle, to provoke and win a decisive battle with the RAF. On so-called 'Black Thursday' it lost 72 aircraft. Ten days later RAF Bomber Command flew its first raid on Berlin. In retaliation, Hitler sanctioned the bombing of London, which began on 7 September. On 15 September the Luftwaffe suffered another major reverse in the skies over the British capital, when two heavily escorted waves of bombers ran into nearly 300 British fighters. Air superiority had been denied to the Luftwaffe; on 12 October Hitler ordered the indefinite postponement of Operation Sealion. The bombing of Britain's cities was thereafter prosecuted by night.

Hawker Hurricane In popular imagination, the Hurricane has often been overshadowed by the Supermarine Spitfire. But this rugged fighter bore the brunt of the fighting in the Battle of Britain, equipping over 60 per cent of fighter squadrons. Fighter Command's top-scoring squadron in the battle, No. 303, flew Hurricanes and is credited with 126 and a half confirmed victories (a half victory is a confirmed victory shared with another pilot).

❝In the Battle [of Britain] we had to rely on our own human eyes. The British fighter pilots could depend on the radar eye, which was far more reliable and had a longer range.❞
Lieutenant-General Adolf Galland, commander of II/JG26 (fighter group) in the Battle of Britain, *The First and the Last* (1955)

Designed by Sir Sydney Camm, the Hurricane was the RAF's first monoplane fighter and the first of its aircraft to exceed 300 miles per hour (483 kph). The Hurricane, which first flew in November 1935 and went into service in 1937, was a straightforward and immensely tough machine. Its fabric covering and fixed-pitch two-blade wooden propeller were backward-looking, but its monoplane design, retractable landing gear and Rolls-Royce Merlin engine were at the cutting edge, as was its revolutionary armament of eight 0.303-inch (7.7-mm) Browning machine guns. It handled well, could absorb a huge amount of battle damage and, thanks to the foresight of the Hawker management, who laid down a production line for 1,000 Hurricanes before they had a single order, there were plenty available at the outbreak of war. By September 1939, 500 Hurricanes had been delivered to RAF Fighter Command.

❝When you saw a squadron of Hurricanes taking off, you knew we couldn't lose.❞

E.H. 'Basher' Gumbrill, armourer with No. 111 Squadron, RAF, *Daily Telegraph Battle of Britain,* 1990

In the Battle of Britain, Hurricanes shot down more enemy aircraft than all other aircraft and anti-aircraft guns combined. While the faster Spitfires engaged the single-seat Me 109 fighter escorts flying top cover, the Hurricane engaged the Luftwaffe bombers and their twin-engined Me 110 escorts. The heavily armed Me 110, which had been designed to spearhead the Luftwaffe attacks, was in many ways a more technologically advanced aircraft than the Hurricane, but in battle it proved no match for the British fighter and eventually suffered the indignity of being provided with its own escorts.

The Hurricane's roomy cockpit, excellent all-round visibility, wide-track undercarriage, responsive flying characteristics and reliable engine and hydraulic system made it a superb flying machine, a true pilot's aeroplane and one that earned the respect and affection of all who flew and maintained it.

During the war the Hurricane went through a number of modifications, particularly improving armament, and it was also produced as the Sea Hurricane for catapult launching from armed merchant ships and for carrier use.

the condensed idea
Radar provided the narrow margin in the Battle of Britain

34 Strategic bombing 1921–45

In the First World War dedicated bombing aircraft had played a minor role, although the Zeppelin raids on London in 1915–18 had caused much public outrage. In the 1920s, the Italian airman General Giulio Douhet and his US counterpart General William Mitchell became apostles of air power. Douhet argued that in any future war victory would be secured by the nation that could dominate the skies and bring an enemy to its knees by bombing its industries and cities.

In 1930 Mitchell, a passionate advocate of a long-range bombing force, observed, 'In future the mere threat of bombing a town by an air force will cause it to be evacuated, and all work in the factories to be stopped.' In the 1930s the bomber cast a long shadow over Europe. It was feared that a 'knockout blow' on London might leave up to 100,000 of its citizens dead within 24 hours.

> **In short, normal life would be impossible in this constant nightmare of imminent death and destruction.**
>
> **General Giulio Douhet,**
> *The Command of the Air* (1921)

Blitz When war came, the apocalypse was averted. Although some 40,000 civilians died in the Blitz on Britain's cities between September 1940 and May 1941, and more than a million homes were destroyed, morale did not crack, nor did the nation's war industries falter. In the Blitz, the Luftwaffe's twin-engined bombers lacked the payload to level London and Britain's industrial heartlands. Nor was the Royal Air Force's Bomber Command better placed to win the war by bombing alone. In the opening months of the war, heavy losses at the

timeline

1937	1940	1942	1942
Bombing of the Spanish city of Guernica by the German Condor Legion in the Spanish Civil War	**7 SEPTEMBER** Luftwaffe begins the Blitz on London	**FEBRUARY** Bomber Command starts the 'area bombing' of Germany with raids of Essen, Duisberg and Cologne	**APRIL** RAF Bomber Command mounts '1,000 Bomber Raid' on Cologne

hands of German fighters caused the suspension of daylight bombing raids. For the next two years, the RAF's bombers, also twin-engined, groped their way blindly over a blacked-out Europe. Even on moonlit nights most of them were dropping their bombs miles from their targets.

Heavy bombers Nevertheless, the bombing campaign remained the only way the British could strike directly at Nazi Germany. The situation improved with the arrival in numbers of four-engined bombers – Short Stirlings, Handley Page Halifaxes and Avro Lancasters – equipped with increasingly sophisticated radio navigation aids. This coincided with a change in Bomber Command policy. Although the destruction of precision targets remained an intermittent, and spectacular, feature of the command's operations, most of its bombs would now fall on 'area' targets. If Bomber Command could not destroy Germany's war factories, it could destroy the cities where their workers lived. Bomber Command's commander-in-chief, Air Chief Marshal Sir Arthur Harris, believed that the systematic destruction of Germany's cities would, by itself, bring an end to the war. He dismissed all other targets, for example those linked with oil or fighter production, as 'mere panaceas'.

The bombing of Germany

In the past 18 months Bomber Command has virtually destroyed 45 out of the leading 60 German cities. In spite of the invasion diversion [Overlord] we have so far managed to keep up and even extend our average of two and a half cities devastated a month . . . There are not many industrial centres of population now left intact. Are we going to abandon this vast task, which the Germans themselves have long admitted to be their worst headache, just as it nears completion?

Air Chief Marshal Sir Arthur Harris, commander-in-chief of Bomber Command, memo to Air Chief Marshal Sir Charles Portal, Chief of Air Staff, 1 November 1944

1942	**1943**	**1943**	**1944**	**1945**
JULY US 8th Air Force arrives in England	Bomber Command introduces H2S airborne radar	**NOVEMBER** Battle of Berlin begins	**MARCH** Battle of Berlin ends	**FEBRUARY** Bomber Command and USAAF devastate Dresden

> **❛Investigation seems to show that having one's house demolished is most damaging to morale. People seem to mind it more than having their friends or even relatives killed.❜**
>
> **Lord Cherwell,** Churchill's scientific adviser, March 1942

The first phase of area bombing reached a climax in July–August 1943, when, in Operation Gomorrah, Bomber Command mounted a series of devastating raids on Hamburg. While Bomber Command flew by night, the United States Army Air Forces' (USAAF) 8th Air Force hit the city by day. A subsequent attempt, in the words of Air Chief Marshal Harris to 'wreck Berlin from end to end', which lasted from November 1943 to March 1944, was abandoned after losses of nearly 500 aircraft. Nevertheless, German air defences were now being steadily degraded, while Bomber Command's range of pathfinding and target-marking techniques was concentrating the maximum number of aircraft over the target in the minimum amount of time. By the end of the war, Germany's cities lay in ruins.

The commanders of the USAAF's 8th Air Force, which arrived in the UK in the summer of 1942, were firm believers in high-level daylight precision bombing by formations of self-defending aircraft. They were not deterred by the fact that earlier in the war both the Luftwaffe and RAF Bomber Command had tried these tactics and failed.

In the skies over Germany the USAAF's theory was tested almost to the point of destruction. B-17 Flying Fortresses and B-24 Liberators, flying in mass formation, sustained increasingly heavy losses at the hands of the Luftwaffe's day fighters. By the late summer of 1943 average losses were running at an unsustainable 10 per cent per mission. The crisis was ended in December 1943 with the introduction of the formidable P-51 Mustang escort fighter (see page 158), capable not only of escorting the bombers all the way to targets deep inside Germany, but also of forming fighting patrols to sweep the skies clear of enemy fighters.

Avro Lancaster   The Lancaster was the RAF's outstanding heavy bomber of the war and the mainstay of the RAF's strategic bombing offensive against Germany. It was derived from its unsatisfactory twin-engined predecessor, the Avro Manchester, and made its operational debut with No. 44 Squadron in March 1942.

On 17 April 1942, 12 Lancasters executed a daring low-level daylight raid on Augsburg during which 7 were lost and 2 Victoria Crosses were won. On 16/17 May 1943, Lancasters of No. 617 Squadron, under the leadership of Wing Commander Guy Gibson, attacked dams on the Ruhr with the

Radar navigation

The first British radio aid to navigation, codenamed Gee, was introduced in the winter of 1941. Gee enabled a bomber's navigator to fix his position by reference to radio pulses transmitted from three stations in England. It was easy for the Germans to jam Gee, and by the end of 1942 it had been phased out. Oboe, introduced in the winter of 1942, was a blind bombing system that was difficult to jam, but with a range limited by the curvature of the earth to some 350 miles (565 km). It was used in the high-altitude Mosquitoes of Bomber Command's Pathfinder Force. Their task was to deliver incendiaries, at which the following main force bombers would aim. H2S radar, introduced in 1943, was independent of control by ground stations. It was an advanced downward-looking radar housed in the bomber's belly that scanned the ground below. The returning echoes, displayed on a cathode ray tube, gave a continuous picture over the terrain below.

'bouncing bomb' designed by Barnes Wallis. As the war neared its end, Bomber Command was able to deploy all the professionalism and technique it had acquired since 1939.

On 12 November 1944, Lancasters of No. 617 Squadron sank the German battleship *Tirpitz* with Barnes Wallis's 5,443-kilogram (12,000-lb) 'Tallboy' bombs. On 14 March 1945, the huge Bielefeld railway viaduct linking Hamm and Hanover was destroyed by 14 specially modified Lancasters of No. 617 Squadron carrying the 9,779-kilogram (22,000-lb) 'Grand Slam' bomb, also designed by Barnes Wallis. Against a shattered Luftwaffe, Lancasters were once again flying by day in loose formations or 'gaggles'.

The Lancaster's four 1,460-horsepower Rolls-Royce Merlin engines gave it a top speed of 275 miles per hour (443 kph). It had a crew of seven and defensive armament of ten .303 machine guns. Its standard bomb load was 6,350 kilograms (14,000 lb) over a range of 1,660 miles (2,671 km).

the condensed idea
Heavy bombers can devastate cities but cannot secure ground

35 Armoured warfare 1940–5

From the summer of 1941, when the European Soviet Union was overrun by the Östheer (the German army in the East), the Red Army underwent a wholesale reorganization. Nowhere was this more apparent than in its tank arm.

In the 1930s the Soviet Union had been a leader in the development of large armoured formations, and several mechanized corps had been formed on the urging of Marshal N. Tukhachevsky, Stalin's chief of staff. However, Tukhachevsky was shot in the 1937 purge of the Soviet military leadership and his reforms slammed into reverse. In 1940 the mechanized corps were broken up.

Sense began to reassert itself in the Red Army war games of early 1940, in which General Georgi Zhukov's Western Force roundly defeated General Dimitri Pavlov's Eastern Force in a remarkable projection of some aspects of the German plans for Operation Barbarossa. Using similar tactics, Zhukov had inflicted a mauling on the Japanese in the 1939 conflict with that country (the Khalkhin-Gol incident).

The war game led directly to Zhukov's appointment as Stalin's chief of general staff. The decision was taken to recreate the disbanded tank formations as a matter of urgency, but by the end of 1941, with the Östheer closing on Moscow, all the large Red Army armoured units had been chewed up and replaced by smaller units acting in an infantry-support role.

timeline

1940	1941	1943	1943	1944
T-34 enters service with Red Army	Evacuation of Soviet tank industry to east of Urals	Red Army forms tank armies	**JULY** The Battle of Kursk, the greatest tank battle in history	**JUNE** The Red Army launches Operation Bagration, which results in the destruction of German Army Group Centre, considered by Soviet military historians to be the decisive battle of the Great Patriotic War

Red Army revival In the battles around Moscow in the winter of 1941, the Red Army lacked the armour to encircle and trap large German formations. The Stavka (Soviet general staff) concluded that there was little chance of transforming tactical advantage into operational success without the addition of larger tank and mechanized corps. These formations duly appeared in the summer of 1942, only to be destroyed in 'cauldron' battles in the southern Soviet Union.

Control by infantry officers unused to armour, tactical rigidity and superior German battlefield reflexes once again threw a question mark over the future of the Red Army's tank arm, but now there was a sufficient number of able and experienced corps commanders to convince Stavka that there could be no turning back. Early in 1943 Stalin authorized the creation of five tank armies.

T-34s in action

The T-34's broad tracks reduced ground pressure to a minimum, and it was fast and agile even in the toughest conditions – the mud that characterized the Russian spring and autumn seasons (*rasputitsa*) and the deep snow of winter. A rugged all-weather diesel engine gave it an excellent power-to-weight ratio and a range of 186 miles (299 km), nearly twice that of the German PzKpfw V (Panther) battle tank and PzKpfwVI (Tiger I and II) heavy battle tanks, which was of huge importance in the great spaces of the Soviet Union.

T-34/76 The mainstay of the Soviet tank armies was the T-34/76 medium tank, which entered service in the summer of 1940 and was a weapon of such basic excellence that it fought throughout the Second World War without major modification. The balance it struck between mobility, protection and firepower is widely regarded as the foundation of modern tank design.

The T-34's sloping armour increased resistance to shell penetration – a feature that was copied in the PzKpfw V Panther – and an innovatory long-barrelled high-velocity gun completed a well-balanced design that

1944	1944	1945	1950–1	1953	1956
Introduction of the T-34/85	Tank armies now contain two or three tank corps and a corps of mechanized infantry – 900 tanks, 850 artillery pieces and 50,000 men	Introduction of T-54 series which was in production until 1981	T-34s form the armoured spearhead of the North Korean army	T-34s used in suppression of East German uprising	T-34s help put down Hungarian uprising

was complemented by its mass production and easy maintenance in the field – in the Second World War, some 68 per cent of the Red Army's tanks were T-34s.

Crew comfort In true Soviet style, the T-34 made few if any concessions to crew comfort. Initially it lacked a radio and a turret with an all-round sight for its commander, who also doubled as the gunner. In battle the commander had his work cut out, shouting directions by microphone to the driver, who only had a restricted view, bellowing orders to the loader about the types of ammunition he wanted, ducking down to the periscope sight to lay the gun, working out the range, opening fire and then keeping himself well clear of the 76.2-millimetre (3-in) gun as it lunged back a full 35 centimetres (14 in) on recoil.

The loader was also a busy man. Of the 77 rounds carried by the T-34/76 (on average, 19 rounds armour-piercing, 53 high-explosive and 5 shrapnel), only 9 were immediately accessible – 6 on racks on the left-hand wall for the fighting compartment and 3 on the right. The remaining 68 rounds were distributed in eight metal bins at the bottom of the turret, covered by rubber matting, which formed the turret floor. In any action in which more than a handful of rounds were fired without an appreciable pause, the loader had to start uncovering and dismantling the turret floor in order to replenish the gun. Struggling in a tangle of bins and matting, he faced an extra hazard every time the gun was fired, discharging a very hot shell case into the debris.

Soviet tank formations

In stark contrast to the multiplicity of vehicles fielded by a German armoured division – often as many as 12 different types of armoured vehicle and 20 types of other vehicle – the Soviet mechanized formations relied on just two: the T-34 and the American Dodge truck, nearly 140,000 of which had been supplied by the United States by the summer of 1943. American Lend-Lease enabled Stalin's war factories to concentrate almost exclusively on the production of battle equipment. Stalin himself told Churchill that he wanted trucks more than tanks.

> ❝We had one advantage – mobility. They were like a herd of buffalo which does not have the freedom of movement enjoyed by the leopards which prowl around the flanks of the herd – and we were the leopards.❞
>
> **Tank crew member, 6th Panzer Division**

On the battlefield, Red Army tactics still lagged behind the adaptability of the Östheer. The moment the fighting became fluid, Russian armoured formations were always likely to be shot up by experienced German units, even when the latter were heavily outnumbered.

Battleworthy By January 1945, the roles had been radically reversed. Soviet tank armies were gouging great chunks out of the frontiers of the Third Reich. On 20 January 1945 the tanks and lorries of the elite Soviet 5th Guards Tank Army thrust deep into the underbelly of East Prussia. The army had been brought up at speed from the rear, where it had remained undetected by the Germans. Three days later 3rd Battalion of 29th Tank Corps burst into the town of Elbing, camouflaging its seven tanks among the hordes of fleeing civilians.

They raced to the centre of the city, headlights blazing in the winter gloom. At first the T-34s were mistaken for training units by shoppers who only that day had been assured that the front had been stabilized. They were disabused when the T-34s began to fire at targets of opportunity. The city's scratch garrison managed to put four of the T-34s out of action, but the remaining three pressed on while behind them the 5th Guards Tank Army closed on the Baltic coast. East Prussia was now cut off from the rest of the Third Reich.

the condensed idea
The T-34 was the template for modern tank design

36 The U-boat war 1939–43

Winston Churchill, Britain's wartime prime minister, believed that the Battle of the Atlantic was the 'dominating factor all through the war. Never could we forget that everything depended on its outcome.' He spoke the truth. Without the Atlantic supply chain stretching from North America to Britain, the British would have struggled to stay in the war. For them, the Battle of the Atlantic was the longest campaign of the war, fought from its very first day, 3 September 1939, when the *U-30* sank the liner SS *Athenia*, to the last, 7 May 1945, when the Kriegsmarine (German navy) surrendered.

In the First World War, German submarines – known as U-boats (from the German *Unterseeboot*) – came close to starving Britain into surrender by cutting the Atlantic supply line. In the Second World War they threatened to do the same, but at the height of the battle were defeated by Allied technology. However, it was a close-run thing. From the summer of 1940, the acquisition of bases in Norway and on the French Atlantic coast enabled U-boats, elements of the German surface fleet and long-range reconnaissance aircraft to broaden the scope of their operations and gave them immediate access to disputed waters. It also facilitated the refuelling of the U-boats by supply submarines known as 'milch cows'.

In contrast, the British – who still feared a cross-Channel invasion – could not supply sufficient escort cover for the Atlantic convoys. Seizing their chance, the U-boats began operating in 'wolf packs', shadowing convoys

timeline

1939	1940	1940	1940	1941	1941
15 SEPTEMBER First U-boat sinking of ship in Atlantic convoy	**5 MAY** Germans capture British submarine *Seal* with complete set of naval ciphers	**JULY** First U-boat base in France is established at Lorient	**AUGUST** Hitler announces 'total blockade' of Britain	**JULY** U-boats concentrate in mid-Atlantic	**SEPTEMBER** US Navy supplies escort for British ships as far as Iceland

during the day and launching surface attacks by night. The period between July and October 1940 was dubbed the 'Happy Time' by U-boat crews, who sank 217 ships for the loss of just two U-boats.

Detection and destruction In many ways the technological problems posed by the Battle of the Atlantic resembled those in the air war. To defeat the U-boats, the Allies needed the equipment to detect and destroy them in huge expanses of ocean. Initially their equipment was not up to the task. The radar sets installed in convoy escorts in 1940 could only detect surfaced submarines at short range. Equally unreliable was the sonar (also called Asdic), the sound equivalent of radar, which detected a submerged submarine by bouncing a sound signal off its hull. Sonar readings were often distorted by wrecks, shoals of fish and changes in underwater temperature.

After the US joined the war in December 1941 the U-boats enjoyed a second 'Happy Time', during which they sank 65 ships in February 1942, 86 in March, 69 in April and 111 in May. The Battle of the Atlantic reached crisis point at the beginning of 1943. U-boats sank 203,000 tons of shipping in January, 359,000 tons in February and 627,000 tons in March. Ships were being sunk at twice the rate they were being built, while for every U-boat sunk two were launched.

Science versus submarine At this point science began to work in favour of the Allies. The most important technical breakthrough came with the development of a powerful new centimetric radar based on a British invention: the cavity magnetron valve. Its accuracy was demonstrated in April 1941 when it detected a surfaced submarine at a range of 10 miles (16 km) and a periscope at 1,200 metres (3,937 ft). It was immediately clear that long-range patrol aircraft equipped with centimetric radar would prove a handful for U-boats.

> ❝We all felt like schoolchildren at Christmas-time.❞
> U-boat ace Kapitänleutnant Otto Kretschmer, *Battle of the Atlantic*, Terry Hughes and John Costello (1977)

1942	1942	1942	1943	1943
US introduces convoy system off East Coast	**NOVEMBER** Transfer of many escorts to support Torch landings in North Africa leads to heaviest monthly loss to U-boats	**DECEMBER** Introduction by Royal Navy of Hedgehog depth-charge mortars	**MAY** Record losses of U-boats (36) in course of month	**24 MAY** Dönitz withdraws U-boats from North Atlantic

Air-to-Surface (ASV) radar was introduced in the spring of 1943. Aircraft equipped with ASV, searchlights and depth charges were able to detect and destroy surfaced U-boats at night. In May 1943 aircraft accounted for 22 of the 36 U-boats sunk by the Allies. Eventually the Germans retrieved a cavity magnetron from a radar set in a crashed British aircraft (the device was almost indestructible) and unpicked its secrets. U-boats were fitted with an antenna that picked up centimetric radar transmissions at a range of up to 9.3 miles (15 km) and, later, 30 miles (45 km), which gave the submarine a chance to dive.

Crew conditions

Space for the crew, of which there were 44, was very cramped. The submariners slept where they could, next to machinery and torpedo tubes. They shared a single lavatory and usually eschewed washing and shaving once they were at sea, because of the shortage of fresh water. Discomfort was at first mitigated by good rations and the intense camaraderie shared on operations, a mixture of forced intimacy and shared danger.

New anti-submarine weapons came thick and fast. High-frequency direction finding ('huff-duff') enabled escorts to pinpoint and shadow U-boats when they were transmitting signals back to base. American Very Long Range (VLR) Liberator bombers, armed with acoustic torpedoes, closed the gap in the mid-Atlantic in which U-boats had operated free from air attack. Hunter-killer support groups built around fast escort carriers took a heavy toll of U-boats.

By mid-summer 1943, for the first time in the war the tonnage of Allied shipping launched exceeded that lost. The German withdrawal from France after the D-Day landings deprived the Kriegsmarine of its best operational bases and thereafter most U-boat activity was confined to the approaches and coastal waters of the British Isles. The introduction of the Type XXI U-boat, the ancestor of all modern submarines, with its increased battery capacity, streamlined hull and increased underwater range of up to 310 miles (500 km) came too late to turn the tide. From 1939 to 1945, the number of German submariners numbered 40,900, of whom 28,000 went down with their boats, a casualty rate of nearly 70 per cent, a loss rate unmatched by any other service in any country.

Type VII U-boat The Type VII was one of the Kriegsmarine's two standard U-boats of the Second World War – the other was the Type IX – and was hardly more sophisticated than its First World War predecessors.

Its diesel/electric engine gave it a speed of up to 17 knots on the surface and a range, at lower average speed, of 16,000 miles (25,750 km) on electric motors. Submerged speed, driven by batteries, which the diesel recharged, was seven knots.

Schnorchel From 1943, underwater endurance and speed were improved by the *Schnorchel* (dubbed the 'snort' by Allied seamen), essentially an air tube leading from a submarine to the surface, enabling the boat to run submerged on its diesel engines. The upper end of the tube was fitted with a valve that closed automatically when water entered. The principal drawbacks to the *Schnorchel* were that, like a periscope, it left a telltale plume of spray, and in rough seas the frequent closing of the waterproof valve often reduced the available air in the boat to dangerously low levels. Nevertheless, the *Schnorchel* was of particular value when the U-boat was leaving or returning to its base in closely patrolled waters. The U-boat's main armament was 14 electrically driven torpedoes (the Type IX carried 19), which left no telltale wake and were launched through four bow and one stern tube (the Type IX had two stern tubes).

Tactics Almost all the U-boat's time at sea was spent on the surface, watching for convoy positions designated by U-boat headquarters, located from March 1942 in Berlin after a British commando attack on the previous HQ at Saint-Nazaire. U-boats usually submerged only when they had taken a position ahead of a convoy's predicted track, waiting until darkness enabled them to surface and launch an attack. The U-boat captain often launched his attack from beyond the escort screen, evading the escort ships' counter-manoeuvres to engage Allied ships from within the convoy itself, where the radar echoes of the merchantmen would be confused with those of the U-boat.

the condensed idea
In two world wars the U-boat threatened to cut Britain's transatlantic lifeline

37 D-Day
1942–4

On 6 June 1944, the invasion of Normandy in northwest France was launched by the Allies. Codenamed Overlord, it was the greatest amphibious operation in history. By midnight on 6 June, over 150,000 US, British and Canadian troops had been landed in France by sea and air.

Never before had a major military operation involved so much scientific preparation and invention. At every level in the planning and mounting of Overlord, scientists played a key role. By this stage in the war, they were able to analyse battlefield experience to devise new weapons and tactics, and improve existing ones, to meet the challenge presented by Overlord.

Nothing was left to chance. The invasion beaches – codenamed Utah, Omaha, Gold, Juno and Sword – were chosen by Allied planners after extensive analysis of sand samples brought back from Normandy by special commando units. Every inch of the invasion area was photographed by Allied reconnaissance aircraft. Solly Zuckerman, chief scientific adviser to the Allied invasion force, studied the results of the photograph mosaics to devise the Transportation Plan, which preceded Overlord.

Transportation plan The plan was a scheme for Allied heavy and tactical bombers to destroy the railway systems in western Germany and France that the Germans would use to reinforce their formations in Normandy after the Allies came ashore. As part of a complex Allied deception plan, many of the bombs fell on the Pas-de-Calais, where the Channel is at its narrowest, to reinforce the German belief that the Allies intended to land there and not in Normandy.

timeline

1943	1943	1943	1943
JANUARY Allies begin planning for landings in northwest Europe	**MAY** Allies launch deception plan to mislead German high command on site of landings	**3 NOVEMBER** In Führer Directive 51, Hitler anticipates an Allied landing in northwest Europe	**DECEMBER** Erwin Rommel arrives in France to take command of Army Group B

Accurate weather forecasts were vital to the success of Overlord. A window of fair weather was predicted to open on 6 June, and on this advice the decision was taken to launch Overlord. As the Allied armada of 5,000 ships headed across the Channel, an electronic deception operation was mounted to reinforce German preconceptions about the landing beaches.

> **‘He told me that if Overlord failed, the United States would have lost a battle, but for the British it would be the end of their military capability.’**
>
> **US Presidential envoy Averell Harriman on a meeting with Churchill, May 1944**

Naval launches headed towards Calais and Boulogne. Each towed balloons fitted with special reflectors that produced radar echoes similar to those made by large troop ships. Overhead, bombers dropped huge streams of calibrated metal strips (codenamed 'Window' by the British and 'chaff' by the Americans), creating more false radar signals. The phantom invasion force convinced German radar operators that huge air and sea fleets were heading for the Pas-de-Calais.

Decoy tips the balance

As part of the deception plan, a double agent controlled by the British, Juan Pujol García ('Garbo'), informed his handlers in German intelligence that the landings in Normandy were merely a feint – the *Schwerpunkt* would be in the Pas-de-Calais. The Germans trusted Garbo, and from 1942 had clandestinely sent him some £350,000 to fund the entirely imaginary network he claimed to have established. German intelligence swallowed the bait, and their divisions remained in the Pas-de-Calais. On 6 June their presence in Normandy might have tipped the balance. Instead, the Germans awarded Garbo the Iron Cross, in absentia.

1944	**1944**	**1944**	**1944**
6 JUNE Allies land in Normandy	**9 JUNE** Two Mulberries are in place at Omaha Beach and Arromanches	**19 JUNE** Storms damage Mulberry at Omaha Beach	**20 JUNE** Units of the US Ghost Army create a fake Mulberry to draw German artillery fire

> **❝Piers for use on the beaches. They must float up and down with the tide. The anchor problem must be mastered. Let me have the best solution worked out. Don't argue the matter. The difficulties will argue for themselves.❞**
>
> **Winston Churchill, 30 May 1942**

Mulberry harbour During the early stages of planning Operation Overlord, the Allies were keenly aware that they could not rely upon seizing a port in full working order to funnel supplies to their forces in Normandy. They decided to create two artificial harbours off the Normandy coast, one to service the American beaches and the other to supply the British. The prefabricated parts of these harbours would be towed across the English Channel and assembled after bridgeheads had been established in Normandy. It was envisaged that the harbours would handle a combined daily total of 14,000 tons of supplies.

Codenamed Mulberries, the harbours consisted of a breakwater and an outer wall constructed 2 miles (3.2 km) offshore by sinking 70 blockships and 200 colossal caissons (codenamed Phoenix). These were hollow floating blocks, some of which displaced 6,000 tons and were the size of five-storey buildings. This created an area of calm water, inside which

Dissenting voices

Not everyone enthused about the Mulberries:

I think it is the biggest waste of manpower and equipment I have ever seen. I can unload a thousand LSTs [Landing Ship, Tank] at a time over the open beaches. Why give me something that anybody who has ever seen the sea act upon 150-ton concrete blocks at Casablanca knows the first storm will destroy? What's the use of building them just to have them destroyed and litter up the beaches?

Admiral John Leslie Hall, US Navy

piers were built and connected to the shore by 10 miles (16 km) of floating roadways (codenamed Whales) that were made of sections of articulated steel. The construction of the Mulberries consumed 2 million tons of steel and reinforced concrete. The cross-Channel towing operation involved more than 10,000 men and 160 ocean-going tugs.

The components of the Mulberry harbours began their passage to France on D-Day itself, five days after the blockships set sail from Oban in Scotland. It was planned that the Mulberries would be complete and functioning within days of the landings – the port of Cherbourg did not surrender until 29 June. However, the plan began to unravel on 19 June with the arrival of four days of stormy weather. In the worst gale for 40 years, both harbours were damaged. The American Mulberry at Omaha Beach, which had not been securely anchored to the sea bed, was put out of action, but the British harbour at Arromanches, popularly known as 'Port Winston', was patched together and in the ten months after D-Day was used to land over 2.5 million men, 500,000 vehicles and 4 million tons of supplies. It had been designed for three months' use, but with a reinforced breakwater lasted another seven, more than justifying the original concept.

the condensed idea
D-Day was the most significant amphibious operation in history

38 Nazi secret weapons 1939–45

In the small hours of 13 June 1944, a pilotless aircraft with a wingspan of 5 metres (16.5 ft) flew from France to England. Crossing the English coast at a speed of about 400 miles per hour (650 kph), it continued towards London, making a strange swishing sound and sending a jet of flaming exhaust from its rear.

As it passed overhead, the sound the aircraft made changed to a chugging, which one observer likened to a Model-T Ford climbing a steep hill. At 4.20 a.m., the sinister aircraft's engine cut out. There was a short silence and then it plunged to earth near the village of Swanscombe, 20 miles (32 km) east of London. There was a huge explosion but no casualties. The first of Hitler's *Vergeltungswaffen* ('revenge weapons') had arrived in England.

Rocket men The story of Germany's pilotless weapons programme began in the late 1920s when a 19-year-old student at the Berlin Technical College, Wernher von Braun, joined the German Amateur Rocket Society. The Society's work impressed a German artillery officer, Walter Dornberger, and he and von Braun began to develop a large transportable military rocket. This was intended to be a substitute for the conventional long-range artillery forbidden to the German army by the Treaty of Versailles (1919).

Funded by the German army, Dornberger established an experimental station at Peenemünde on a remote island in the Baltic. By the summer of 1942, Dornberger was ready for a test firing of von Braun's A-4 rocket, which was to become known to the Allies as the V-2.

timeline

1939
British intelligence is alerted to German missile research programme

1942
28 OCTOBER First glide test flight of V-1 at Peenemünde

1943
AUGUST 17/18 RAF Bomber Command raids the development site of the V-2 at Peenemünde

1944
12/13 JUNE Germans launch their V-1 campaign

The Luftwaffe programme Meanwhile, the Luftwaffe had developed a pilotless weapon of its own. Near Peenemünde it was preparing to test its FZG-76 flying bomb, the V-1. The V-1 had a number of significant advantages over its rocket rival. It was cheap and easy to produce and burned low-grade petrol instead of the scarce liquid oxygen and high-grade alcohol needed to power the V-2. Unknown to the Germans, the British had got wind of the V-weapon programme, and on the night of 17/18 August 1943 nearly 600 heavy bombers pounded the plant at Peenemünde, setting back the V-2 programme by at least two months. It was the only time in the war when the full power of Bomber Command was thrown against such a small target.

The Luftwaffe planned to launch the V-weapon campaign by hitting London with 500 V-1s per day, making the city uninhabitable, something it had failed to do in the Blitz of 1940–1. Once again Allied bombers intervened. From December 1943 they dropped thousands of tons of bombs on the conspicuous concrete and steel ramps built to launch V-1s from sites in northern France. The V-1 offensive did not start until a week after the Allied invasion of northwest Europe on D-Day, 6 June 1944.

The 'doodlebugs', as the V-Is were quickly dubbed, thrust Londoners back into the front line for the first time since the Blitz. They were not particularly accurate, but London was a very big target and the Germans intended the effect of the V-1s to be indiscriminate. By the end of August 1944, they had killed or seriously injured some 21,000 people in the London region. A quarter of a million young mothers and children were evacuated and another million left the city of their own accord. At night thousands sheltered in London's Underground stations.

The psychological effect of the V-1 was unnerving. On the ground, Londoners could hear it approaching. It had no radio control – to avoid jamming – but

> **‘There are serious indications that Germany has been developing bacterial warfare gases, flame weapons, glider bombs and pilotless aircraft . . . and it is recommended that necessary provisions should be taken.’**
>
> **Report by the scientific adviser to the Secret Intelligence Service, November 1939**

1944	1944	1944	1945
14/15 JUNE First airborne interception of a V-1 by Flight Lt. J.G. Musgrave of No. 605 Squadron	**8 SEPTEMBER** First V-2 lands in Chiswick, London	**25 NOVEMBER** A V-2 hits a Woolworths in New Cross, London, killing 106 and seriously injuring 108	**27 MARCH** Last V-2 falls on London. A British deception scheme, using German agents turned by the Double Cross system, has ensured that the flight of V-2s is recalibrated by the Germans so that many fall in the capital's suburbs and Kent rather than in central London

> **❛Doodlebug, doodlebug,
> Where have you been?
> I've been to London
> To bomb the Queen.❜**
>
> Schoolboy rhyme

was guided by a gyroscopic automatic pilot monitored by a magnetic compass, and its dive on the target at a measured distance was determined by the revolutions of a small propeller. When it told the V-1's pulse jet to stop, there was an ominous 15 seconds' silence before it plunged to earth to explode with a force that could destroy a whole city block. If the engine cut out after the V-1 flew overhead, you were safe. If not, the 15 seconds of silence might be your last.

Mastering the V-1 menace By the autumn of 1944, the V-1 threat had been neutralized. Assembled on the south coast and the approaches to London were massed anti-aircraft batteries firing shells armed with proximity fuses, which exploded near their targets. Fast fighter aircraft, including the newly introduced Gloster Meteor jet, shot down the V-1s at close range or, in a dangerous manoeuvre, nudged them off course. On 28 August the defences brought down 93 of the 98 V-1s that approached or crossed the English coastline. Two had been downed by the cables on barrage balloons, 23 by fighters and the remainder by anti-aircraft guns.

At the beginning of September 1944, the worst of the V-1 offensive was over. The launching sites in northern France had been captured by the Allies, forcing the Germans to fire the V-1s at longer ranges from Holland

Air-launching the V-1

A Luftwaffe unit, Gruppe III of Kampfgeschwader 3, was tasked with firing V-1s suspended below their inner wing between the fuselage and their port or starboard engine. He 111 bombers, based in Holland, took off with a ton of high explosive and petrol slung precariously beneath the fuselage and flew about 90 metres (300 ft) above the waves to avoid radar detection. They climbed to 450 metres (1,500 ft) before firing the V-1's sparking plugs via the cable linking it to the carrying aircraft. Often the missile was reluctant to unstick. Once the engine had started, it sometimes threatened to send aircraft and missile straight into the sea. KG 3 launched around 400 V-1s by this perilous method, of which some 160 crossed the coast. Only about 50 got anywhere near London. Other targets escaped unscathed.

or air-launch them from converted bombers. Success came at a price. It has been estimated that for every pound that the Germans spent on the V-1 programme, the British spent five in combating it – the combined cost of casualties, air defence and damage repair (some 23,000 homes were destroyed and about a million damaged).

The V-2 There was no relief for Londoners. On 8 September the first V-2 rocket, fired only minutes before from a site in Holland, fell on the London suburb of Chiswick with a shattering roar that could be heard all over the city. Rumours quickly spread that the explosion had been caused by a gas main catching fire. The War Cabinet, fearful of mass panic, did not reveal the existence of the V-2 until November 1944.

> **❝I crossed the road and, between the clouds, sure enough, right over our heads, was a horrible black thing. It gave me quite a turn . . .❞**
> **Diary of Vera Hodgson,** 7 July 1944

Each V-2 was about 20 times as expensive as the V-1, but unlike the doodlebug the V-2 gave no warning of its approach and could not be intercepted after it had been launched. It climbed to a height of about 80–100 kilometres (50–60 miles) before hurtling to earth at four times the speed of sound (2,500 mph/4,000 kph) to deliver a ton of high explosive. Transported on a vehicle that was also its launcher, it could be fired from almost any level piece of ground. Its launching sites were regularly changed to avoid detection from the air.

The V-2 offensive reached a climax in February 1945, during which 232 fell on southern England. On 8 March a V-2 fell on London's Smithfield Market, killing 233 people. In all, 1,115 V-2s fell on England, 517 of them in the London area, killing 2,754 people and injuring 6,523. Over 1,000 V-2s were also fired at the port of Antwerp, in an attempt to deny the Allies the use of its harbour during the closing months of the war.

the condensed idea
The V-1 was the first cruise missile and the V-2 the forerunner of mobile ballistic missiles

39 Escort fighter 1941–5

In the Second World War the bedrock of US strategic bombing tactics in Europe was formation flying in a self-defending 54-aircraft combat wing, which was both dangerous and physically exhausting. Extreme physical effort was required from the pilot to keep station in the turbulence generated by hundreds of propellers. The pilots flying in wing positions depended on the skill of element leaders right up to combat wing level. Poor flying by the leaders, and the constant seesawing of positions, added to pilot fatigue and ran the risk of collisions or breaking the formation, thus providing Luftwaffe day fighters with 'cold meat' – isolated aircraft.

Flying consisted of sliding the B-17 Flying Fortress and B-24 Liberator bombers around to maintain the integrity of the formation. Banking was dangerous because of the close proximity of other aircraft. Frequent throttle changes were required, which could lead to excessive fuel consumption, particularly by aircraft flying in high groups. By the spring of 1943, heavy losses to German fighters had forced the USAAF's 8th Air Force to adopt the 'tucked-in wing' formation of three 18-aircraft squadrons stacked closely together with one squadron flying lead, one high and one low.

A combat wing, dubbed a *Pulk* (herd) by the Luftwaffe, deployed formidable defensive power and was a daunting sight to novice fighter pilots. The B-17G's defensive armament consisted of thirteen .50 machine

timeline

1941	1942	1942	1942	1943	1943
7 DECEMBER US enters the war after the Japanese bomb Pearl Harbor	**6 JULY** First B-17s of 97th Bombardment Group (BG) arrive in England	**17 AUGUST** US 8th Air Force flies its first raid in Europe	**DECEMBER** 8th Air Force introduces first combat wing formation	**APRIL** 8th Air Force issues the Pointblank Directive after the Casablanca Conference	**AUGUST** 8th Air Force fields six BGs in England, some 288 aircraft

6 . . . the progressive destruction of and dislocation of the German military, industrial and economic system, and the undermining of the morale of the German people to a point where their capacity for armed resistance is fatally weakened. 9

Directive on the air war issued by the Western Allies
after the Casablanca Conference, January 1943

guns. A combat wing could bring to bear 648 machine guns firing
14 rounds a second with an effective range of 600 yards (548 m). The
two-ounce bullets remained lethal on the human body at ranges of up
to 4 miles (6.5 km).

Self-defending fallacy The USAAF began to make shallow
penetrations into Germany in January 1943, and from February losses
began to mount steadily. The Luftwaffe's day fighters were as well armed
as the US bombers, and by autumn 1943 they were carrying 30-millimetre
(1.2-in) heavy cannon and 210-millimetre (8.3-in) rockets. The latter
were not particularly accurate, but were effective in loosening up the
bomber formations.

Heavy losses over Germany became the norm. The attrition reached a
peak on 17 August when the 8th Air Force attacked the fighter assembly
plant at Regensburg and the ball-bearing factories at Schweinfurt. Of the
376 aircraft despatched on the double raid, 60 were lost and many more
written off. A second raid on Schweinfurt in October cost the Americans
77 aircraft lost and another 133 damaged out of 291 despatched. After the
second Schweinfurt raid, bombing operations were temporarily suspended.
It was brutally clear that the bombers would have to be escorted to and
from targets deep in Germany. However, there were no aircraft capable
of fulfilling this role.

1943	**1943**	**1944**	**1944**	**1944**	**1945**
17 AUGUST 8th Air Force mounts the double raid on Schweinfurt-Regensburg	**DECEMBER** P-51B enters service with 8th Air Force	**MARCH–JUNE** Anglo-American combined bomber offensive against Germany is switched to preparations for the D-Day landings	**MAY** P-51D begins operations with 8th Air Force	**NOVEMBER** German oil production halted by renewed combined bomber offensive	**FEBRUARY** 8th Air Force and Bomber Command mount crushing day/night raids on the city of Dresden

The USAAF's P-38 Lightning and P-47 Thunderbolt fighters lacked the performance to meet enemy fighters on equal terms and the range to escort the bombers over Germany. The Luftwaffe could now choose the time and place to attack, even when the P-47's range was extended by 490-litre (108-gallon) drop tanks. German fighters would often draw the P-47s into combat, at which point they would have to jettison their drop tanks and reduce their escort range. The P-38 had a longer range but poor performance over 6,000 metres (20,000 ft), the altitude at which most combats over Germany took place.

Enter the Mustang The crisis was resolved with the arrival of the North American P-51B Mustang in December 1943. Powered by the Rolls-Royce Merlin and fitted with a 340-litre (75-gallon) drop tank, the P-51B had a range of 1,000 miles (1.6 km), enabling it to fly escort to such targets as Emden, Kiel and Bremen. The bubble-canopied P-51D, which arrived in May 1944, had a boosted performance with reinforced wings, allowing exceptional fuel loads and, with drop tank, a range of 1,500 miles (2,400 km) sufficient for escort to any target and even for the shuttle missions that flew to the Soviet Union.

Air supremacy battles

On 30 May 1944, 8th Air Force Mustang ace Major George Preddy wrote in his combat report:

As the bombers were approaching . . . Magdeburg, I was leading a section of seven ships giving close escort to the rear box which was quite a distance behind the main formation. I noticed 20 to 30 single-engined fighters attacking the front boxes, so we dropped our tanks and headed towards them. We came up behind three Me 109s in rather tight formation. I opened fire on one from 300 yards and closed to 150 yards. The 109 burst into flames and went down. I slipped behind the second 109 and fired while closing from 200 to 100 yards. He started burning and disintegrated immediately. He went down spinning. The third enemy aircraft saw us and broke down. I followed him in a steep turn, diving and zooming. I got in many deflection shots, getting hits on the wing and tail section. I ran out of ammunition, so my element leader, Lt. Whisner, continued the attack getting in several good hits. At about 7,000 feet the pilot baled out.

The P-51D matched the Me 109G in level manoeuvring flight and had the edge in climb and dive. Only the rate of roll left the German fighter on equal terms. It could remain in the air for over nine hours. In the P-51D the USAAF possessed a superb escort fighter that it could use to provoke and win a series of air supremacy battles. In January 1944, the Americans had introduced a modified bomber support relay system, which remained standard for the rest of the war. Rather than flying to a predetermined rendezvous point and then accompanying part of the bomber stream until relieved by another unit, a group was allocated an area along the route, which it patrolled while the bomber stream passed through.

The most experienced P-47 groups were assigned those sectors where enemy opposition was anticipated, while the target leg of the bomber route was flown by P-38s and P-51s. The arrival of the Mustangs prompted another tactical adjustment of the bomber formations. They were reduced to three squadrons of 12 aircraft, with the lead squadron in the centre and the trail squadrons formed up above and below. Although overall strength had been cut by one-third, the new formation occupied 17 per cent more air space than its predecessor, reducing the strain on pilots and making it easier for the Mustangs to provide escort. The Mustangs were employed not only as escorts, hugging the bomber formation as had the German Me 109s in the Battle of Britain, but as fighting patrols whose role was to seek out and destroy the enemy.

the condensed idea
The outstanding long-range fighter of the Second World War

40 Aircraft carrier
1941–5

In the war fought across the Pacific Ocean between 1942 and 1945, the United States combined technology and technique to push naval warfare into a new realm. In the First World War battleships had ruled the seas, slugging it out over ranges of 20,000 yards (18.3 km). In the vast expanses of the Pacific, however, the most important ship was the aircraft carrier, whose dive- and torpedo-bombers could strike at an enemy hundreds of miles away.

The aircraft carrier was the descendant of the seaplane carriers of the First World War. The first true aircraft carrier, capable of launching an aircraft from an unobstructed flight deck while at sea, was the Royal Navy's modified seaplane carrier HMS *Argus*, which entered service in October 1918. In the post-war years, the British were followed into the carrier race by the two pre-eminent Pacific naval powers, the United States and Japan, both of which by 1921 operated three carriers. By the spring of 1941, a 'carrier gap' had opened – the Japanese enjoyed a decisive advantage of ten carriers to the four deployed by the US Navy.

Pearl Harbor Nevertheless, with ten battleships apiece, both the US and Japanese navies envisaged a decisive role for what was still considered to be the arbiter of naval power. Pearl Harbor was to change all that. On 26 November 1941 the Japanese fleet, with six carriers at its heart, left harbour. Maintaining radio silence, and under the cover of clouds and squalls, it sailed to its attack position 200 miles (322 km) from the US Navy's Pacific base at Pearl Harbor on the Hawaiian island of Oahu. The Americans were aware of Japanese intentions, as they had

timeline

1941	1942	1942	1942	1942	1942
7 DECEMBER Japanese attack Pearl Harbor	**2 JANUARY** Japanese seize Manila, forcing US and Filipino troops into the Bataan peninsula	**20 JANUARY** Japanese push into Burma	**15 FEBRUARY** British surrender in Singapore	**30 MARCH** Southwest Pacific under General MacArthur and Central Pacific under Admiral Nimitz	**18 APRIL** Doolittle Raid, first US carrier raid on Japanese home islands

been intercepting and reading Japanese diplomatic messages for months. However, they were ignorant of Japan's precise plans.

At 7.55 a.m. on 7 December the Japanese struck, achieving total surprise. Aircraft from its carriers sank or disabled eight of the battleships anchored at Pearl Harbor and destroyed over 300 aircraft on the ground. But the Japanese did not destroy Pearl Harbor's dock and oil storage facilities, which would have forced the Pacific Fleet back to America's West Coast; and two of the US Navy's carriers were not at Pearl Harbor, but on a training cruise, while a third was under repair in California. The blow at Pearl Harbor had brutally settled the carrier-versus-battleship debate in favour of the carrier.

A new era Six months later, at the Battle of the Coral Sea (4–8 May 1942), a new era in naval warfare opened. The first large-scale aircraft carrier clash was fought without either surface fleet sighting the enemy. At Coral Sea the Japanese sank the US carrier *Lexington* and damaged another, *Yorktown*. Believing that both carriers had been sunk, the Japanese pressed on with their plan to capture the Pacific island of Midway, which offered a base within striking distance of Hawaii.

The Americans now possessed a priceless advantage. They had cracked the Japanese naval code, JN-25, and had positioned their fleet to defeat the strong task force that the Japanese had assembled to take Midway. In the ensuing carrier battle – one of the truly decisive encounters of the Second World War – American dive-bombers destroyed four Japanese

> **❝You will not only be unable to make up your losses but you will grow weaker as time goes on . . . we will not only make up our losses but will grow stronger as time goes on. It is inevitable that we shall crush you before we are through with you.❞**
>
> Admiral Harold Stark, **Chief of Naval Operations, to Admiral Kichisaburo Nomura, Japanese ambassador to the United States, 1941**

1942	**1942**	**1942**	**1942–3**	**1944**	**1945**
4–8 MAY Battle of the Coral Sea	**20 MAY** Allies withdraw from Burma into India	**4–6 JUNE** Battle of Midway	Land and naval battles for Guadalcanal (August 1942–February 1943)	**OCTOBER** Battle of Leyte Gulf	**FEBRUARY–MARCH** Capture of Iwo Jima

carriers and reversed the balance of power in the Pacific. The Japanese were now forced to defend a vast and swiftly acquired ocean empire from attack at any point the Americans might choose.

Pacific drive The American Pacific drive, which began with the clearing of the island of Guadalcanal (August 1942–February 1943) witnessed a series of savage air, land and sea battles, a war of attrition that bled Japan white. By mid-1944, all 15 of the Japanese aircraft carriers brought into service since 1941 had been sunk or irreparably damaged, while of 27 fleet carriers added to the US Navy, only one had been sunk. In the Battle of the Philippine Sea (June 1944) the reformed Japanese carrier fleets emerged relatively intact, but by August they had lost over 750 aircraft in what became known as the 'Great Marianas Turkey Shoot'.

> **❝Scratch one flattop, Dixon to carrier. Scratch one flattop!❞**
>
> **Dauntless pilot Lt.-Commander Bob Dixon to the US carrier *Lexington* on the sinking of the Japanese carrier *Shoho* at Coral Sea**

At Leyte Gulf in October 1944, four Japanese carriers were sent to the bottom. New Japanese fighters were entering service but there were no carriers from which they could fly.

From October 1944 the recurring theme of the Japanese air effort was the *kamikaze* suicide attack. The largest single *kamikaze* was the 78,000-ton battleship *Yamato*, which on 6 April 1945 sailed from the Inland Sea to attack the landings on Okinawa. She carried sufficient fuel only for a one-way trip, and the plan was to run her aground on Okinawa to bombard US positions. On 7 April *Yamato* and her screening destroyers were located and attacked by waves of aircraft from the US carrier fleet. At the cost of only ten aircraft the largest battleship ever built was sent to the bottom.

Essex-class carrier Conceived in mid-1939, the Essex-class US Navy carriers, of which 24 were finally built, constituted the 20th century's most numerous class of capital ships. In the Pacific war the Essex class was the mainstay of the Pacific Fleet's combat strength and continued to serve until the 1970s.

The Second World War carriers displaced 272,000 tons and were 250 metres (820 ft) long. Their four Westinghouse geared turbines produced 150,000 horsepower, driving the carrier at 32 knots. Defensive firepower was formidable, with twelve 5-inch (12.7-cm) guns controlled by two Mark 37

Directors and forty 40-millimetre (1.5-in) anti-aircraft guns with Mark 51 Directors. Close defence was provided by fifty-five 20-millimetre (0.79-in) guns.

The carriers' famous 'Sunday Punch' was provided by its complement of 36 fighters, 36 dive-bombers and 18 torpedo-bombers. Standard fighters were F6F Hellcats, big beefy aircraft that were more than a match for the Japanese; the dive-bombers were heavily armed Curtiss SB2C Helldiver two-seaters, the most numerous Allied dive-bombers of the Second World War; the torpedo-bombers were exceptionally well engineered and robust TBF Avengers. Together they were a deadly combination.

The carriers were packed with advanced technological equipment: air and surface search and fire-control radars; a plan position indicator (PPI) display kept track of ships and enabled a multi-carrier force to maintain a high-speed formation at night or in heavy weather when identification friend or foe (IFF) identified hostile ships and aircraft.

Dive-bombers

The Curtiss SB2C Helldiver was a powerful two-seat dive-bomber that carried a 455-kilogram (1,000-lb) bombload with a defensive armament of four wing-mounted 0.5-inch (12-mm) Brownings and two 0.3-inch (8-mm) Brownings on flexible mountings in the rear cockpit. The Helldiver had a top speed of 281 miles per hour (452 kph) at 3,810 metres (12,500 ft), service ceiling of 7,620 metres (25,000 ft) and range of 1,100 miles (1,770 km). It made its operational debut in the Pacific in November 1943 and became the most numerous Allied dive-bomber of the Second World War, although, as its nickname 'Son of a Bitch Second Class' suggests, it was never wholly popular with aircrew because of poor handling qualities.

None of the Essex carriers was lost in the Second World War, during which they played a key role in the Pacific, participating in the 1943 landings on Tarawa in the Gilbert Islands, bombing the Japanese home islands, protecting the Pacific Fleet and transporting aircraft and troops. Eleven Essex-class carriers took part in the Korean War and 13 in the Vietnam War, although creeping obsolescence latterly limited their role to that of helicopter and anti-submarine platforms.

the condensed idea
The key to victory in the Pacific

41 Codebreaking
1923–45

One of the greatest Allied technical triumphs of the Second World War was achieved not on the battlefield but in the Buckinghamshire countryside at a Victorian mansion, Bletchley Park, the home of the British Government Code and Cypher School (GCCS).

It was here that the British decrypted the top-secret German signals encoded on the Enigma machine. The machine had been invented and marketed in the 1920s by a German, Arthur Scherbius. He saw the machine as a way of keeping business correspondence secret, but the German armed forces quickly spotted its military potential. By 1935, Enigma had been adopted as standard equipment by all branches of the German armed forces and intelligence services.

Polish breakthrough However, in the 1930s early forms of the Enigma code had been broken by a team working for Polish military intelligence. Before the outbreak of war in September 1939, the Poles shared their knowledge with the British and presented them with an Enigma machine. Mathematicians at Bletchley Park immediately began working on the later, modified Enigma codes that had defeated the Poles. By the end of the war, there were some 10,000 people at Bletchley, housed in a hotchpotch of temporary offices built in the grounds.

It was a very British organization, full of brilliant eccentrics and misfits; among them were the mathematician Alan Turing, one of the fathers of the computer, and Roy Jenkins, a future home secretary. Security was

timeline

1935	1938	1940
Enigma is in use by all branches of the German armed forces	Codebreaking and eavesdropping station established at Bletchley Park	Ultra plays an important part in revealing the Luftwaffe order of battle in the Battle of Britain

very tight, and the story behind Bletchley Park remained a secret until the 1970s. The codename for Enigma decrypts was 'Ultra'.

Knowing how the Enigma machine worked was not enough. It was vital to discover the Enigma keys, the settings that were changed as often as three times a day. Using extra-sensitive US-built receivers, the Y Service, a top-secret British radio interception network, listened in to the apparently meaningless groups of letters transmitted in Morse code. They were taken down and then sent to Bletchley, where the Enigma key was unlocked.

Bombes The principal weapons originally used by the British cryptanalysts were electro-mechanical computers, known as Bombes, in large part designed by Alan Turing, which were matched to the electric wiring of the Enigma machine. German carelessness then entered the picture. Because of the need to indicate to a receiving station the way

> **The geese which laid the golden eggs but which never cackled.**
>
> **Winston Churchill on the Bletchley Park cryptanalysts**

Enigma

The Enigma machine looked like a cross between a portable typewriter and a cash register. Inside was a complex system of gears, electric wiring and a series of drums. Each of the drums carried an alphabet on the outside. Any letter typed by the Enigma operator on the keyboard could be transposed into an infinite variety of different letters, in theory 158 trillion. When A was struck on the keyboard it might be transposed to M. When M was struck on an Enigma deciphering machine, it would be transposed back to A. The settings were frequently altered, but as long as both machines were altered at the same time, the system continued to work. Encoded messages, seemingly random groups of letters, were sent in Morse code, protecting German radio communications from eavesdroppers. The Germans were convinced that Enigma was unbreakable.

1941	1941	1942–3	1943	1944
The British supply Stalin with Ultra-derived information of plans for Barbarossa without revealing the source	**8 MAY** Capture of Enigma code book from *U-110*	Ultra-derived information is given to the Allied high command in North Africa	Bletchley breaks back into German naval codes at the crisis in the Battle of the Atlantic	Ultra proves key to the success of Operation Overlord

in which the Enigma setting machine had been geared to transmit, its operator was obliged to preface each message with a repeated sequence of the same letters. This established a pattern that could provide a trained mathematician with the chance to break into a message and thus into its whole meaning. Luftwaffe keys proved far easier to break into than army, navy (Kriegsmarine) or intelligence keys.

Colossus In 1941 the Germans introduced a method of transmitting non-Morse teleprinter messages. The fiendishly complex 12-rotor Lorenz machine could encipher and decipher messages and transmit them with the aid of perforated tapes at the rate of 25 letters per second. It was more secure than Enigma and was beyond the capacity of a Bombe to decipher rapidly. Enigma contained traffic ranging from routine orders to detailed battle plans, as in the build-up to Kursk in 1943. Lorenz, which Bletchley called 'Tunny' and its ciphers 'Fish', was crucially confined to communications between the German army's high command and army group commanders in the field.

Allied secrets

The British shared the Ultra secret with their American allies, but only provided their Soviet allies with summaries of Ultra-derived information carefully laundered to disguise its source. But there was at least one Soviet spy at Bletchley. This was John Cairncross, who in the early summer of 1943 provided Soviet intelligence with raw decrypts of the lengthy German deliberations in the protracted build-up to the Battle of Kursk (1943).

The brilliant cryptanalyst John Tiltman broke into Fish messages in 1941, using hand-methods that relied on statistical analysis, but modifications subsequently introduced by the Germans made this method impossible. In May 1943, following the capture of two Lorenz machines in North Africa, a semi-electronic machine containing fewer than 100 valves was devised and dubbed a 'Robinson', after Heath Robinson, because of its hastily improvised nature. It was soon followed by a more powerful machine, Colossus, developed by Max Newman and T.H. Flowers of the British General Post Office (GPO) Research Station. It contained 1,500 valves rather than electro-magnetic relays, and at the beginning of 1944 began deciphering the Fish cipher.

The GPO team was then ordered to produce an even more powerful version, Colossus II, in three months, which they accomplished by building it on site at Bletchley. Equipped with 2,400 valves, it also incorporated a loop of

cracking codes

The Bletchley codebreakers were able only intermittently to break into the Kriegsmarine codes. For the months, between February 1941 and December 1942, they were unable to penetrate the code used by U-boats. The Bombes helped them to break back in. The codebreakers and Allied naval technology ensured that within six months the crisis in the Battle of the Atlantic (see chapter 36) was over. However, the Gestapo keys were never penetrated by Bletchley's cryptanalysts. In spite of these setbacks, by the end of the war much Enigma traffic was being read at the same speed by the British as the Germans.

friction-driven perforated tape, which was read photo-electrically and provided a limited memory. Colossus II was the world's first programmable electronic digital computer, and it entered service at a critical time, 1 June 1944.

As Germany's position deteriorated and its communications networks were degraded, its high command was increasingly forced to rely heavily on Fish traffic. Via Colossus, this yielded a harvest of vital intelligence to the British and Americans. During the battle of Normandy, Bletchley was able to supply Field Marshal Montgomery with information on day-to-day German strengths at the battlefront and the effects of Allied air strikes. Bletchley knew in advance of Hitler's intention to counterattack the flank of US General George S. Patton's Normandy breakout at Mortain, a disclosure that led to the encirclement of 50,000 retreating German troops in the Falaise Pocket. By May 1945, there were ten Colossus machines at Bletchley. They were all destroyed at the end of the war.

the condensed idea
Britain's greatest technical triumph of the Second World War

42 The atom bomb 1934–45

It is a grand irony that the introduction of a weapon that has cast a pall over the world since 1945 had its origins in 19th-century medical research. Discovery of the means to heal led to the development of the means to kill.

The origins of the atomic bomb lay in the discovery in the late 19th century of radioactivity by Henri Becquerel, of radium by Pierre and Marie Curie, of X-rays by Wihelm Röngten, and the coherent understanding of the penetrative alpha and beta rays outlined by Ernest Rutherford in 1900. In 1934 the Hungarian-born physicist Leo Szilard, later a Jewish refugee from Nazi Germany, discovered that the nuclei of certain atoms could be split by bombarding them with atomic particles known as neutrons. In turn this would release more neutrons, which would split more nuclei, and so on in a chain reaction releasing huge amounts of energy.

Scientists realized that the energy could be used to create a bomb of enormous power. In Britain two more refugees from Nazi Germany, Otto Frisch and Rudolf Peierls, found that a rare form of uranium – uranium-235 – was required to produce an instantaneous explosive chain reaction of the type required for a bomb. Meanwhile physicists working in France discovered that an artificial element, plutonium, could also be used to make an atomic bomb.

Einstein's intervention Atomic research was also underway in Germany. Many scientists were fearful of the consequences of an atomic bomb being placed in the hands of Adolf Hitler. In the United States in

timeline

1939	1941	1941	1942	1942	1944
Leo Szilard prompts Albert Einstein to write to President Roosevelt, warning of the German programme to develop an atom bomb	**MAY** US government places order for 250 B-29 Superfortresses	**7 DECEMBER** United States enters the war after Japanese attack on Pearl Harbor	Szilard, working with Enrico Fermi, starts first self-sustaining nuclear reaction	Manhattan Project transfers joint US–UK work on the A-bomb to the United States	**MAY** B-29 enters service

1939, Albert Einstein, the leading physicist of the day and another refugee from Nazi Germany, warned President Roosevelt that Germany might be planning to build an atomic weapon. Prompted by Szilard, Einstein proposed an American research programme to develop an atomic bomb, adding that the bomb should never be used.

Roosevelt responded by setting up a Uranium Committee, which reported in 1941 that it would be possible to design and build an atomic bomb. The committee concluded that its use would be 'determining'. The British, who were working on their own nuclear weapon project, codenamed Tube Alloys, pooled their resources with the Americans after the latter entered the war in December 1941. Joint research was transferred to the USA under the codename of Manhattan Project. Many of the Allies' most brilliant scientific minds were gathered together in a specially built laboratory complex at Los Alamos, New Mexico. In charge of the

Germany's nuclear ambitions

The crowning mercy of the Second World War was that Germany did not produce an atomic bomb. In the 1930s, Hitler's persecution of the Jews had driven much German scientific talent abroad and into the hands of the Allies. The chaotic and competitive nature of the Nazi state, with its myriad rival empires, also militated against the concentration of effort that characterized the Manhattan Project. By 1944, Hitler himself had become obsessed by the development of a bewildering range of conventional weapons with which he hoped to turn the tide of war, but which Nazi Germany could no longer sustain. The Führer had been advised of the possibility of an atomic weapon in 1942, but the Germans failed to separate U-235 (the essential fissile element of the bomb). By the summer of 1944, German scientists had only reached a point at which they were aware of the almost insuperable difficulties that lay ahead if they were to build an atomic pile, the preliminary to developing an atomic weapon.

1944	**1945**	**1945**	**1945**	**1945**	**1945**
JULY United States capture Saipan in the Mariana Islands, in the central Pacific and within bombing range of Japan	**FEBRUARY** USAAF launches fire raids on Tokyo	**JULY–AUGUST** Assembly of Little Boy is completed in Tinian. Authorization for the dropping of the A-bomb is given	**6 AUGUST** Little Boy is dropped on Hiroshima	**9 AUGUST** Fat Man is dropped on Nagasaki	**2 SEPTEMBER** Japan surrenders

construction of facilities, the procurement of raw materials and equipment, the provision of accommodation and testing facilities for the bomb was a hard-driving US army engineer, General Leslie Groves. The scientific director of the Manhattan Project was J. Robert Oppenheimer.

Only the Americans had the resources to throw almost unlimited funds at the Manhattan Project – by the spring of 1945 there were some 129,000 people engaged in the nuclear programme, working on 30 sites in North America. One of the most important was at Oak Ridge, Tennessee, the principal uranium separation plant for the production of fissionable material for the atomic bomb. By October 1945 the programme had cost nearly $2 billion, 90 per cent of which had been absorbed by building plants and producing fissionable materials. The original budget for the plants had been $90 million.

By the early summer of 1945 there was little doubt that the atomic bomb would be dropped on Japan. From November 1944, Boeing B-29 Superfortress bombers of US XX and XXI Commands, the supreme expression of Second World War aviation technology, had reduced Japan's major cities to rubble in a devastating series of fire raids. The bombers were running out of targets to attack. Modifications to the B-29 to carry an atomic bomb had begun in the summer of 1943, and in the summer of 1944 a special unit, 509th Composite Group, began training to drop it.

> **'We must now accept the fact that [our] pioneering work is a dwindling asset and that, unless we capitalize it quickly we shall be outstripped.'**
>
> **Sir John Anderson, British home secretary**

General George C. Marshall, the US army's chief of staff, was convinced that the continuing naval blockade of Japan, and a military intervention by the Soviet Union, would force a Japanese surrender; but the new US President, Harry S. Truman, had already made up his mind. Once the bomb had been produced, at so great a cost, he felt bound to use it, and in so doing send the clearest of messages to America's wartime ally, the Soviet Union, about the shape of the post-war world.

Little Boy and Fat Man Two types of bomb had been developed by scientists working on the Manhattan Project. The first, torpedo-shaped and relying for its chain reaction on uranium, was nicknamed 'Little Boy'.

The A-bomb attacks

The B-29 chosen for the mission was commanded by Col. Paul W. Tibbets. It was called *Enola Gay* after Tibbets's mother. The B-29 had been blessed by a Catholic priest and a pin-up of Rita Hayworth had been attached to Little Boy. On 6 August, the B-29 approached Hiroshima. At 08:15:17 hours, the B-29's bomb bay doors opened and Little Boy began its descent from an altitude of 9,500 metres (31,000 ft), detonating some 600 metres (2,000 ft) above the aiming point.

As *Enola Gay* pulled away, the crew saw a vivid flash, then felt a double shockwave as it struck the aircraft. Below them, some 15 miles (24 km) away, a ball of fire seethed skyward as the bomb detonated with a force equal to 29,000 tons of conventional explosive, devastating 5 square miles (13 sq km) of Hiroshima and killing some 75,000 human beings.

The Japanese did not surrender and on 9 August Fat Man was dropped on Nagasaki. Approximately 35,000 people died. On 2 September 1945 Japan surrendered. The atomic era had been born.

The second, bulbous and using plutonium, was called 'Fat Man'. In July 1945, 509th Composite Group was transferred to the island of Tinian, in the Marianas chain. On 16 July, the Manhattan scientists successfully exploded the first atomic device at Alamogordo in the New Mexico desert.

On 24 July a mission directive was issued by General Spaatz, commander of the newly formed US Strategic Air Forces in the Pacific. He ordered 509th Group to 'deliver its first special bomb as soon as weather will permit visual bombing after 3 August on one of the targets: Hiroshima, Kokura, Niigata and Nagasaki'. By 2 August Little Boy had been assembled on Tinian and on that day Hiroshima, an undamaged industrial centre and port, was chosen as the primary target.

the condensed idea
A step towards global annihilation

43 Ballistic missiles 1955–2012

In the Second World War the Germans experimented with submarine-launched missiles, and in the immediate post-war period US naval shipbuilding programmes included projects for a 'submersible missile barge' in which a fleet submarine could tow and then fire a V-2 missile. In another project, the fleet submarine *Cusk* was modified to carry and fire a Loon (US-built V-1) cruise missile. The concept was seductive, as a submarine could approach an enemy coast undetected. The drawback was that it could deliver only a fraction of the firepower of a carrier group, but the development in the late 1950s of nuclear warheads transformed the situation.

In the early 1950s the United States had matched the numerical superiority of the Soviet Union and communist China with advanced technology. The US military-industrial complex told successive governments that anything was possible, at a price. In the case of the nuclear-powered submarine, the price came very high, but it was one that politicians believed was worth paying.

> **❛Underway on nuclear power.❜**
> Signal from *Nautilus*,
> 17 January 1955

Nuclear world By 1954 nuclear energy as a source of industrial power seemed the key to the future, and in the USA, Britain and, ominously, the Soviet Union, reactors were generating power for civilian purposes. In 1955 the US Navy completed the world's first operational nuclear-powered submarine, USS *Nautilus*, namesake of the submarine in Jules Verne's *Twenty*

timeline

1955	1959	1960	1962
US Navy completes the world's first operational nuclear-powered submarine, *Nautilus*	The Soviet Union introduces the 'Hotel' class nuclear-powered ballistic missile submarine	USS *George Washington* launches the first Polaris submarine	The first version of Polaris, the A-1, is tested in the Pacific

Thousand Leagues Under the Sea and the successor of a submarine that had served with distinction in the Second World War.

Nautilus heralded the dawn of a new naval era every bit as revolutionary as that of the dreadnought. She had the ability to stay at sea to the limits of her food supply and her crew's endurance; and her specially strengthened and streamlined hull allowed her to dive to depths below 300 metres (1,000 ft), travel at speeds well over 20 knots and, by re-circulating air through carbon-dioxide scrubbers, remain submerged indefinitely. On her sea trials in January 1955, she remained submerged throughout a journey of 1,100 nautical miles (2,000 km) from New London to San Juan, Puerto Rico, in less than 90 hours, at the time the longest submerged cruise by a submarine.

Soviet Missiles

When the Soviet Union overran Germany in 1945, it discovered huge containers designed to be towed behind U-boats. Each one would have fired a V-2 rocket at New York from positions off the American eastern seaboard. Initially the Soviets designed a similar plan, codenamed Golem, but discarded it in favour of missiles launched from within submarines. In 1955–6 the 'Zulu' class of submarines were rebuilt to accommodate a 'Sark' missile. The 'Hotel' class carried three SS-N-4 short-range missiles.

Polaris   The US Navy's original plans for a submarine-based missile force got off to a false start with the Regulus and Jupiter projects. It had initially intended to use cruise missile systems in a strategic role, but the sheer size of Jupiter and Regulus and, more importantly, the need for

> **❝The skill, professional competency and courage of the officers and crew of *Nautilus* were in keeping with the highest traditions of the Armed Forces of the United States and the pioneering spirit which has long characterized our country.❞**
>
> US Presidential citation after *Nautilus's* voyage under the polar ice cap

1971	**1979**	**1994**
Second-generation US SLBM, Poseidon, becomes operational	Trident SLBM, Poseidon's replacement, becomes operational	Trident replaces Poseidon in Britain's SSBNs

The Cold War

Nautilus continued to set performance records that rendered the anti-submarine warfare (ASW) milestones of the Second World War redundant. She was immensely difficult to detect by sonar in the lower depths beneath successive temperature layers of water; she was invisible to radar; and she was fast enough to elude most hunters on the surface. *Nautilus* was not nuclear-armed, but in the spring of 1958 she played an important role in the US response to the Soviet intercontinental ballistic missile (ICBM) threat posed by the launching in 1957 of the first satellite, Sputnik. At the time the Soviets had no submarine-launched ballistic missile (SLBM) capability while the US SLBM programme was well advanced. The launching of Sputnik had opened a new phase in the Cold War, and the US responded by despatching *Nautilus* on Operation Sunshine, navigating beneath the ice cap of the North Pole. It was a preliminary to the introduction of the Polaris two-stage solid-fuel nuclear-armed SLBM in the early 1960s.

the submarine to surface to fire them, rendered the systems impractical. Submarines are at their most vulnerable when surfaced, and this vulnerability was increased with a fully or partially fuelled missile on deck.

Polaris and its successors were a much more attractive proposition. The US Navy had initiated the Polaris programme in 1956 and the USS *George Washington*, the first US SSBN (submarine, ballistic missile, nuclear-powered) launched the first missile while submerged in July 1960. Each of *George Washington*'s 16 Polaris missiles was enclosed in its own tube and could be serviced, adjusted and fired from beneath the surface from a position precisely fixed by inertial navigation and programmed to its target by small computers in the submarine and in the missile itself.

The A-1 The first version of Polaris, the A-1, had a range of 1,000 nautical miles (1,850 km) and a single 600-kiloton W47 nuclear warhead. In May 1962, in Operation Dominic, a Polaris missile with a live W47 warhead (with reduced yield) was tested in the central Pacific, the only incidence of an American test of a live strategic nuclear missile. The A-1 was a strategic asset designed to complement the limited number of land-based medium-range systems deployed by the United States in Europe. The medium-range systems lacked the range to attack major Soviet targets, and

Polaris, with its forward bases in the UK and Spain, had been developed specifically to reinforce this aspect of nuclear deterrence.

Later versions of Polaris were larger and had a longer range. The A-3 was fitted with multiple re-entry vehicles (MIRVs), which spread over a single target; the B-3, which evolved into the Poseidon missile, had up to 14 high-speed and hardened re-entry vehicles designed to overwhelm Soviet anti-ballistic missile (ABM) defences.

British Polaris The British became interested in Polaris after the cancellation of their Blue Streak ICBM programme in 1960 and the US abandonment in 1962 of the Skybolt air-launched missile programme, which Britain's Conservative government had hoped to buy. At a meeting in the Bahamas between President John F. Kennedy and Prime Minister Harold Macmillan, it was agreed that Britain should be supplied with Polaris missiles (minus the warheads, which the British would make) for the Royal Navy's Resolution-class nuclear-powered submarines. In return the British ceded control over the targeting of the Polaris missiles to the Supreme Allied Commander Europe, who was always an American. In order to enable Polaris to penetrate the Soviet ABM defences around Moscow, the British embarked on the enormously expensive Chevaline project, which gave the missile a range of countermeasures, including chaff and multiple decoys. The Royal Navy's submarines are now armed with Polaris's successor, the larger, longer-ranged Trident.

SSBNs

SSBNs are floating missile silos made super-mobile by their nuclear power plants. Because they are mobile they are largely immune from the pre-emptive strikes that threaten land-based missiles. In the days when the theory of mutual assured destruction (MAD) held sway, SSBNs were the ultimate expression of deterrence, as they could not be eliminated in a first strike and their accurate, second-generation multiple independently targetable re-entry vehicles (MIRVs) could deliver a crippling riposte to a nuclear aggressor.

the condensed idea
The mainstay of nuclear deterrence

44 Helicopters
1941–2012

The rotor-wing aircraft is a far from ideal military platform. It is noisy, fuel- and maintenance-hungry, vulnerable to hits and mechanical breakdown and far slower than its fixed-wing counterparts. Nevertheless, in the last 60 years the combat helicopter has been one of the most significant additions to military inventories and has transformed the face of the battlefield.

In 1941 the Germans were the first to use helicopters on military operations – the Focke-Achgelis Fa 223 Darche (Dragon), designed as a pre-war transport and passenger aircraft, and the smaller Flettner Fl 282. Both were used to transport senior officers, carry equipment between ships, and perform reconnaissance and artillery spotting duties. The Luftwaffe was impressed and planned to extend the helicopters' functions to sowing mines, casualty evacuation and ground attack roles. However, the programme was overtaken by defeat in 1945.

Casualty evacuation The US had also identified the potential of the helicopter, introducing a limited number of small Sikorsky R-4 Hoverflies as casualty-evacuation (CASEVAC) vehicles. In the Korean War (1950–3), the helicopter's CASEVAC role continued along with a limited reconnaissance function. In the early and mid-1950s the French took up the helicopter torch in colonial wars in Vietnam and Algeria. In the latter, Sikorsky S-55s and Sud Alouettes flew against nationalist guerrillas over rugged terrain armed with fixed forward-firing machine guns, rocket pods and, later, wire-guided missiles.

timeline

1941	1954–62	1955	1961–75
Germany introduces helicopters to battlefield operations	Helicopters given improvised attack role in Algerian war	Introduction of turboshaft engine	Vietnam War transforms the role of the helicopter on the battlefield

Between 1961 and 1975 the war in Vietnam proved to be the forcing bed for new combat helicopter tactics. By 1966 the special demands of counter-insurgency warfare resulted in the presence in the theatre of some 1,500 Bell UH-1 'Huey' utility transports, many of which rapidly modified to carry weapons. By the mid-1960s, the standard complement of a US army UH-1 company comprised nine armed UH-1s (gunships or 'hogs') and 16 unarmed troop carriers ('slicks'). In the early days of operations in Vietnam, the heavier and slower-moving helicopter gunships would arrive over the landing zone shortly before the main body and lace the area with suppressive fire and rockets before the approach of the lighter and more vulnerable troop carriers.

'Air cavalry'

A milestone in the development of the combat helicopter came in 1955 when the turboshaft engine (in which the turbine drives a shaft that turns the blades) superseded the turbojet engine (in which the turbine compresses air to generate thrust) with greatly improved power-to-weight ratio. By 1957 the US army was developing the concept of 'air cavalry' units to go into battle carried by rotor rather than wheeled vehicles. This led to the transformation of the 7292nd Aerial Combat Reconnaissance (ACR) Company, formed in 1958, into the US army's 1st Cavalry Division (Airmobile), which arrived in Vietnam in August 1965.

Attack helicopters The first purpose-built attack helicopter, the Bell AH-1 HueyCobra, arrived in Vietnam in September 1967. The HueyCobra was the result of a crash programme to meet the US army's requirement for a fast, well-armed helicopter to provide escort and fire support for the Boeing-Vertol CH-47A Chinook medium transport helicopter, the workhorse of the Vietnam War, capable of carrying up to 44 troops into battle, of evacuating 24 wounded men, or ferrying in up to 12,700 kilograms (28,000 lb) of supplies on an external cargo hook.

Hard-hitting and immensely robust, Cobras flew over a million operational hours in Vietnam and Cambodia, attacking enemy ground positions and armour, and flying escort to unarmed transports. Its crew

1965	**1967**	**1982**	**1989**	**2003**
AUGUST Arrival in Vietnam of US army's 1st Cavalry Division (Airmobile)	**SEPTEMBER** Arrival in Vietnam of Bell AH-1 HueyCobra	AH-64 Apache enters full production	Apache makes its combat debut in Operation Just Cause	Apache suffers first setback in Operation Iraqi Freedom when lured into a 'flak trap'

refined what were dubbed 'nap of the earth' techniques, taking advantage of natural cover, including trees, hills or buildings, while 'popping up' only for a brief reconnaissance or strike. Helicopters operate in a markedly different environment as regards speed and space from fixed-wing aircraft, which gives them a degree of immunity from air-to-air interception but makes them vulnerable to ground and rocket fire.

McDonnell Douglas AH-64 Apache

Following the 1972 cancellation of the AH-56 Cheyenne attack helicopter in favour of USAF and Marine Corps projects like the A-10 Thunderbolt close-support attack aircraft and the AV-8B Harrier II multi-role attack fighter, the US army sought an aircraft to fill an anti-armour role, and which would remain under its command. In 1973 the army issued a requirement for an Advanced Attack Helicopter (AAH), which shifted the emphasis from helicopters as aerial platforms for counter-insurgency operations to a machine that would fly and fight in high-intensity conflict – in all weathers, against heavy enemy ground fire and against hardened targets.

The result was the heavily armoured Apache – the US army uses Native North American names for its helicopters – which entered full production in 1982. In its anti-tank role the Apache has a range of 300 miles and an endurance of some two hours.

High-intensity battle

One of the Apache's key features was a helmet-mounted display, the Integrated Helmet and Display Sighting System (IHADSS). This enables the pilot or gunner to slave the helicopter's 30-millimetre (1.2-in) automatic M230 Chain Gun to his helmet, making the gun track his head movements. The Apache is built to endure high-intensity battle conditions, operates in bad weather and uses advanced avionics to function by day or night. Its M230 Chain Gun is carried between its main landing gear and it is configured to carry a customizable weapons load, typically a combination of AGM-114 Hellfire anti-tank missiles and Hydra 70 general-purpose unguided 70-millimetre (2.75-in) rockets.

'Flying tanks'

The Cobra's anti-tank capability, demonstrated in Vietnam in 1972, prompted many strategists in the US and the Soviet Union to describe attack helicopters as lightly armoured flying tanks, unconstrained by considerations of terrain. With the end of the war in Vietnam, the Cobra fleet was adapted to carry TOW (Tube-launched, Optically-tracked, Wire-guided) missiles and three-barrelled 20-millimetre (0.79-in) cannon while work was underway on a successor attack helicopter.

❛**You could fire that Hellfire missile through a window from four miles away at night.**❜

General Carl Stiner, commander of Operation Just Cause

The Apache's FLIR (forward-looking infrared) system, housed in its nose sight, gives it a deep strike capability hundreds of miles beyond the front line of friendly troops. This capacity is enhanced by its Ultra High Frequency (UHF) radio system, which it shares with the USAF, facilitating joint air attack strikes with A-10s and Harrier fixed-wing aircraft, which often act as target designators.

The Apache made its combat debut in 1989, during Operation Just Cause, the invasion of Panama. During the First Gulf War, some 280 Apaches saw combat, destroying over 500 tanks and losing just one helicopter to an Iraqi rocket-propelled grenade (RPG).

In March 2003, during Operation Iraqi Freedom, the Second Gulf War, the Apache suffered a setback. Thirty-three helicopters were despatched to attack a brigade of Republican Guard tanks halted in open country near Karbala. They had been lured into a 'flak trap' laced with anti-aircraft guns, which brought down one Apache and damaged 30 others. From 2001, Apaches have been serving in Afghanistan in Operation Enduring Freedom.

the condensed idea
The most adaptable addition to the modern battlefield

45 Assault rifle
1906–2012

Assault rifles are selective fire rifles or carbines that typically fire ammunition with muzzle energies and sizes intermediate between those of handguns and more traditionally high-powered rifle ammunition. They fall into a category between light machine guns, intended more for sustained automatic fire in a support role, and sub-machine guns, which fire a handgun cartridge rather than a rifle cartridge.

Assault rifles are the standard small arms in most of today's modern armies, having largely replaced or supplanted larger, more powerful rifles such as the American Garand of the Second World War. Belt-fed weapons, or those with very limited capacity fixed magazines, are generally not considered to be assault rifles.

The origins of the assault rifle can be traced back to before the First World War. In 1906 the Russian Captain Vladimir Fyodorov designed a small-bore selective fire rifle with a detachable box magazine, the Avtomat. He also designed the small-calibre 6.5mm cartridges for the rifle, but in the First World War the Avtomat was chambered for the more readily available 6.5-millimetre (0.25-in) Japanese Arisaka rifle cartridge. The Avtomat entered service with the Imperial Army in 1915–16, although only in small numbers, and later served with the Red Army.

Storm rifle   The first assault rifle to see general deployment was the German StG 44 (*Sturmgewehr* 44, meaning 'storm' or 'assault rifle' from 1944). The name 'storm rifle' had apparently been dreamed up by Adolf Hitler. By the end of the war, some 426,000 StG 44 variants of all types

timeline

1906	1915	1944	1946	1947
In Russia Captain Fyodorov designs a small-bore selective fire rifle, the Avtomat	The Avtomat enters service with the Russian Imperial Army	The Germans introduce the first assault rifle, the StG 44, on the Eastern Front. Kalashnikov designs a gas-operated carbine, the starting point for the AK-47	Kalashnikov is persuaded to make radical changes to his original design of the AK-47	The AK-47 makes its debut

had been produced, proving particularly useful on the Eastern Front, where they performed well in conditions of extreme cold with a rate of fire of between 500 and 600 rounds per minute. One of their principal uses was against mass-produced Red Army PPS and PPSh-41 sub-machine guns with drum magazines. One exotic variant of the StG 44 was the *Krumlauf* – a bent barrel attachment for rifles with a periscope facility for shooting around corners from a safe position. Another version was used by tank crews when engaging infantry in the 'dead' areas around their vehicle. Yet another was equipped with an early version of an infrared aiming device.

> ❝My work is my life, and my life is my work. I invented this assault rifle to defend my country.❞
>
> **Mikhail Kalashnikov**

AK-47 The most widely produced and famous of assault rifles is the AK-47 (Avtomat Kalashnikova model 1947), the selective fire, gas-operated weapon universally known by the name of its inventor, the Soviet weapons designer Mikhail Kalashnikov.

Increasing firepower

The StG 44 had a considerable post-war influence on Soviet and American designers of assault rifles, as is evidenced by the AK-47 designed by Mikhail Kalashnikov and the American M16 and its variants. In 1948 the US army made a detailed study of battlefield injuries in the First and Second World Wars and concluded that combat often takes place unexpectedly and at short ranges, which preclude deliberate 'aiming'. It also concluded that as many as two US infantrymen out of every three never fired their rifles in combat. Equipping soldiers with rapid-fire weapons would make it more likely that they would use them. To achieve this, a fully automatic weapon was needed to increase the firepower of regular soldiers. The result was the M16, which underwent a trial by fire with the USAF in Vietnam in the early 1960s, and by 1967 appeared in its M16A1 configuration, which is the standard service rifle of the US army. The M16A2 now equips 15 NATO countries and 80 more worldwide.

1956	1959	1980–90	2004	2007
The Red Army receives large quantities of the AK-47	A modified version of the AK-47 is introduced which is produced in larger quantities than any other	Soviet Union becomes principal supplier of arms to countries and movements embargoed by the West	Kalashnikov museum opens in Izhevsk in the Urals	Publication of Larry Kahaner's *AK-47: The Weapon that Changed the Face of War* cements the assault rifle's iconic status

Kalashnikov was conscripted into the Red Army in 1938 and was a tank sergeant in June 1941 when Germany invaded the Soviet Union. In October 1941 he was wounded in the defence of Bryansk and while convalescing began designing a sub-machine gun. His skill as a weapons engineer was quickly recognized, and in 1944 Kalashnikov designed a gas-operated carbine heavily influenced by the American M1 Garand rifle. In 1945 this design provided the basis for the work he began on the Kalashnikov assault rifle. It was gas-operated, with a breech-block mechanism similar to his 1944 rifle, and a curved 30-round magazine.

> **It is the Germans who are responsible for the fact that I became a fabricator of arms. If not for them, I would have constructed agricultural machines.**
> **Mikhail Kalashnikov**

In 1946, while Kalashnikov's rifle was undergoing competitive testing, a colleague, Aleksandr Zaytsev, persuaded him to make substantial changes to his rifle, and in the subsequent trials it exhibited many of the qualities, including durability and ease of use, for which it has become famous. Kalashnikov's creation can best be described as a hybrid blend of rifle technologies to which its designer had ample access: the trigger, double-locking lugs and unlocking raceway of the M1 carbine; the safety mechanism of the Remington Model 8 rifle; and the gas system and layout of the StG 44, although he denied the last.

AK-47s worldwide

In the latter half of the 20th century the AK-47 became the weapon choice of guerrillas worldwide. In the brutal jockeying of the Cold War, in which proxy wars were fought by the United States and the Soviet Union, the Kalashnikov's cheapness and rugged simplicity scored heavily over the more expensive and over-engineered weaponry supplied to its proxies by the United States. If well looked after, the AK-47 will enjoy a service life of up to 40 years, depending on the conditions to which it has been exposed. Approximately 75 million AK-47s have been built and another 100 million AK-type rifles have been produced from Albania to Venezuela. In the 1980s the mujahideen guerrillas fighting in Afghanistan were supplied with the Chinese Type 56 AK-47 derivatives.

Because of initial production problems, it was not until 1956 that the Red Army began receiving the AK-47 in large quantities. In 1959 an upgraded, lighter version was introduced with a stamped sheet metal receiver and a slanted muzzle brake to offset muzzle rise under recoil. This model was produced in greater quantities than any other. The Kalashnikov's principal advantages encapsulate the very best of Soviet design since the 1930s: it is simple, compact, easy to maintain, and capable of withstanding much careless handling and fouling without ceasing to function. This is helped by its chromium-plated bore and chamber, gas pistons and gas cylinder interior, which is important because in the 20th century most military-production ammunition (and virtually all former Soviet and Warsaw Pact ammunition) contained potassium chlorate. On firing, this converted to corrosive and hygroscopic potassium chloride, which required constant cleaning to avoid permanent damage. Today, many military parts are chrome-plated.

> **‘Anything that is complex is not useful and anything that is useful is simple. This has been my whole life's motto.’**
> **Mikhail Kalashnikov**

In the 65 years since it was developed, the AK-47 has acquired a unique cultural status, certainly equal to that enjoyed by Second World War weapons such as the Spitfire or the T-34. It adorns the flag of Mozambique and the coat of arms of East Timor. It is to be found on the flag of Hezbollah and forms the logo of the Iranian Islamic Revolutionary Guard Corps. It straddles the cultural divide of the post-Cold War world. For those in the West, it has become the weapon of the terrorist, the urban guerrilla and the drugs cartel. In the developing world it is seen as the weapon of the freedom fighter.

the condensed idea
The most significant item in the small arms inventory of the post-war world

46 Jet fighter
1953–90

Over Europe in the closing months of the Second World War, the Luftwaffe introduced the first jet fighter to combat: the Messerschmitt Me 262. However, it was not until the Korean War (1950–3) that the first jet-against-jet combats took place.

The new combat environment – in which greater speeds and more sophisticated instrumentation required acutely sensitive flying skills – produced a new breed of pilot. Moreover, the speeds and heights achieved by jet fighters prompted a wholesale tactical revolution. It was predicted that the day of the dogfight was over.

Veteran American fighter pilots of the Second World War who flew in the Korean War discovered that the announcement of the death of the dogfight was premature. Twelve years after the end of the Korean War, the same forecasts were being made about the air war over Vietnam.

In the intervening years there had been another radical change in aircraft and weaponry. Browning .50-calibre machine guns had been replaced by 20-millimetre (0.79-in) cannon and air-to-air missiles. Missile-guidance systems, on-board radar and in-flight refuelling were some of the fundamentals that pilots flying over Vietnam had to master, along with the skill of surviving in a dogfight.

McDonnell Douglas F-4E Phantom II In the Korean War the outstanding jet fighter was the F-86 Sabre. In Vietnam it was the F-4 Phantom, a big 25-ton brute of an aircraft flown by a crew of two, a pilot and radar intercept officer (RIO). It had been designed as an air superiority

timeline

1953	1958	1960	1962	1963	1966–73	1967
The US Navy begins work on a new attack fighter	**27 MAY** Phantom makes it maiden flight	Phantom adopted by the US Navy	US Marine Corps receives its first F-4Bs	**27 MAY** Maiden flight of first USAF Phantom	Phantoms fly in Vietnam War	Phantom production rises to 75 a month

fighter, seeking its prey over hostile territory rather than engaging hostile aircraft over home territory, as part of Defense Secretary Robert McNamara's drive to create a unified fighter for all branches of the US military.

The Phantom entered service with the US Navy as an interceptor in 1960, and its adaptability led to its adoption by the Marine Corps and USAF. The latter emphasized the Phantom's fighter-bomber role. By the mid-1960s the Phantom had become a major component in all three wings. Eventually 5,195 were built, making it the most numerous American supersonic military aircraft.

The Phantom was equipped with powerful Pulse-Doppler radar and was armed with four Sparrow and four Sidewinder missiles. Early versions had no guns, but the F-4E carried an internally mounted 20-millimetre (0.79-in) M61 Vulcan rotary cannon. Sidewinder homed in on infrared emissions from the target aircraft. When it was activated in combat, the pilot would pick up a growling sound in his earphones. As the pilot approached the target, the growl grew louder. Once it was strong enough, the missile was fired. In three seconds the Sidewinder accelerated to Mach 2.5 as it sped towards its target. It had a range of some 2 miles (3.2 km) and was detonated by a proximity fuse when it was within killing distance.

Sidewinder missiles were not wholly reliable, as heat from the sun or generated from the ground when the Phantom was flying at low level – by a factory, for example – could deflect them. The missile was most effective in a tail chase when it homed in on the exhaust pipe of the target aircraft. The Sparrow was a radar-guided missile and its initial speed on firing was

Flying the Phantom

Air-to-air missiles gave our fighters a tremendous capability relative to the MiG-17, which carried only cannon and rockets. But fighting a MiG with a gunless F-4 is like fighting a guy with a dagger when he's got a sword, or maybe vice versa. A fighter without a gun, which is the most versatile air-to-air weapon, is like an aeroplane without a wing. Five or six times, when I had fired all my missiles, I might have been able to hit a MiG if I'd had a cannon, because I was so close his motion was stopped in my gunsight.

Col. Robin Olds

1967	1972	1972	1983	1986	1991
OCTOBER First F-4E delivered to Tactical Air Command with internal gun and powerful J79 engine, the first of 949 delivered from 1967 to 1977	**10 MAY** Lieutenant Randy 'Duke' Cunningham and Lieutenant William P. Driscoll become the first fighter aces of the Vietnam War	**9 SEPTEMBER** WSO Captain Charles B. DeBellevue becomes the highest-scoring ace of the Vietnam War	Navy F-4N Phantoms are replaced by F-14 Tomcats	Navy F-4S Phantoms are replaced by F/A-18 Hornets	Phantoms fly 'Wild Weasel' (radar suppression) missions in Operation Desert Storm

❝The triumph of thrust over dynamics.❞

Phantom crews' ironic description of their aircraft

Mach 3.7 over a range of 25–28 miles (40–45 km), but a pilot needed to be certain that his target was hostile. In Vietnam, rules of engagement precluded long-range missile attacks, as visual identification was normally required.

In addition, the rules of engagement for American and South Vietnamese pilots did not permit them to cross the North Vietnamese border with China, where the North Vietnamese MiGs gained height. The MiGs tended to limit their attacks to aircraft engaged in strike or reconnaissance roles and rarely took on fighters flying MiG Combat Air Patrols (MiGCAP).

With the arrival of the MiG-21 in late 1965, the Phantom could be outpaced and out-turned but not out-climbed. MiG pilots would wait at low altitudes, where they were difficult to detect on the Americans' radar. As US strike forces headed for their target area, the MiGs would dart in to pick off any trailing aircraft with cannon or Atoll missiles.

A trap was set for them. On 2 January 1967, 56 Phantoms, led by Col. Robin Olds, flew towards Hanoi in a strike formation. Radar-jamming and reconnaissance aircraft accompanied them to confuse the North

The MiG

The MiG-21 was an all-weather interceptor with a maximum speed at high altitude (18,900 metres/62,000 feet) of 1,320 miles per hour (2,124 kph) or Mach 2. Early versions were armed with one or two 30-millimetre (1.2-in) guns, later versions with one rapid-fire 23-millimetre (0.9-in) gun and two air-to-air missiles. The MiG-21 did not have the long-range radar or heavy bombing payload of the Phantom F-4, but in the hands of an experienced pilot it was a challenging opponent, particularly at high and low altitudes. One tactic used by US pilots was the barrel roll manoeuvre. The Phantom pilot, unable to stay with a faster-turning MiG, would cut the corner by flying a high barrel roll away from the target, then would pull down and below to lock on and fire a Sidewinder. The MiG, flying in a horizontal plane, was stymied by a three-dimensional manoeuvre.

Vietnamese. The group flew towards Phuc Yen airfield, where most of the MiGs were stationed, and then flew to and fro at 2,100 metres (7,000 ft) above a layer of cloud, to entice them up.

The MiGs swallowed the bait and emerged through the cloud. Col. Olds's rearman, Lt. Charles Clifton, locked his radar on to a MiG and Olds fired two Sparrows at close range, both of which missed. He missed with a Sidewinder as his enemy disappeared into cloud. Seeing another MiG ahead, Olds barrel-rolled to the right, held his position above the MiG and, as he came within range, completed the roll and dropped behind his enemy. He activated two Sidewinders and, as the growl grew louder, fired. The first Sidewinder struck home and the MiG exploded, the first of six North Vietnamese fighters downed that day.

In 1990, F-4Fs flew air-defence suppression and reconnaissance missions in the First Gulf War. From the 1980s, in all three US services the Phantom was replaced by a new generation of aircraft. It was operated by 11 other air forces worldwide and saw extensive combat with the Israel Defense Forces in the Arab–Israeli wars and with the Iranian air force in the Iran–Iraq War (1980–8).

> ❛. . . dogfighting today is surprisingly like our experiences in World War II and Korea. We found ourselves doing the things that people in the services swore would never be done again.❜
>
> **Colonel (later General) Robin Olds**

the condensed idea
From 1960 to 1980 the Phantom was the world's number one all-round combat aircraft

47 Stealth

1943–2012

Stealth or low observable (LO) technology is a quality and design goal affecting the configuration of many large items of military kit. Although it is a pressing preoccupation of today's weapons designers and engineers, stealth technology – in effect a combination of technologies – has a history stretching back to the development by the British of radio direction finding (RDF) or, as the Americans later called it, radar (see page 132). Bomber aircraft and surface ships could be easily detected by radar, and submarines by its sound equivalent, sonar, the sending and receiving of sound impulses through water. Stealth technology aims to reduce or eliminate this vulnerability.

In July 1943, RAF Bomber Command aircraft dropped foil strips, codenamed Window, to form half-wave reflectors for German radar signals. Dropped in massive quantities, the strips jammed the radar by cluttering its tubes with false returns, swamping the echoes from genuine aircraft.

The German navy, the Kriegsmarine, incorporated stealth elements in an experimental Type VIIC submarine, *U-480*, which began its operational career in 1944. The U-boat's synthetic rubber coating consisted of a perforated inner rubber layer and a smooth outer one that enabled it to avoid detection by Allied sonar.

The Luftwaffe also experimented with primitive stealth technology. The Horten Ho 229, a jet configured like a 'flying wing', first flew in January 1945 but never became operational. The Ho 229 had a lower radar reflection than conventional aircraft with their tailplanes and round fuselages. Its innovatory design was later reflected in the post-war eight-engined Northrop YB-49, a project that was cancelled by the USAF in 1949. The YB-49's direct descendant, the Northrop Grumman B-2 stealth bomber, made its first flight in the summer of 1989.

Radar cross-section In the 1950s, military aircraft designers on both sides of the Iron Curtain developed ways of reducing radar cross-section (RCS), the measure of a target's apparent size on radar. The British Avro Vulcan V bomber, which was a delta-winged distant relative of the YB-49 and entered service in 1960, had a remarkably small RCS. In 1964 Clarence 'Kelly' Johnson and his team at Lockheed's 'Skunk Works' produced the SR-71 Blackbird spy plane designed to operate at heights and speeds beyond radar detection. In the 1980s, aspects of stealth technology were incorporated in the Rockwell B-1B strategic bomber, reducing its radar cross-section to less than 1 per cent of the B-52 Superfortress, ageing mainstay of USAF's strategic bombing force from 1955.

'Be quick, be quiet and be on time.'
Clarence 'Kelly' Johnson's motto at Lockheed Martin's 'Skunk Works'

Computers A paper written in 1962 by Soviet physicist Pyotr Ufimtsev, 'Method of Edge Waves in the Physical Theory of Diffraction', was extremely influential in the development of stealth technology in the United Sates. The paper, a theoretical examination of the reduction of RCS, was seized upon by the USAF in the 1970s and, with the aid of a new generation of computers, its findings were channelled into the development of the first true stealth warplanes. Radar detection and radar guidance of missile defences depends upon the reflection of radar energy by the target. Using carefully selected synthetic materials with low reflectivity and a shape that reduces the area of reflecting surfaces, an aircraft could now be designed with a very low 'radar signature', enabling it to remain invisible to radar at ranges where other aircraft would be detected. Design and the selection of appropriate materials also plays a vital part in reducing the aircraft's infrared signature generated by its engines.

1983
Lockheed F-117 Nighthawk enters service

1997
Northrop Grumman B-2 Spirit attains operational capability

2009
The B-2 becomes part of the USAF's Global Strike Command

2011
2 MAY Helicopters incorporating stealth elements fly on mission by US Navy SEALs to kill Osama bin Laden in Pakistan

Nighthawk The first stealth aircraft was the single-seat Lockheed F-117 Nighthawk, another product of the Skunk Works, which entered service in October 1983, although it was not unveiled to the public until 1988. Its multi-faceted airframe was designed to deflect radar signals and was powered by two non-afterburning turbofans. To save money, many of the avionics, fly-by-wire systems and other parts were borrowed from the F-16 Fighting Falcon, F/A-18 Hornet and F-15E Eagle. Because of the project's secrecy, the parts were described as spares for the donor aircraft.

The penalty imposed by the stealth design restricted the Nighthawk to subsonic speeds. While designated as a fighter, the Nighthawk was actually a fighter-bomber. It carried no radar, which lowered emissions from the cross-section. A typical 2,270-kilogram (5,000-lb) bomb load consisted of Paveway laser-guided bombs, penetration bombs or two Joint Direct Attack Munitions (JDAMs) and a guided stand-off bomb. It first saw action in the US invasion of Panama in 1989. During the First Gulf War of 1991, although constituting 2.5 per cent of the US aircraft in the theatre, F-117s hit over 40 per cent of the USAF's strategic targets.

Only one F-117 has been lost to enemy action. In March 1999, while flying a mission against the Serbian army in the former Yugoslavia, a Nighthawk was detected by radar operating on unusually long wavelengths and downed at a range of some 8 miles (13 km) by Serbian surface-to-air missiles (SAMs). The wreckage was later inspected by the Soviet military. The F-117's stealthily faceted airframe required a huge amount of maintenance and was eventually rendered obsolescent by the more streamlined design of the B-2 Spirit bomber. In 2008 the Nighthawk was retired.

> **With the launch of these great aircraft today, the circle comes to a close – their service to our nation's defense fulfilled, their mission accomplished . . .**
>
> Brigadier-General David Goldfein, commander of USAF 49th Fighter Wing, bidding farewell to Nighthawk, March 2007

Northrop Grumman B-2 Spirit The B-2 is a stealth heavy bomber designed to penetrate deep anti-aircraft defences to deliver conventional and nuclear weapons. It made its first public flight in the summer of 1989, and the original USAF procurement programme envisaged a force of 132 aircraft. However, the collapse of the Soviet Union in the early 1990s eliminated the B-2's primary Cold War mission, and its subsequent history has been dominated by Congressional wrangling and defence cuts that have limited production to a handful of aircraft. At today's prices the cost of each B-2 is estimated at just over a billion dollars.

The B-2's stealth characteristics stem from its reduced acoustic, infrared, visual and radar signatures. Its four non-afterburning turbofan engines are buried in its wing to minimize their exhaust signature. The bomber is made of radar-absorbent composite materials and its flying wing design reduces the number of leading edges, making its contoured shape all but invisible to radar.

The B-2 attained operational capability in January 1997 and made its combat debut two years later in the Kosovo war, bombing one-third of selected Serbian targets in the first two months of the conflict. On these missions the B-2s flew nonstop on a round trip from their home base in Whiteman, Missouri. One of the B-2's longest missions, against Taliban targets in Afghanistan during Operation Enduring Freedom, was accomplished with the support of aerial refuelling.

In 2003, during Operation Iraqi Freedom, B-2s flew from Whiteman Air Force Base, Missouri, the island of Diego Garcia in the Indian Ocean and an undisclosed forward operating location. The last may have been Andersen Air Force Base in Guam or RAF Fairford in Britain, both of which have climate-controlled hangars. In September 2009 the B-2s became part of the USAF's Global Strike Command, and in March 2011 flew the first strikes in Operation Odyssey Dawn, the UN-mandated enforcement of the no-fly zone in Libya.

The B-2

The B-2's two-man crew can fly over an operational range of some 6,900 miles (11,100 km). At 12,200 metres (40,000 ft), some 3,050 metres (10,000 ft) below its service ceiling, the maximum speed is 630 miles per hour (1,000 kph). The B-2 combines a GPS Aided Targeting System (GATS) with GPS-aided bombs such as JDAM. It can bomb 16 targets in a single pass when armed with 450- or 900-kilogram (1,000- or 2,000-lb) bombs or up to 80 when carrying 225-kilogram (500-lb) bombs.

the condensed idea
The B-2 is most expensive warplane in history

48 Cruise missile
1909–2012

Cruise missiles are the descendants of the German V-1 of the Second World War, although the concept can be traced back to the 1909 movie *The Airship Destroyer* directed by Walter R. Booth, a British equivalent of the French cinema pioneer Georges Méliès. In *The Airship Destroyer* a German airship invasion of England is thwarted by a radio-controlled 'aerial torpedo'.

In the interwar years there were a number of abortive experiments with weapons similar to the 'aerial torpedo', including a Soviet boost-glide rocket fitted with a gyroscopic guidance system. A similar guidance system was installed in the German FZG-76, launched from a ramp or the belly of an aircraft and better known as the V-1 flying bomb.

In the post-war years US military planners grappled with the difficulty of penetrating heavily defended Soviet air space to strike at distant targets. One solution was a self-propelled bomb carried close to the target and then released, enabling the 'stand off' carrier aircraft to turn for home.

In May 1947 the USAAF awarded the Bell Aircraft Company a contract for the construction of a supersonic air-to-surface missile compatible with the B-29, the B-36 Peacemaker and the B-52 Stratofortress. The result was the GAM-63 Rascal, the acronym for RAdar SCAnning Link, the missile's guidance system.

timeline

1944	**1957**	**1961**	**1972**
JUNE Start of V-1 campaign against Britain	The Rascal enters service with the USAF	Rascal is succeeded by Hound Dog	SRAMs arm B-52 strategic bombers

Rascal Rascal did not enter service with the USAF until 1957. It was propelled by a liquid-fuel rocket system and used inertial guidance, having been pre-programmed with the target's location. Two of its three available warheads were nuclear. Rascal's service career was abruptly curtailed in 1958 after the collapse of its testing programme, and in 1961 it was succeeded by the AGM-28 Hound Dog, which was two-thirds the weight of the Rascal and carried a more powerful warhead. Driven by a turbojet engine, Hound Dog had a range of over 700 miles (1,125 km), enabling the bomber to stay well clear of Soviet defences, and also incorporated the latest TERCOM (terrain-contour matching) guidance system, which gave the missile a detailed plan of its flight path. Hound Dog constantly compared this with the ground over which it passed, correcting as necessary to maintain the prescribed flight path.

Advances in American miniaturization technology in the 1960s led to the development of SRAMs (short-range attack missiles). In 1972 they became the armament of B-52 bombers, which employed a rotary launching device in the bomb bay capable of carrying eight missiles, each with a 200-kiloton warhead and a range of 100 miles (160 km). Inertially guided and rocket-propelled, they were said to have a radar signature 'no bigger than a bullet'.

The SRAMs were originally meant to be launched simultaneously with SCADs (subsonic cruise armed decoys) carrying radar-jamming and other electronic systems to lure the defences away from the SRAMs. The air planners also intended to square the confusion by arming the SCAD with

> **❝I would stop short of calling it a boondoggle, as it does seem to be getting the job done, just at a very high cost.❞**
> **William Hartung,** director of Arms and Security Initiative at the New America Foundation, on the cost/hit ratio of Tomahawk, 2011

1983	1991	1999	2001	2004	2011
Tomahawk enters service with the US Navy	**JANUARY** Tomahawks are fired in the first salvo of the Gulf War	Tomahawks are fired against targets in the former Yugoslavia in Operation Allied Force	**OCTOBER** Tomahawks are launched at Afghanistan at the opening of Operation Enduring Freedom	'Tactical Tomahawk' enters service	**MARCH** Tomahawks open Operation Odyssey Dawn against the Gaddafi regime in Libya

a nuclear warhead, but political opposition obliged the planners to recast the idea under another name, ALCM (air-launched cruise missile). ALCM incorporated a new inertial guidance system updated by TERCOM and, in the AGM-68 version, was armed with a 200-kiloton warhead.

At the same time the US Navy developed its own ALCM, Tomahawk, as an anti-ship missile. The navy and air force systems were compatible, but the US Navy also developed Tomahawk as a ship-or submarine-launched missile for use against surface vessels or land targets.

Tomahawk Tomahawk is a long-range, all-weather subsonic missile developed in the 1970s and currently in service with surface ships and submarines of the US Navy and the Royal Navy. Tomahawk blasts off with the aid of a rocket then switches to a turbofan engine, which emits little heat, making it hard to be spotted by infrared detectors. It 'cruises' to its target over a maximum range of 700 miles at extremely low altitudes at high subsonic speeds and is piloted over an evasive route by a number of mission-tailored guidance systems.

The 'Tactical Tomahawk', which entered service in 2004, is a component in the 'networked force' being implemented by the Pentagon. It uses data from multiple sources (aircraft, unmanned air vehicles, satellites, ships and tanks, and soldiers on the ground) to find its target while simultaneously sending data from its sensors to these platforms. The Tomahawk Land Attack Missile (TLAM) is equipped with a TV camera for loitering capability, enabling commanders to

Tomahawks' impact

Of the 297 Tomahawks fired in the First Gulf War, 282 flew their mission successfully, 9 failed to leave the tube and 6 fell into the water after leaving the tube. At least two (and possibly as many as six) were shot down, most or all of them in a single quickly arranged stream attack, as the missiles had to fly a single mission profile most of the way to the target.

❛In the real world you're just not going to have the sort of precise intelligence that would tell you, after you launch the Tomahawk, and it's halfway there, that now there's a bus full of widows and orphans. That just doesn't happen.❜

John Pike, director of GlobalSecurity.org

assess damage to a target and to redirect the missile to another target if required. During flight it can be reprogrammed to attack any one of 15 pre-designated targets with GPS (global positioning satellite) co-ordinates stored in its memory or any other GPS co-ordinates.

Tomahawk can carry a 200-kiloton nuclear warhead, a 455-kilogram (1000-lb) conventional warhead or, in the case of the TLAM-D, 24 canisters of sub-munitions. In the First Gulf War, 297 Tomahawks were launched. The first salvo of the conflict was fired by the cruiser USS *San Jacinto* on 17 January 1991, followed by the attack submarines USS *Pittsburgh* and USS *Louisville*.

During Operation Allied Force in 1999, 218 Tomahawks were fired by US ships and a British submarine, HMS *Splendid*, against targets in the former Yugoslavia. In October 2001, in the opening hours of Operation Enduring Freedom, some 50 Tomahawks struck terrorist targets in Afghanistan. In the 2003 invasion of Iraq, over 725 Tomahawks were fired at Iraqi targets. On 19 March 2011, 124 Tomahawks were fired by US and British forces (122 US, 2 British) against some 20 Libyan targets around Tripoli and Misrata in the opening phase of Operation Odyssey Dawn against the Libyan dictator Muammar Gaddafi.

the condensed idea
Costly, controversial and often ineffective

49 Unmanned aerial combat
1987–2012

By 2030, up to a third of the aircraft flying in the Royal Air Force could be remotely piloted by aircrew sitting in front of screens thousands of miles from the combat zone. These new weapons stem from over 20 years of development by the USAF of unmanned aerial vehicles (UAVs), originally conceived as reconnaissance and forward observation platforms but now deployed as unmanned combat aerial vehicles (UCAVs), formidable offensive weapons in their own right.

The Central Intelligence Agency (CIA) and Pentagon began experimenting with reconnaissance drones, originally called 'Gnats', in the 1980s, and awarded General Atomics Aeronautical Systems a contract to develop the Predator UAV in January 1994. In the spring of 1995 the first Predator was deployed to the Balkans for operations in the former Yugoslavia. By 2001, when the USAF began operations in Afghanistan, it had acquired 60 Predators, of which 20 were lost in action, principally because of bad weather. Subsequent modifications included improved de-icing systems and avionics.

Hellfire After the Balkans campaign, Predator was further modified to undertake a strike role firing Hellfire missiles. Given that Predator was exceptionally quiet and the Hellfire travels at supersonic speed, this was

timeline

1987	1990–2007	1994	1995
Hellfire enters service	30,000 Hellfire missiles stockpiled	First flight of Predator	Predator enters service with USAF

a potent combination. Initially, the Predator's pilot controlled the UCAV from a van parked near its operating base. However, by 2000 improvements in communications systems made it possible to fly Predator remotely from great distances. From 2007, RAF Predators were flown from the USAF's Creech Air Force Base, Nevada.

❝One drone may kill 10 or so civilians for every militant killed.❞

Daniel Byman,
Brookings Institute

By the spring of 2009, the USAF deployed 195 Predators and 28 larger and more capable General Atomics Reapers. In Iraq and Afghanistan in 2007–8, the Predators fired their Hellfire missiles 244 times. By 2009 the USAF had lost 70 Predators on operations – the unit cost of a Predator was $4.5 million. Fifty-five were lost to equipment failure, operator error or bad weather. Four were shot down in Bosnia, Kosovo and Iraq, and 11 more were the casualties of operational accidents on combat missions. In March 2011 the USAF took delivery of its last Predator.

Predators in action

Predators were used successfully in operations against important al-Qaeda operatives in Afghanistan, Pakistan and Yemen, but not without sparking controversy. The way that the Americans used Predators and Reapers in Pakistan has raised fears that the CIA is running a targeted assassination programme, which often causes heavy collateral damage.

Pakistan, the United States's ally, has complained that between 2006 and 2009 operations that eliminated 14 al-Qaeda militants also killed nearly 700 civilians. According to the New America Foundation think tank, at least one in four killed by American UCAVs since 2004 has been an innocent civilian. Other sources, such as the Brookings Institute, put the ratio higher.

2000	**2007**	**2007**	**2007**	**2007**	**2009**
Predator achieves ability to be flown from great distances	General Atomics Reaper introduced	Reaper deployed to Iraq	**OCTOBER** Reaper makes first kill in Afghanistan	423rd Wing USAF activated to operate Reaper	**SEPTEMBER** An F-15E Strike Eagle shoots down a straying Reaper as it heads for Tajikistan. Reapers are deployed to the Seychelles in the Indian Ocean on anti-piracy patrols

> **❝Since assuming office, Barack Obama has authorized nearly four times as many drone strikes as did the Bush administration throughout its entire term in office . . . on an average of one strike every four days, compared with one every 40 days under Bush.❞**
>
> Peter Bergen and Katherine Tiedemann in *Foreign Affairs*

The growth in the number of UCAVs has been exponential. In 2011 the Pentagon and CIA will purchase more unmanned aircraft than manned, and more personnel will be trained to fly them than the total number training to fly bomber and fighter aircraft.

General Atomics MQ-9 Reaper The MQ-9 Reaper is the first hunter-killer UCAV designed for endurance and high-altitude surveillance. Its 950-horsepower turboprop engine is more powerful than Predator's, which enables it to carry a payload 15 times greater and cruise three times faster than its predecessor. Fully loaded, it has an endurance of 14 hours, and with extra fuel tanks and reduced weapons payload this can be extended to 42 hours. Reaper can carry a variety of weaponry,

Hellfire

The AGM-14 Hellfire is an ASM (air-to-surface missile) initially designed for use against armour, although it now boasts a multi-mission, multi-target, precision-strike capability and can be launched from air, sea and ground platforms. Its name derives from its original specification as a HELicopter-Launched FIRE-and-forget weapon. Hellfire II, developed in the 1990s, has spawned a number of semi-active laser variants that home in on a reflected laser beam aimed at the target from the launching platform. Hellfire II, weighing 48 kilograms (106 lb) with a 9-kilogram (20-lb) warhead, has a range of 3 miles (4.8 km) and is carried by Predator and Reaper.

including Hellfire missiles, 225-kilogram (500-lb) laser-guided bombs and Joint Direct Attack Munitions (JDAMs), whose guidance kit turns 'dumb' unguided bombs into all-weather 'smart' munitions.

With a range of 3,200 nautical miles (5,900 km) and an operational altitude of 15,240 metres (50,000 ft), Reaper is particularly well suited for 'loitering' operations in support of ground troops or reconnaissance. Added capability comes at a price – each Reaper costs twice as much as a Predator. Reaper operators stationed at bases like Creech near Las Vegas can hunt for targets and observe terrain using a number of sensors including a thermal camera. Reaper's on-board camera can read a licence plate at a range of 2 miles (3.2 km). An operator's command takes a fraction over one second to reach Reaper via a satellite link.

> **❛The United States Air Force must recognize the enormous strategic and cultural implications of the vast expansion in remotely piloted vehicles.❜**
> **Robert Gates, US Secretary of State for Defense, March 2011**

The MQ-9 Reaper was deployed to Iraq in September 2007 and achieved its first kill a month later against Afghan insurgents in the mountainous Oruzgan province. It is fully integrated into USAF operations and often flies missions alongside manned aircraft. A hint of the future came in 2008 when the New York National Guard 174th Fighter Wing began to convert from F-16 fighters to Reapers, in the process becoming the first fighter squadron to become an all-UCAV unit. By March 2011 the USAF was training more pilots for advanced unmanned aerial vehicles than for any other single weapon system.

the condensed idea
The UCAV is the warplane of the future

50 Cyberwar
1982–2012

In the 21st century, warfare has been transformed by the computer revolution, a phenomenon that has reached into every aspect of contemporary life. In similar fashion, during the 19th-century Industrial Revolution, the torrent of technological innovation was eagerly harnessed by the world's modern military machines.

The survival of today's advanced societies – and their industrial, power, financial, transportation, communications, health and security infrastructures – is now heavily dependent on information technology, which is itself immensely vulnerable to blitzkrieg attack from external enemies and hostile agencies. Cyberspace, characterized as the fifth domain of warfare after land, sea, air and space, is an arena in which nation states remain the major but by no means the exclusive players. Indeed, in China, which devotes huge resources to the cyberspace domain, the state allegedly operates hand-in-glove with criminal surrogates.

Internet By 2011 approximately one in three of the world's population was an Internet user, an arena in which it is sometimes difficult to distinguish friend from foe. Moreover, the Internet remains a potentially fragile instrument. Over 90 per cent of digital traffic travels through undersea fibre-optic cables, which are crammed into a number of vulnerable choke points – among them the waters off New York, the Red Sea and in the Luzon Strait in the Philippines.

The origins of the cyberspace battlefield can be traced back to June 1982, when the CIA sabotaged computer-control software stolen by Soviet spies

1982	2001	2007	2008	2008
CIA sabotages Soviet software in first cyber conflict	US spy plane's collision with Chinese jet sparks superpower jostling in cyberspace	Estonia comes under cyber attack from Russia	Russia launches cyber attacks to coincide with troop movements in South Ossetia war	Mumbai massacre

from a Canadian firm and used to regulate gas pipelines. It was an early demonstration of a so-called 'logic bomb'. Pump and valve settings went haywire, causing a huge blast in Siberia, which was monitored by the US early-warning satellites.

Cyberwars The first so-called cyberwar is often cited as the aftermath of an April 2001 incident in which an American EP-3 Aries II spy plane collided with a Chinese jet over the South China Sea. In the following weeks thousands of websites in China and the United States were subjected to defacement and hacker attacks.

> **If there had been a world wide web in the days of the Blitz, then the Germans would have been attacking us on the net as well as from the air and we'd have been doing the same back to them.**
>
> **Dr David Betz,** Department of War Studies, King's College, London, 2008

The stakes are higher when government agencies, or their surrogates, step in. Cyberwar played a significant part in Israel's 2006 incursion into Lebanon to deal with Hezbollah, the militant Shia Muslim faction. Using black propaganda tactics, the intelligence arm of the Israel Defense Forces (IDF) compromised Hezbollah-backed TV and radio stations and launched denial-of-service attacks on Hezbollah websites.

In April 2007, Estonia came under cyber attack from Russia after the relocation of a controversial war memorial, the Bronze Soldier of Tallinn, erected by the Soviet Union in 1947. Estonian ministries, banks and the national media were the principal targets. In August 2008, during the brief South Ossetia war, cyber attacks were launched by the Russian military to coincide with air strikes and troop movements against the former Soviet republic of Georgia.

The United States is not immune from attack. In April 2009 reports surfaced that China and Russia had penetrated the US electrical grid, leaving behind software programs with the potential to disrupt the system. President Barack Obama declared that the United States's digital infrastructure was a 'strategic national asset', and in May 2010 the Pentagon established the Cyber Command (CYBERCOM) under Gen. Keith

2009	2009	2010	2011
China hacks into US Joint Strike Fighter Project	United States and Israel release Stuxnet to disrupt Iran's nuclear enrichment programme	Indian Cyber Army hacks into sites controlled by the Pakistani army	China launches cyber attack on Britain's Foreign Office

> ❝The People's Liberation Army is using "information warfare units" to develop viruses to attack enemy computer systems and networks, and those units include civilian computer professionals.❞
>
> **Pentagon report, 2010**

Alexander, director of the National Security Agency (NSA). His brief was to establish 'full spectrum' operations – to defend US military networks and to attack the systems of other nations, although precisely how remains secret. The UK has its own cyber-security apparatus, based at GCHQ (Government Communications Headquarters), the British equivalent of the NSA. After the 2007 Bronze Soldier incident, NATO set up a Cooperative Cyber Defence Centre of Excellence in Tallinn, the capital of Estonia.

Chinese cyber-spies China aims to attain cyber supremacy by the end of the 21st century, although it vehemently denies involvement in cyber-spying. Nevertheless, few doubt that in 2009 the Chinese successfully hacked into the USAF's $300 billion Joint Strike Fighter Project. In the breakneck Chinese drive for growth, it is clear that their intelligence services have more to gain from penetrating the US military and industrial establishments than the Americans have in penetrating theirs. Nevertheless, there are sound geopolitical reasons for American intelligence to keep a close eye on its Chinese counterparts.

Subcontinental cyberwar

Regional rivalries on the Indian subcontinent have led to an outbreak of cyber warfare. In November 2010 a group calling itself the Indian Cyber Army hacked websites controlled by the Pakistani army and a number of Pakistani ministries. The attack was launched as a response to the involvement of Pakistani terrorists in the 2008 Mumbai massacre. A month later, the so-called Pakistani Cyber Army hit back by hacking into the website of India's leading investigative agency, the Central Bureau of Investigation (CBI).

For military commanders, modern technology is both a blessing and a curse. Cruise missiles and smart bombs are guided by GPS satellites; drones are piloted remotely against the Taliban in Afghanistan from bases in Nevada; warplanes and warships are huge data-processing centres; even

The e-threat

The blurring of the lines between criminality and war is a sinister phenomenon but hardly a new one. Inevitably, experts are divided on the threat posed by cyberwar. Some predict the galloping collapse of modern societies under sustained e-attack, a scenario that recalls governments' apprehension in the 1930s of the devastating effect of strategic bombing raids on European capital cities. Then, it was affirmed that 'the bomber will always get through'. Today the hacker, often with little more than a laptop, poses a similar threat. Nevertheless, it is equally likely that cyber attack will not be a decisive weapon but a means of disrupting and delaying the enemy's response to achieve a limited objective. One scenario frequently advanced in this context is the Chinese seizure of Taiwan without having to engage the United States in a shooting war.

the 'poor bloody infantry' are being wired up. Yet exponentially increasing connectivity over an insecure Internet multiplies the avenues for e-attack.

Stuxnet Malware, an abbreviation of 'malicious software', is a form of programming designed to disrupt or destroy target computer systems or infiltrate them to harvest information. The Stuxnet worm is an example of complex malware that is programmed to spy on and subvert specific industrial systems, operating like a sniper rifle rather than a blunderbuss.

In 2009–10 Stuxnet's principal targets were the Iranian uranium enrichment facilities at Natanz, ostensibly part of a civilian energy programme but suspected of being the preliminary to the development of nuclear weapons. Stuxnet, probably introduced via infected memory sticks, altered the speed of Natanz's centrifuges, of which approximately 1,000 were eventually dismantled and removed. The effect has been to push back the Iranian nuclear programme by two or three years. Israeli intelligence, with US help, was behind the attack.

the condensed idea
Cyberwarfare is war in the fifth dimension

Index

Quercus Editions Ltd
55 Baker Street
7th floor, south block
London
W1U 8EW

First published in 2012

A catalogue record of this book is available from the British Library

UK and associated territories: ISBN 978 1 78087 264 3
Canada: ISBN 978 1 84866 195 0

Printed and bound in China

10 9 8 7 6 5 4 3 2 1